Coups from Below

Coups from Below

Armed Subalterns and State Power in West Africa

Jimmy D. Kandeh

First published in 2004 by
PALGRAVE MACMILLAN™
175 Fifth Avenue, New York, N.Y. 10010 and
Houndmills, Basingstoke, Hampshire, England RG21 6XS
Companies and representatives throughout the world

PALGRAVE MACMILLAN is the global academic imprint of the Palgrave Macmillan division of St. Martin's Press, LLC and of Palgrave Macmillan Ltd. Macmillan® is a registered trademark in the United States, United Kingdom and other countries. Palgrave is a registered trademark in the European Union and other countries.

ISBN 1–4039–6715–6

Library of Congress Cataloging-in-Publication Data

Kandeh, Jimmy D. (Jimmy David), 1959–
Coups from below : armed subalterns and state power in West Africa / Jimmy D. Kandeh.
p. cm.
Includes bibliographical references and index.
ISBN 1–4039–6715–6
1. Civil-military relations—Africa, West. 2. Military government—Africa, West. 3. Coups d tat—Africa, West. I. Title.

JQ2998.A38C584 2004
332′.5′0966—dc22 2004049755

A catalogue record for this book is available from the British Library.

Design by Newgen Imaging Systems (P) Ltd., Chennai, India.

First edition: November 2004

10 9 8 7 6 5 4 3 2 1

Printed in the United States of America.

Contents

List of Tables

Preface

This study interrogates the subalternization of politics in West Africa. Among the topics explored are the changing dynamics of military coups, the specificities of subaltern coups and dictatorships, the conjunction of violence and accumulation, the politics of military disengagement, and the relationship between armed subalterns and popular sectors. Subaltern coups are broadly symptomatic of protracted state failures, especially the inability of political leaders to institutionalize power, eradicate mass poverty and promote socioeconomic development. Although these interventions are often directed at senior officers and/or civilian political incumbents, and despite the populist rhetoric adopted by their leaders when first in power, subaltern dictatorships have mostly failed to pursue transformative goals or create new mobilizational political structures. Instead, they have been marked by unprecedented levels of violence, instability, corruption, human rights abuses, and in two cases (Liberia and Sierra Leone) by state collapse and the outbreak or continuation of armed conflict.

The idea to undertake this project stemmed from three articles I published in the *Review of African Political Economy* during the 1990s. The first essay was on the "Contradictory Class Functionality of the 'Soft' State," in which I argued that the malleability and functional contraction of the state in Sierra Leone and elsewhere in the region threatened the reproduction of ruling class dominance. In the absence of any commitment to legitimize political power, and given the rapacity of political classes and their dependence on violence to maintain political order, it was only a matter of time before those called upon to enforce state power would usurp it. The recurrent intrusion of armed subalterns in the politics of West African states led me to expand the compass of my inquiry to include this substratum, with special focus on its protest repertoire, differentiation from other subordinate strata, relation to ruling sectors, and liberating potential. This effort resulted in the publication of "What Does the Militariat Do When it Rules? Military

Regimes in The Gambia, Sierra Leone and Liberia." A third article, titled "Ransoming the State: Elite Origins of Subaltern Terror in Sierra Leone," refocused analysis on the political class as the ultimate source of political violence by armed subalterns. Together, these three essays set the stage for this study of armed regulars and state power in West Africa.

Along the way, I was invited to present papers at seminars (Freetown, 2001, 2002), workshops (Jos, 2000), and conferences (Woodrow Wilson, 2001; Abuja, 2001; Oxford University, 2000; US State Department, 2000) that provided unique opportunities to learn from others and refine some of my arguments. It was in Jos, Nigeria, that I met Robin Luckham, whose pioneering work on the military in Africa has influenced legions of African students, myself included. Robin offered useful suggestions for my project, as did Zaya Yeebo who was also in Jos at the time and whose insights into the Rawlings era in Ghana are unparalleled. Also in attendance at the Jos workshop was George Kieh, who is currently seeking the Liberian presidency, and Alaric Tokpa; both men suffered greatly under Doe and I was fortunate to listen to their accounts of what transpired in Doe's Liberia. Writing solicited papers delayed the completion of this project but improved the final product.

A sabbatical grant from the United States Institute of Peace (USIP) in 1998–1999 and a series of faculty research grants from my employer, the University of Richmond, made possible the research upon which this study is based. To the USIP and the University of Richmond, I wish to extend my appreciation and gratitude. I also want to take this opportunity to acknowledge my former professors at the University of Wisconsin-Madison (Fred Hayward, Crawford Young, Patrick Riley, Murray Edelman, Erik Olin Wright, Ivan Szelenyi) and at Fourah Bay College, University of Sierra Leone (George Carew, Ahmed Dumbuya, Eustace Palmer, Clarence Johnson, Dale Webster), without whose intellectual guidance and encouragement this book would never have been conceived. I cannot begin to thank the many individuals who helped bring this project to fruition but to all of them, especially Gabriella Pearce and Erin Ivy, editors at Palgrave Macmillan, I wish to extend my heartfelt gratitude and thanks.

Introduction

A significant number of military interventions in West Africa have been carried out not by disaffected senior officers but by subaltern ranks or the militariat, who occupy a class position in the army that is analogous to the working class in society. In no other subregion of the world have armed subalterns seized power with such regularity and dispatch as in West Africa. Ghana (1979, 1981), Liberia (1980), Burkina Faso (1983), Sierra Leone (1968, 1992, 1997), and Gambia (1994) exemplify, to varying degrees, this pattern of military *coups from below*. These interventions represent a different type of coup d'etat whose implications for the transformation of praetorian violence from a tool of domination to a means of criminal expropriation remain largely unexplored. What the change in rank and social background of coup leaders in West Africa signifies, how it is to be understood and explained, and what happens when armed marginals seize control of the state are the broad foci of this study.

Subaltern coups are to be distinguished from those orchestrated by senior officers. Discontinuities with respect to class location, rationalizations for intervention, patterns of mobilization (vertical for senior officers, horizontal for subalterns), targets of grievances, and coup ramifications separate these two types of intervention. Whereas, for example, intra-class tensions and intrigues may prompt senior officers to stage coups, subaltern interventions are more likely to express inter-class antagonisms. Coups by armed regulars have in many instances started as pay strikes and mutinies directed at top military officers and/or civilian political incumbents. Where subaltern coup leaders tend to espouse some variant of populist ideology—with the usual emphasis on fighting corruption, alleviating poverty and returning power to the people—usurpations by senior officers are typically conservative affairs devoid of any emancipatory or transformative agenda. What is perhaps most distinctive about subaltern coups is the duality of the usurpations they set in motion—both the command structure of the army and broader patterns of political leadership in society are inverted when armed marginals capture state power. Restoring rank discipline under such circumstances has often turned out to be more elusive than compelling public acquiescence to subaltern military rule.

The emergence of the militariat as contender for political power in West Africa nailed the coffin of earlier myths that saw African armies as "puritanical, decisive, efficient and self-sacrificing" agents of development.[1] In his modernist outfitting of the professional soldier, Lucian Pye portrayed African armies "as one of the more modernized of the authoritative agencies of government."[2] Marion Levy went so far as to hail the military as the institution most capable of "combining maximum rates of modernization with maximum levels of stability and control."[3] The military was in essence depicted as a cohesive organization, a stabilizing force, and an agent of development. Nothing imploded these myths more assuredly than the sudden transformation of armed subalterns into heads of state or, as Sierra Leoneans took to calling them, "foot of state."[4]

That the African soldiery failed to minimally approximate the lofty billing of its modernist invention cannot be overstated. Rather than provide security, order, and political stability, the military has become a primary source of instability, lawlessness, banditry, and disorder in many parts of Africa. Even under the best of circumstances, military establishments have routinely acted "to maintain or increase their . . . prerogatives even when these values conflict with the aspirations and interests of larger segments within . . . society."[5] Socially unproductive military expenditures have stifled economic growth and limited the availability of social, health, and welfare services for ordinary citizens. And in situations of chronic disorder or where armed subalterns wield state power, "tonton-macoutization" directly connects the soldiery to the world of crime as "looting, confiscation and pillage" become "the favored means of acquiring and consuming wealth."[6]

Armed regulars, or the subaltern ranks of African armies, are not professional soldiers. Rather, they belong to what Samuel Huntington identified as the "organizational bureaucracy"—distinct from the "professional bureaucracy"—whose members "have neither the intellectual skills nor the professional responsibility of the officer."[7] Military professionalism, according to liberal orthodoxy, is a composite of expertise, organizational discipline, political neutrality, and client (society) protection.[8] Seen from this perspective, a soldier's "employment of his expertise promiscuously for his own advantage would wreck havoc on society."[9] Irrespective of the rank of coup leaders, interventions by the military in political processes tend to compromise military professionalism because, as Amos Perlmutter argued, "when the soldier delves into politics, he (unlike laborers, farmers, and industrialists) threatens the very reason for his corporate existence, becoming a political master instead of a political instrument."[10]

Subaltern coups are especially destructive of political power. Violence, to paraphrase Hannah Arendt, destroys power as it graduates into terror and terror "is the form of government that comes into being when violence, having destroyed all power, does not abdicate, but on the contrary remains in full control."[11] Violence can be justified but not legitimized while power, on the other hand, requires legitimation for its effective exercise. The more political leaders rely on violence to reproduce their dominance, the greater the likelihood that violence could spiral out of control, destroy power, and consume not only its purveyors and beneficiaries but also society as a whole. In a very real sense, therefore, the origins of subaltern coups can be traced to the predatory or spoils logic of political domination in West Africa.

In the pages that follow, I argue that armed subalterns in West Africa represent a retrograde political force that is more likely to terrorize society and felonize the state than rescue the latter from decomposition or establish legitimate political institutions. The degenerate propensities of subaltern ranks derive from their lumpen social background and historical alienation from popular sectors. "Lumpenity" is textured by chronic material deprivation, social alienation, violence, thuggery, criminality, and the absence of collective consciousness or any coherent liberating discourse. The debasement of humanity that pervades the "life world" of lumpens is often displaced onto the public domain when the militariat takes charge of the state.

Problematizing Subaltern Violence

The massive intrusion of violence into the politics of African states in the postindependence era cannot be understood independent of the interests and practices of ruling sectors determined to impose rather than legitimate their dominance. This primacy of domination over legitimation, or repression over consent, suggests the absence of hegemonic ruling classes capable of promoting material and institutional development. As Robert Fatton contends,

> . . . ruling classes exist throughout Africa but have yet to become hegemonic. They dominate more by threatening and/or using direct violence than by providing moral, material and intellectual leadership. Politics in Africa is not consensual but Hobbesian, and the rule of the ruling classes is not democratic but dictatorial. The absence of hegemonic ruling classes thus explains African despotism.[12]

The intersection of predatory accumulation and violence favored the political ascendancy of armed subalterns, as ruling class appropriation of lumpen violence and subaltern mimicry of ruling class pillage transformed state power into a tool of criminal extraction.

A major consequence of predatory domination in West Africa has been erosion of the state's protective, extractive, allocative, and regulative capacities. This functional retreat or progressive disqualification has invited unprecedented levels of violence and insecurity throughout the subregion. In the seasoned perspective of Basil Davidson, it is precisely "when the state is no longer prepared to enhance life-chances, no longer willing to sustain large scale patronage, and no longer capable of paying salaries to the lower echelons of its personnel" that a "country becomes a hellish environment" in "which soldiers wantonly fire bazookas into population centers . . . rape mothers, wives and daughters . . . steal livestock, crops and money."[13] Under these conditions, accumulation and violence become inseparable as "the realm of clientelism and the world of crime overlap."[14]

The absence of any discernible and coherent political agenda separates subaltern violence from ruling class violence. In the case of the latter, violence and repression provide access to public offices and resources but they do not serve as means of directly extorting private citizens. Expropriation by the militariat, on the other hand, makes no distinction between public and private property; what elites misappropriate or embezzle, armed subalterns simply pillage. Violence by armed subalterns has thus served not only to terrify mass publics into submission and flight; it has also created opportunities for accumulation by its leaders and patrons. This extension of predatory violence from the public to the private realm is, though common to dictatorships of the militariat, rooted in elite practices that valorize pillage and privatize violence.

Subaltern political violence, or what David Keen has termed "bottom-up" violence, as distinct from "top-down" elite violence, was, in the early years of independence, driven not by subaltern deprivation or greed but by the struggle among competing fractions of political classes for access and control of state offices and resources.[15] As instruments of oppression, armed subalterns in "normal times" function to reproduce relations of domination in society. This is what Flight Lieutenant Jerry Rawlings of Ghana had in mind when he acknowledged, "For five years I used my weapons to protect them [senior officers] while they raped the country."[16] Enforcing state power seldom serves the interest of the militariat as a substratum but it nonetheless draws its personnel closer to the corridors of power. The violent usurpation of the power they are routinely called upon to enforce occurs largely in response to bad governance and the degeneracy of political classes in West Africa. Insurgencies, including those initiated by armed regulars, can, as Christopher Clapham writes, "be ascribed to an experience of postindependence government so bad as to lead to a resistance born of desperation, and to the consequences of prolonged immiseration, exploitation and state decay."[17] It is, in other words, the cumulative effect of elite pillage and repression that, in many cases, creates the conditions that favor the extension of lumpen violence from the fringes of society to the mainstream of politics in West Africa.

Thandika Mkandawire takes this argument a step further in his analysis of the urban origins of rebel violence and mayhem in Africa. While noting that not all cases of neopatrimonial collapse have resulted in violence, Mkandawire takes issue with apocalyptic (Kaplan, 1994), culturalist (Ellis, 1998), neopatrimonial (Bratton and Van de Walle, 1998), and rational-choice (Richards, 1995; Collier, 2002) accounts of insurgent violence in Africa that are either overly pessimistic or are misguided caricatures of painful realities. Departing from these approaches, Mkandawire provides an alternative explanation of insurgent violence that emphasizes its urban origins and rural displacement. According to him,

> The roots of revolt in most African countries lie in the cities, and more specifically, the capital cities. Most guerrillas are merely "passing through" the countryside on their way to capture power in the city, or some natural resource deemed necessary for the prosecution of war. This, together with the movements' unclear political agendas, the apathy or hostility of local communities, and the complexities and peculiarities of the African rural societies, produces a volatile combination that has led to so much unnecessary suffering. . . . One clear message for rebel movements . . . is that rural Africa is a treacherous environment, which will not only erode their political agenda but also reduce them to despicable criminals and bandits.[18]

Cases of subaltern insurgent violence not only originate in the cities; they are also for the most part intra-elite conflicts "writ large." Subalterns engage in wanton violence not because they have lost their heads or are driven by insatiable criminal appetites but because they are products of political systems that have failed them and the rest of society.

Leadership corruption and repression are the real progenitors of subaltern political violence in West Africa. Corruption, violence, and insecurity are closely intertwined. Rampant official corruption enfeebles the state, alienates popular sectors and deprives governments of the resources and active public support needed to ward off threats to society. As Charles Tilly reminds us, "the threats against which a given government protects its citizens . . . are consequences of its own activities."[19] Stated differently, the principal threats to state security in West Africa are rooted in predatory repression and mass poverty.

Historicity of Subaltern Coups

Several factors help explain the subalternization of politics in the West African subregion. The conjunction of accumulation and domination, the identical class location of political incumbents and senior military officers, the privatization of violence and the functional contraction of the state, have been major contributing factors. Far from being the cause of state decomposition, the irruption of armed subalterns on the political scene is symptomatic of broader leadership failures in the postindependence period.

The first subaltern coup to succeed in West Africa was the Togolese coup of 1963, which toppled the government of Sylvanus Olympio. This usurpation bucked the trend of the 1960s and 1970s, which saw mainly senior officers, not sergeants or noncommissioned officers, staging coups and becoming heads of state. Since the Rawlings coup of 1979 in Ghana, however, there has been a dramatic increase in the number of attempted and successful subaltern coups. Increasingly, political leadership in contemporary West Africa is as likely to come from the ranks of the military underclass as from senior military officers and civilian politicians.

A key variable in fomenting subaltern coups is the degree to which the exercise of political power overlaps with wealth accumulation. The centrality of the state to processes of class formation undermines the formal separation of power and wealth and deprives society of an independent business class whose autonomy from the state can help transform and democratize state power. Where the class functionality of state power is formative, immediate and direct, it is difficult, if not impossible, for state institutions to reproduce the dominance of political classes precisely because the resources and relative autonomy needed to do so are respectively siphoned-off and undermined by elite rapacity and greed. Given the relative neglect of the other ranks by affluent politicians and senior military officers, it is not surprising that armed regulars have frequently resolved to "pay themselves" by looting public and private property.

A second reason why coups by the militariat are more prevalent today than in the past has to do with the complementary class location, interests, and ethnic identity of senior military officers and political incumbents. Clientelization of senior officers by civilian political incumbents reduced the likelihood of coups from above while increasing its chances from below. Senior officers may be less inclined to move against their civilian patrons because they share common interests based on class, ethnicity, and other affective ties. Ethnoclientelism, however, can exacerbate class tensions in the army even as its upper echelon is co-opted. Ordinary soldiers observe and take exception to the sudden embourgeoisment of their officers, which many have rightly come to believe occurs at their expense. Resentment based upon perceptions that senior officers are "stiffing" the ranks, "chopping them small," and siphoning their supplies has often been at the center of the grievance narratives of subaltern mutineers and insurgents.

A third factor to consider regarding the historicity of subaltern coups is that they have typically succeeded in countries facing acute economic and political crisis. Economic problems in Africa did not take a turn for the worse until the 1970s, when the continent was hit by the oil price shocks of 1973 and 1979. From the 1970s onward, many African states have had to deal with huge balance of trade deficits, which forced them to seek assistance from the International Monetary Fund (IMF), in addition to borrowing from other multilateral and private financial sources. IMF conditionalities imposed severe hardships on the population of most African states but failed in the majority of cases to reverse negative growth trends. Governments laid-off hordes of workers who could not be absorbed into private sectors that were also contracting and shedding excess capacity. Soaring unemployment combined with the collapse of educational systems to create a veritable youth crisis throughout much of the continent. As economies nose-dived and political institutions atrophied, an opening was created for unconventional claimants of power to emerge. The informalization of both politics and the economy sanctioned predatory accumulation, multiplied contenders for power, and increased the probability of coups by armed regulars.

Organization of Study

The five countries examined in this study have, to varying degrees, experienced subaltern coups and dictatorships. For purposes of this study, at least two of three conditions must be met for a military intervention to qualify as a subaltern coup. First, the planning and execution of the intervention must be the work of armed regulars. Although junior officers may find themselves in leadership roles, they are ultimately answerable to the ranks.[20] Second, senior military officers must be among the principal targets of the coup. It is often by virtue of the actions taken against senior officers that subaltern coups showcase their incipient class character. Third, the inaugural rhetoric of coup leaders must be populist. The seven coups covered in this study targeted senior officers, all but one (the 1997 coup in Sierra Leone) initially espoused some form of populist goals and three (Ghana in 1979, Liberia in 1980, Sierra Leone in 1997) were initiated by subaltern ranks. Although coups in Ghana (1981), Burkina Faso (1983), Sierra Leone (1992), and Gambia (1994) did not have their origins in the militariat, the junior officers who masterminded them initially espoused some form of populist ideology that sought to link the interests and aspirations of armed regulars with those of popular sectors. Thus, the Rawlings and Sankara dictatorships are included in this study largely on account of their populist orientation and stance against corrupt senior officers and other ruling class elements.

Five of the eight chapters in this book are case studies of subaltern coups and dictatorships in Ghana, Liberia, Burkina Faso, Sierra Leone, and Gambia. The first three chapters address issues of theoretical and historical significance. Chapter 1 explores the class implications of military coups, the conjuncture between the class structure of society and the hierarchy of military establishments, and the growing convergence of violence and accumulation in Africa. Although coups may implicate class antagonisms, they are by no means uniquely determined by class factors. How class and other cleavages interact to influence military coups and the impact of these interventions on class relations are some of the issues engaged in this chapter.

Chapter 2 examines the class location and politics of the militariat. The political agency of this substratum, the contradiction between its subordinate location and positional centrality, and the factors that distinguish its protest register from those of other subordinate strata, are explored. Since armed subalterns play a critical role in the reproduction of political domination, their relationship to both ruling sectors and other subordinate strata tends to be inherently ambivalent, contradictory, and conflictual. More often than not, armed subalterns have been politically aligned with ruling sectors and against popular forces.

Chapter 3 traces the historical origins of the militariat and provides a chronology of subaltern coups in West Africa. The militarization of politics in Africa has strong imperial antecedents and public antipathy toward standing armies did not recede with the dawn of independence; to the contrary, in most countries where armed subalterns usurped power, the hostility of mass publics toward armed forces intensified. Situating dictatorships of the militariat in the engendering context of colonial militarism and postcolonial accumulation and repression is critical to understanding the enhanced role of armed subalterns in the politics of contemporary West African states.

Chapter 4 offers a review of subaltern coups and dictatorships in Ghana. More than any other prior intervention, the Rawlings coup of 1979 in Ghana set the tone and stage for subsequent interventions by elements of the military underclass in West Africa. Marked by unprecedented levels of violence, indiscipline, harassment, and humiliation of senior officers and civilians, the "first coming" of Rawlings in 1979 sounded some of the populist themes that were to reverberate in Liberia, Burkina Faso, Sierra Leone, and Gambia. Although the "second coming" of Rawlings in 1981 was inspired and organized by leftist radicals, this usurpation was an undisguised sequel to the earlier AFRC coup. What Rawlings's leadership of the militariat suggests, among other things, is the possibility of a progressive or at least moderate alternative to the abiding degeneracy that has so often afflicted subaltern dictatorships.

Chapter 5 examines one of the most brutal subaltern dictatorships to emerge in Africa, namely the Samuel Kenyon Doe regime (1980–1989) of Liberia. The combustible mix of class and ethnic grievances that gave rise to this lumpen dictatorship partly accounts for the extraordinarily gruesome atrocities that marked Doe's ascendancy and demise. Doe's false populism and his transformation of the People's Redemption Council (PRC) into a brutal, self-serving personal dictatorship, sets the Liberian experience apart from those of Ghana and Burkina Faso. Doe's agenda did not remotely envisage a populist transformation of Liberian society and, lacking any charisma, he vastly exceeded Sankara and Rawlings in the degree to which he personalized power. The warning issued by his supplicants that there would be no Liberia without their benefactor ("No Doe, No Liberia") turned out to be quite prophetic, at least in the short term. Not unlike their counterparts in the AFRC of Sierra Leone, Doe and his retinue of Krahn vandals, as well as those who took up arms against him, were perfectly content to destroy the Liberian state if they could no longer control its offices or lay hands on its resources.

Thomas Sankara's leadership of the militariat in Burkina Faso is the subject of chapter 6. Though petty-bourgeois in composition, the leadership of the *Conseil Nationale de la Revolution* (CNR) sought to work with, among, and for the downtrodden, with the overriding goal of uplifting and transforming society in the process. Sankara's charisma, anti-imperialist rhetoric, identification with the peasantry, and defiance of the West endeared him to youth and radical elements throughout sub-Saharan Africa. The sincerity of his populist commitment and the extent of his efforts to make the peasantry the social base of the CNR's transformative project remain unparalleled in West Africa. With his tragic assassination on the orders of Blaise Compaore, the current leader of Burkina Faso, Sankara joined the pantheon of martyred revolutionary leaders in Africa—alongside Amilcar Cabral, Eduardo Mondlane, Solomon Mahlangu, Steve Biko, and Samora Machel. More significant is what Sankara's brief tenure at the helm of Burkinabe politics demonstrates—that it is quite possible to reorient the militariat and redirect its energies away from the pursuit of parochial agendas toward the achievement of emancipatory goals.

Chapter 7 offers an analysis of the National Provisional Ruling Council (NPRC) and Armed Forces Revolutionary Council (AFRC) coups and dictatorships in Sierra Leone. With more subaltern takeovers of government than any other country in the subregion, Sierra Leone offers compelling insights into the politics of the military underclass in West Africa. Although the leaders of the NPRC and AFRC came from different ethnoregional backgrounds, they nonetheless shared a common predatory agenda. Like the Provisional National Defense Council (PNDC) coup in Ghana, the AFRC coup in Sierra Leone was a rerun of the earlier NPRC takeover, albeit with a slightly different caste of characters. Roughly half the members of the AFRC served in the NPRC and although the NPRC relinquished power in 1996, both dictatorships were opposed to the democratic aspirations of popular sectors. Compared to other subaltern coups in the subregion, the 1997 coup in Sierra Leone is to date the most unpopular. For the first time in independent Africa, the combination of domestic armed resistance, civil disobedience, and regional military intervention succeeded in reversing the 1997 coup and reinstating the ousted government.

Chapter 8 looks at the Armed Forces People's Revolutionary Council (AFPRC) coup and dictatorship in Gambia. As one of three subaltern coups to overthrow a democratically elected government in West Africa, the AFPRC coup was unmistakably influenced by events in Sierra Leone. But where the NPRC's Valentine Strasser could not prolong his incumbency, the AFPRC's Yayah Abdul-Aziz Jamus Junkung Jammeh succeeded himself by contesting and "winning" multiparty elections in 1996. How the processes of self-succession in Gambia compared to those in Liberia and Ghana, and why the AFPRC was able to remain in power—albeit in the guise of an "elected" but despotic government—are among some of the comparative issues addressed in this chapter.

The conclusion summarizes the key points and arguments of the preceding chapters, provides a comparative summary of the seven coups and dictatorships, and explores strategies for permanently relegating soldiers to their barracks. Although popular legitimation of political authority does not always discourage or prevent subaltern coups, as evidenced by the 1981 coup in Ghana and the 1997 coup in Sierra Leone, it is perhaps the best safeguard against coups of any kind. Moreover, as Pat MCGowan and Thomas Johnson have warned, "until the political-economic problems associated with under-development are successfully resolved," the trend toward increased military intervention in the politics of African states "will not be stopped, much less reversed."[21]

CHAPTER 1

Class Dimensions of Military Coups

Conventional scholarship on the military in Africa tends to focus almost exclusively on the causes of military coups, civil–military relations, the developmental role of the military, and military disengagement from politics. Institutionalist narratives, for example, attribute military coups to low levels of military professionalism and political institutionalization. Typical of this approach are studies by Samuel Huntington, Amos Perlmutter, and Samuel Finer, which, *inter alia*, extolled the virtues of military neutrality in politics.[1] Morris Janowitz explained military coups in terms of the corporate interests of soldiers while Samuel Decalo stressed the role of personal ambition and idiosyncratic variables in these takeovers.[2] Others, like Pat McGowan and Julius Ihonvbere, sought to relate military coups to social contradictions, economic stagnation, and declining real incomes.[3] None of these accounts, however, fully incorporated class variables into their overall explanatory frameworks.

Studies of military interventions that emphasize internal conflicts within armed forces have mostly described tensions between senior and junior officers or among ethnic groups in the army. Relatively few studies have engaged the issue of class relations inside military establishments and their relevance to understanding political action by the military. Ruth First and Roger Murray were, in this regard, among the first to draw attention to the relevance of class in understanding military coups in Africa. A common thread in their analyses is the perception of senior military officers as part of the ruling elite or the military fraction of the political class in Africa. Ruth First, for example, argued that "the interests of the officer corps lie in preserving the inflated standards of the African elite; in retaining or increasing the army's share of the budget; and in steadying the state when it shakes under stress, since it has itself such a large group stake in the budget and the economy."[4] Linking military and civilian political elites helped shed light on the erosion of professionalism in African armies but said very little about the internal repercussions of this erosion and the relationship between senior officers and the military underclass, or between the latter and other subordinate strata.

Only in the works of Robin Luckham, Eboe Hutchful and Emmanuel Hansen do we begin to see serious attempts at analyzing class relations within African armies. Luckham compared military hierarchies to labor processes and outlined a structural division of labor between military management (the officer corps) and military labor (ranks).[5] Hutchful's study of the 1979 and 1981 coups in Ghana highlighted the significance of class antagonisms and corporate interests in explaining these interventions.[6] Hansen perhaps went farthest in formulating a "class theory" of the military in Africa. He viewed "personnel in the military as a fractional part of the class forces in civil society" and argued that both senior officers and subaltern ranks are capable of acting as class forces within the military and in the broader society.[7] The military rank structure, in Hanson's analysis, reflected the class structure of society.

Recognizing the conjuncture of military rank structure and the class structure of society does not assume class solidarity across the civilian–military divide. For a variety of reasons, complementarity of interests or class location has not prevented senior officers from ousting civilian incumbents, nor has it drawn armed subalterns any closer to other subordinate strata. Senior officers are ideologically closer to their civilian counterparts than armed subalterns are to workers and peasants. Class solidarities, both within the army and between soldiers and their class equivalents in society are frequently undercut by ethnic loyalties, patronage ties, personal ambition, and, in a few instances, by the corporate interests of the army as a state institution. The degree to which, and under what circumstances, corporate interests override the class interests of soldiers is historically variable and structurally problematic, especially in light of the failure of most African states to professionalize their armed forces.

The class dimensions of military coups in Africa are shaped, first and foremost, by the identical class location of civilian elites and senior military officers, on the one hand, and subordinate strata and the military underclass, on the other. Civilian and military sectors of the political class are united around a predatory mode of accumulation while armed subalterns share conditions of extreme social deprivation with workers, lumpens and peasants. Given the greater class solidarity among competing elements of the political class, coups by senior officers tend to be reproductive of existing structures of domination, exploitation, and accumulation. In cases where senior officers usurp power, intra-class schisms, not class antagonism, are often prominent motivating factors. Tensions and differences frequently crystallize around competing ethnic loyalties and patronage networks that are constantly mobilized to secure control or gain access to public offices and resources. Intra-class schisms pit civilian and military elites against each other, with the result that tensions among civilian elites are often played out among senior military officers.[8]

The relevance of class to the study of military coups in Africa ultimately derives from the state's contradictory functionality as a class apparatus.[9] Malleable state institutions tend to facilitate class formation at the top but endanger the reproduction of ruling class dominance. This is because both the predatory mode of accumulation characteristic of ruling circles and its attendant repression are fundamentally incompatible with the interests and aspirations of mass publics. Predatory repression forecloses political legitimation and the greater the reliance on coercive apparatuses to reproduce dominance, the more pivotal the role of military and paramilitary forces become, either as enforcers or usurpers of state power. On the other hand, higher levels of legitimation and political institutionalization can effectively lessen the role of violence in the political process and reduce the incidence of military coups.

Domination and Accumulation

Since patterns of capital accumulation in Africa vary from those associated with advanced capitalism, it is not surprising that class formation in the continent also deviates from conventional capitalist forms. Defining classes on the basis of the function they perform in production processes is not particularly useful to comprehending the specificity, indeterminacy, and fluidity of class formation in Africa, where domination, rather than ownership of the means of production, is the critical variable in the delineation of class boundaries. Even in advanced capitalist societies, "classes are not given uniquely by any objective positions because they constitute effects of struggles, and these struggles are not determined uniquely by the relations of production."[10]

The conventional wisdom regarding processes of class formation in Africa is that power rather than production relations determine them. Class relations in Africa, Richard Sklar observed, are "at bottom . . . determined by relations of power, not production."[11] More often than not, "it is their relationship to the state which largely enables actors to get rich and dominate the social scene."[12] This explains the "premium on political power," which, in the words of Claude Ake, "is so high that we are prone to take the most extreme measures to win and to maintain" it.[13] The state, in other words, functions as a primary avenue of dominant class formation and is the principal focus of class conflict in Africa.

Dominant class formation in Africa is predicated on the exercise of power. This has undermined both the relative autonomy of the state and its capacity to perform basic tasks. Compounding this problem is the historical and structural disconnect between state and society in Africa. In the words of Goran Hyden,

> The dilemma facing African leaders is that because the state is not structurally tied to society they are not in a position to exercise systemic power. They lack the more subtle institutional means that are at the disposal of a government in societies where the state is firmly rooted in the productive system of the country and where, therefore, it can be used to shape the system at large. Seen in this perspective, the image of the African leader as being extremely powerful is mistaken . . . it is difficult to call the African holding state power a "ruling class". They are not the carriers of a hegemonic "bourgeois" culture and prefer to act as patrons of their respective communities.[14]

Because the class whose formation is made possible by institutional fragility lacks a hegemonic ideology and is largely parasitic in its mode of consumption and accumulation, it is incapable of leading a genuine transformation of African society. Simply put, the interests of Africa's political classes cannot be reconciled with the developmental aspirations of society.

The fragility or "softness" of the state in Africa is not simply a historical inheritance but a "symptom of ruling class interests." According to Robert Fatton,

> To characterize the state as being soft is to miss the class relationships and class struggles that provide the social context which molds and shapes the state itself. Thus, if the state in Africa is relatively weak in terms of its capacity to impose its authority on all sectors of society, it is nonetheless powerful enough to unleash its violence against particular groups and classes. The relative impotence of the state to enforce its own rules is biased impotence. It is an impotence that consistently favors and enhances the power, interests, and status of the well-off and privileged classes.[15]

Departing from Fatton, it can be argued that while the malleability of the state may favor the formation of ruling sectors, it does not guarantee the reproduction of their dominance and may in fact threaten it. The use of state coercion to exploit and terrorize, rather than protect and safeguard, ordinary citizens, has led to the privatization of violence and delegitimation of power. Power becomes fragmented as its exercise is privatized and dissociated from the interests and aspirations of society. Under these circumstances, not only is the state's monopoly over the use of violence called into question, the absence of autonomous rules of political contestation encourage political competitors to resort to the same violent means of gaining power that are used to reproduce political domination.

Violence is not the only component of public power that is privatized by ruling sectors in Africa. Arguably, there is no compelling reason to privatize state violence were it not for the unfettered rapacity of political classes. Predatory accumulation, more than any other single factor, necessitates the privatization of violence. A defining attribute of predatory domination is the "conversion of political power and position into economic wealth for the benefit of the few at the expense of the many."[16] As Sara Berry contends,

> . . . class relations are based partly, but not exclusively, on differential access to the state. Politicians, senior civil servants and military officers exercise a great deal of power over access to foreign and domestic capital and markets, and they have used this power both to accumulate large fortunes and to consolidate their control of the economy. Exploitation . . . occurs not so much through the labor market . . . as through a burgeoining de facto market in government contracts, licenses and offices. Corruption is not a matter of personal ethics but a central mechanism of resource allocation and control.[17]

Control of, and access to, public offices and resources determine the social location of predatory elites. Predatory accumulation impoverishes societies, delegitimizes political institutions and alienates popular sectors from the institutions of government. A mode of accumulation that is so deleterious, regressive, and unproductive cannot provide the basis for social progress, economic development, and political institutionalization. This is what John Lonsdale had in mind when he wrote:

> Modern African regimes, overcrowded at first with power, have used force to narrow the ranks of their collaborators, and may have stifled productive effort in the process. They have strangled the ambition of independent

> capitalists who might become their rivals; they have neglected the peasants on whose labors they depend. Nobody today is being liberated by the process of state formation, save for the growing army of bureaucrats.[18]

Given the convergence of accumulation and domination in Africa, individuals who control or have access to the coercive apparatuses of the state routinely employ violence not only to suppress dissent and opposition but to also expropriate the state and its citizens. This lack of distance between accumulation and domination, or between wealth and power, is a useful starting-point in understanding the political agency of armed subalterns in West Africa.

Subaltern coups are by-products of the intersection of predatory accumulation and violence. Predatory forms of authoritarian rule multiplied prospects for military interventions by all ranks of the military, from the most senior to the lowest subaltern. By politicizing their armies and diverting the loyalties of soldiers away from the state and toward individual patrons, political classes in Africa unwittingly sowed the seeds of their own demise. While involving the army in the political process may not necessarily be a bad thing, assuming this involvement is geared toward the pursuit of a transformative developmental agenda, the results of politicizing the military in Africa have been disastrous. Like their colonial precursors, postcolonial armies in Africa continue to betray a "mercenary" character that sets them apart from, and in opposition to, the rest of society. But even mercenaries, realizing how important they are to the survival of political incumbents, can entertain delusions of grandeur that are sometimes acted upon. It is this centrality of violence to the reproduction of political domination that allows the military underclass to function as both instrument of oppression and contender for power.

Subaltern mimicry of elite modes of accumulation transforms violence from a tool of domination into a means of criminal extraction. How subalterns exercise power is shaped by elite practices that valorize pillage and privatize violence. Violence and pillage texture the life world of lumpens, the stratum from which armed regulars are disproportionately recruited. It is little wonder, therefore, that compradorization of its leadership elements (Doe of Liberia and Jammeh of Gambia come to mind) is usually what happens when armed subalterns capture state power.

Predatory Accumulation and Coups from Above

Depending upon the circumstances, coups by senior officers are sometimes rooted in intra-class competition, rivalries, and tensions among ruling fractions and cliques. Roger Murray saw the first wave of coups (1960s) in Africa as attempts "to stabilize the situation for overseas capital and . . . for national capital."[19] This explained "the post-coup tendency towards . . . more propitious political conditions for capitalist exploitation and development" in countries like Nigeria and The Congo.[20] In a similar analysis of a different period, Shehu Othman attributed the 1983 Nigerian coup to "domestic intra and inter-class conflict, and its relations to the political conditions under which both Nigerian and international capitalism operated."[21] At a more general level, Bjorn Beckman observed that "the army itself has served as a powerful vehicle for bourgeois class formation" in Africa, "with a growing number of senior officers establishing themselves in business, either alongside their army careers or on early retirement."[22]

State intervention in African economies created myriad opportunities for rent-seeking among politicians, bureaucrats and army officers. According to John Mbaku, "since members of excluded groups are unable to gain access to government controlled markets, and cannot compete for rents because of their exclusion from institutionalized political processes, they must resort to the capture of the rent-creating apparatus of government."[23] Mbaku uses evidence from Nigeria to demonstrate how the link between violence and accumulation enhanced the role of the military in resource extraction and allocation. He avers that "since government regulatory activities have either destroyed or rendered private capital accumulation processes ineffective, and allowed the state to have absolute control over resource allocation, only those who control the apparatus of government or have access to it, are capable of accumulating capital." It is this "emerging importance of violence as a rent-seeking tool in sub-Saharan Africa" that "has given the military a very significant role in resource allocation."[24]

Rent-seeking by a kleptocratic political class represents a mode of accumulation that is not only at odds with mass aspirations but is quite different from those associated with foreign capital. As Richard Jeffries puts it,

> It would take a great deal of ingenuity . . . to attempt to calculate the proportion of surplus value respectively appropriated by foreign capital on the one hand and by local state officials on the other. But foreign capital investment and foreign trade can at least . . . have their economically progressive, even productive functions; whereas kleptocracy is wholly regressive in its effects.[25]

Coup leaders, whatever their rank, do not have to be lackeys or unimaginative stooges of foreign capital for their actions to have a class character, meaning, and purpose. Internal processes of class formation have externalities but global capitalism can at best provide only partial insights into the class dynamics of military coups.

Loosely crafted in class terminology, Michael Lofchie's analysis of the 1971 Ugandan coup recites the need to protect foreign capital as an important factor behind this intervention. Central to Lofchie's account is his depiction of the Ugandan army as "a kind of economic class, an elite stratum with a set of economic interests to protect." In this view,

> Uganda soldiers at all ranks were wealthy individuals. If additional military benefits such as housing, food, medical treatment, uniforms, insurance and family allowances are taken into account, the material discrepancy between a Ugandan soldier and an average Ugandan citizen is little short of extraordinary. It amounts to a difference between opposed social classes.[26]

It was, Lofchie argued, in order to protect its relative high salary, huge share of the national budget, and illicit activities that the Ugandan army seized power in 1971.

Lofchie's portrait of the Ugandan army as a homogeneous stratum or "class" is plainly misleading. Ascribing a single class character to the military misreads its corporate identity and fails to account for contradictions among competing solidarities. A general and a private may share common ethnic and social backgrounds but they do not belong to the same class. The general has more in common with a government minister, bureaucrat or wealthy businessman than with subaltern ranks who are materially closer to wage laborers and are culturally lumpen. As William Gutteridge reminds us, the "leadership elite" of the armed forces "is not in many ways significantly differentiated from their opposite numbers in the civil service, state enterprises, commerce and industry."[27] Alongside their counterparts in civilian sectors, top military officers constitute an important fraction of the political class.

Class action by senior military officers can assume a variety of forms. Senior officers act to routinely defend and protect the interests of the political class as a whole. They do this, however, not by promoting the relative autonomy of the army from political processes but by subordinating the army to the predatory agenda of political incumbents. This is a role not unlike that performed by armed subalterns as instruments of oppression. But whereas senior officers are usually motivated by class interests and ethnic loyalties in defending political incumbents, armed subalterns, by contrast, are driven less by class solidarity than by ethnic loyalties and patronage ties.

From a class standpoint, therefore, senior officers have a direct interest in reproducing a system under which they are privileged. One of the factors, however, responsible for the erosion of the corporate integrity and professionalism of African armies is the clientelization of senior officers by political incumbents.

Intra-class action against political incumbents (civilian or military) usually reflects fissures within the political class based on ethnicity, patronage, personal rivalries, and ambitions. These intra-class conflicts have been as important in determining political outcomes as inter-class conflicts pitting the military underclass against senior officers and their civilian counterparts. Beyond issues of ethnicity, personal rivalries and ambition, what is often at stake in coups by senior officers is determination of the "hegemonic" or dominant fraction of the political class. Conflict within the political class is not over the mode of accumulation; it is about who should preside over the spoils regime of the state.

Examples of interventions by senior officers that reflected intra-class tensions, competition and personal rivalries include the 1966 (Afrifa) and 1978 (Akuffo) coups in Ghana; the 1967 (Lansana, Blake) coups in Sierra Leone; the 1983 (Buhari), 1985 (Babangida) and 1994 (Abacha) coups in Nigeria; and the 1966 coup in Burkina Faso (Lamizana), to name a few. Typical of a class-motivated coup by senior officers was the 1978 intervention in Ghana, a palace coup that merely substituted one military leader for another. General Fred Akuffo, who took over from General Ignatius Kutu Acheampong, was more interested in granting senior military officers immunity from prosecution before handing over power to a democratically elected government than holding them accountable for plundering Ghana's resources. Coups in Nigeria have also been predominantly intra-class affairs in which personal ambition and rank opportunism, not to mention the manipulation of ethnic loyalties and tensions, have been major factors. Concerns and loyalties more parochial than class animate the politics of elites (military or civilian) who are after all united on the issue of what to do with state offices and resources but fractured over who should be in charge.

The politicization of the officer corps of African armies eroded their corporate identity, professionalism, and integrity. Restoring the professionalism of these armies, if not disbanding them in cases where they create more insecurity than they prevent, is critical to keeping armies out of politics. This would call for ethnic diversification of both the officer corps and ranks of African armies and their subordination to democratic civilian control. It would also require improving relations between soldiers and civilians, which have become increasingly antagonistic since independence. African states can, perhaps, learn a few lessons from India, where civil–military relations, as described by Rebecca Schiff, are based on "concordance among the military, the political elites, and the citizenry about the role and function of the armed forces."[28]

Predatory Repression and Subaltern Coups

The cleavages that give rise to subaltern coups are embedded in social structure, especially the distribution and access to wealth, state patronage, and mobility opportunities. These cleavages are not unique to the military but are rather shared by the wider social structure. How armed subalterns experience the market as consumers, how they react to their impoverishment or the lack of freedom from want, whom they blame for their privations, and what they make of their role in reproducing domination, are issues that foreground class relations in both the military and society as a whole.

An important class dimension of subaltern coups in West Africa is the extent to which they express deep-seated antagonism toward senior officers and the political establishment. Like most public institutions, the military consists of individuals occupying different locations in the class structure and military hierarchy. This differentiation, as Robin Luckham writes, is common to all armed forces:

> The basic cleavage between a commanding stratum of officers and a subordinated class of ordinary soldiers or policemen is found in all industrialized standing armies. It is deeply entrenched in management practice, labor processes, career structures and class relations. It was also the pattern around which all colonial and post-colonial military establishments were formed, even following national liberation struggles.[29]

Unpacking the multiple "corporate" identities of the military is a necessary first step in analyzing the class character of military coups. Luckham identified three types of corporate or quasi-corporate interventions by the military, two of which are class specific. The first involves coups by senior officers that seek to protect or enhance their "accumulation of power and wealth . . . through privileged access to the state." The second describes those instances where broader professional and corporate interests propel the military to seize power. A third form of "military corporatism" is shaped by the material conditions of subaltern ranks.[30] Although the first and third examples are not, strictly speaking, expressive of military corporatism, they can nonetheless be respectively analyzed from the standpoint of ruling class formation and subordinate class resistance.

Both senior officers and subaltern ranks are capable of class action that is independent of the corporate interests of the military. This is a point made by Emmanuel Hansen, who recognized the importance of understanding the conjuncture of military and social structure and situating it in concrete historical conditions. Hansen saw the military as a class instrument, part of the class forces of society, with senior officers constituting the petty bourgeoisie of the military while the other ranks make up the lower orders. He described the "first coming" of Rawlings in Ghana as both a "rebellion of the men of the ranks first against their officers and then against comparable classes in civil society" and as "a class action on the part of the lower classes to assert themselves."[31] How such class action can be contemplated, executed and sustained in the absence of solidarity with other subaltern strata, poses a problem for any class theorization of political action by armed regulars.

Leaving aside the impact of corporate erosion and loss of prestige in fomenting coups (as in Ghana's 1979 Rawlings coup), it would be overly simplistic to attribute coups by the military underclass to a corporate desire to improve the lot of rank and file soldiers. As "enforcers of class and state power and as consumers of scarce societal resources,"[32] subaltern leaders have been motivated less by a desire to emancipate their substratum than by prospects for personal enrichment and social uplift through the seizure of state power. The sudden and often spectacular transformation of previously destitute marginals into overnight tycoons underscores the changing role of subaltern violence and coups in West Africa.

There are at least two broad senses in which class is relevant to understanding subaltern coups. First, the location of the militariat in the class structure and military hierarchy differentiates subaltern coups from those carried out by senior officers. As noted earlier, coups by the militariat mirror inter-class antagonisms whereas those by senior officers tend to be triggered by intra-class competition, personal rivalries, greed and ambition. In the case of Nigeria, William Graf has shown how the enrichment of military officers and their social detachment from the other ranks fostered "a permanent inter-class struggle in the military itself as well as the larger society of which it is a part."[33] But "to oppose the upper classes," as Eric Nordlinger cautioned, "is not necessarily to support the lower classes, especially . . . in the context of economic scarcity."[34] Given the distance between the militariat and other subordinate strata, it is not surprising that the class issues that often instigate coups by this substratum are obscured at the first taste of power.

A related class dimension of subaltern coups involves the delusions of grandeur and mobility aspirations of armed lumpens. The capture of state power serves the same purpose for leadership elements of the militariat as it does for competing fractions of the political class. Where ruling elements misappropriate, embezzle or divert public funds to personal use, armed subalterns simply extort, ransack, maim and pillage. Violence is an unmediated mode of consumption among armed subalterns who ordinarily lack access to the avenues of bureaucratic misappropriation. The inevitable result of this predatory diffusion of violence is the felonization of the state, as was the case in Sierra Leone and Liberia.[35]

It is, however, important to distinguish violence spawned by need and desperation from violence motivated by greed and rapacity. In those instances where violence is driven by relative deprivation, consumption rather than accumulation is the main objective. This form of equal opportunity violence, which targets everybody (including leadership elements of the militariat), is by definition extortionist and can easily graduate into armed robbery and greed-motivated carnage; rarely, though, has direct looting by subalterns led to the accumulation of significant capital. For leaders of subaltern insurgencies and the political class, on the other hand, violence secures access to the sources of bureaucratic expropriation. Samuel Doe of Liberia and leaders of the National Provisional Ruling Council (NPRC) of Sierra Leone were perfectly content to rely on bureaucratic means of expropriating their respective states while marauding gangs of armed supporters engaged in endless looting of private and public property. The brazen venality of leadership elements of the militariat often makes it impossible to rein-in renegade soldiers who are, after all, behaviorally cued by their compradorized bosses.

Collaboration between armed subalterns and other subordinate strata has been either lacking or at best spasmodic. If ruling sectors are politically fractured by ethnic loyalties and patronage ties, the same is no less true of subordinate classes. But whereas ethnicity and patronage have not prevented the development of a broad sense of class solidarity among ruling sectors, they have helped stifle the development of class-consciousness among subordinate strata. Divisions among senior officers also tend to be replicated among the ranks, a displacement that furthers the disaggregation of the military underclass. Recruited on the basis of ethnicity and patronage, subaltern ranks of African armies have often served as reproductive agents of state power. Although state power does not privilege subordinate class interests, it can favor specific *ethnies*. Neither ethnicity, however, nor patronage, has prevented subaltern ranks from usurping power. Like senior officers, armed subalterns seek control of state power, or access to its offices and resources, not to improve the lot of the marginalized and destitute but to advance the specific interests and life chances of its leadership elements.

Typical of class-based subaltern military interventions were the 1968 coup in Sierra Leone, the 1979 coup in Ghana and the 1980 coup in Liberia, to name a few. Class, however, was not the only source of grievance behind these interventions. Even when subaltern coups have a definite class character, their architects usually exhibit low levels of class-consciousness, which tends to limit their capacity to forge alliances with other subordinate strata. The greater capacity of senior officers to find common cause with their civilian counterparts is, when contrasted with the inability of armed subalterns to forge political alliances with other marginals, suggestive of differentials in levels of class consciousness between ruling and subordinate classes. In the many instances where class had to compete with ethnicity for the loyalty of armed subalterns, ethnicity has often but not always trumped class solidarity.

Low levels of class consciousness among armed subalterns does not mean their political action lacks a class character. How subalterns are impacted by processes of dominant class formation, the group(s) they blame for their social deprivation and what actions they take to promote their collective interests are as important to undersatanding the class character of subaltern coups as are the motives and consequences of these coups. Low levels of class consciousness do not strip subaltern political action of its class content or deny it a class character.

Class conflict is first a "struggle about class before it is a struggle among classes"[36] and the failure of armed subalterns to forge alliances with other subordinate strata limits the possibilities of class action by this substratum. As Nii K. Bentsi-Enchil observed in the case of Ghana, "the basically repressive attitude of soldiers to civilians has not changed, and will not change without an evolution in the lower ranks' political consciousness."[37] The task of raising the level of political consciousness among the ranks has often fallen on the shoulders of junior officers, some of who may espouse a populist ideology but seldom a class-based agenda. Jerry Rawlings, for example, declared in 1979 that he was "neither a communist nor a capitalist," preferring instead to portray himself as a pragmatic populist who could lead a multi-class effort to curb the wrongs and injustices of society.[38] Thomas Sankara in neighboring Burkina Faso was a bit different; more an ideologue than Rawlings, not even he could irrevocably align the Burkinabe militariat with other subordinate strata.

Conclusion

Irrespective of personnel level, "the class origin of military officers and ranks is not a useful or reliable indicator of their class sympathies or ideological inclination."[39] Subaltern origin and location does not necessarily bring the military underclass closer to other subordinate strata or help to overcome other competing solidarities within military establishments. This is not to suggest that subalterns cannot act to further the corporate interests of armies but it is to argue that they tend to do so either when led by senior officers or in opposition to these officers. In the latter case, subaltern political action can simultaneously defend the corporate interests of the army and reflect the class interests of armed regulars. To the degree that they are indistinguishable from their civilian elite counterparts, senior officers, on the other hand, have become progressively less capable of protecting the corporate interests and integrity of military establishments. This is rather odd since officers, as opposed to the enlisted ranks, are supposed to embody, symbolize, and defend the integrity and professionalism of armies.

Subaltern displacement of senior officers as custodians of the corporate interests of armies was evident in Ghana where a combination of corporate and class grievances led to the June 4, 1979 coup. The leaders of this coup wanted not only to rid Ghana of corrupt and oppressive military officers who plundered the country but to also restore "integrity, accountability and a degree of honesty" to the armed forces.[40] In Sierra Leone, a similar mix of class and corporate variables prompted the ranks to temporarily seize power in 1968. Although the main grievance of the coup leaders was neglect of the ranks by senior officers, who were at the time in charge of the government, they also made it known that "soldiers and police have no business running the country."[41]

By and large, senior officers have more in common and are closer to other fractions of the political class than armed subalterns are to other subordinate strata. Armed subalterns share the same class location with workers, lumpens, and peasants but their political interventions tend to threaten the interests of other subordinate strata. In fact, it can be argued, based on the available evidence, that subaltern coups are more likely to subvert the interests of subordinate classes in the long run than the interests of political classes. Doe's dictatorship in Liberia, for example, did more harm to ordinary Liberians than to the entrenched Americo-Liberian ruling class.

In sum, to claim that a military coup has a class dimension is not to suggest that it is reducible to class or can be uniquely explained in class terms. Monocausal accounts of military coups do not take us very far in understanding the complex dynamics of these events. Class is not the only variable implicated in military coups and not all military coups are triggered by class factors. The interaction of class, ethnicity, corporatism, patron-clientelism, and personal ambitions in shaping military coups often makes it very difficult to single out any one factor as the most determinant.

CHAPTER 2

Situating the Militariat

I shoot, therefore I am.
—Chidi Amuta

Primus inter pares within subordinate strata, armed regulars and irregulars have routinely parlayed their guns into means of physical survival, consumption and, in some instances, criminal extraction. Cartesian rationalism may posit a contrary ontology but for the teeming ranks of the militariat in Africa, it is the gun that defines existence, rights, entitlements, and power. Armed subalterns derive a large measure of their self-worth, not to mention political clout, from their weapons. Guns, from this perspective, do not only kill and destroy; they also feed, clothe, house, and enrich those who resort to violence for personal gain. Predicating self-worth on weapons, however, increases the potential for confrontation between armed subalterns and the rest of society. This is because armed marginals, especially when they go on the rampage or during mutinies and coups, frequently act as though their needs and interests supercede those of the rest of society.

Guns and violence have shaped both the self-image of armed subalterns and the overall trajectory of politics in many African states. Proliferation in the number of claimants to power reflects the centrality of violence in reproducing political domination. The swagger of the militariat comes from the knowledge that it can wreak havoc and make life difficult for elites and society as a whole. This dual threat to elites and the rest of society has resulted in uneasy accommodation by the former and hostility from the latter. Elite responsiveness to armed subaltern needs and demands has seldom prevented coups by the militariat while public antagonism has in some cases (Sierra Leone in 1997 comes to mind) triggered subaltern mutinies and usurpations. Given a larger pool of potential copycats, coups by the militariat are more contagious than those orchestrated by senior officers and, with gun-toting high-school dropouts fancying themselves to be leadership material, the remilitarization and debasement of politics in Africa is depressingly reminiscent of the conquest phase of colonial occupation.

The militariat is first and foremost a subaltern or subordinate category. It is a substratum that occupies the lower rungs of class structures, sharing its relative deprivation, subordination, spontaneity, and lack of cohesion with peasants, workers, and lumpens. Armed regulars in West Africa may be disproportionately drawn from the ranks of peasants and lumpens but it is the consciousness and outlook of the latter, in addition to its interaction with ruling sectors, that shapes the insurgent politics of the militariat. Politically, armed subalterns are more likely to act as lumpens than as peasants or workers. Their protest forms, access to coercive resources and proximity to power, however, sets them apart from other subordinate categories, including unarmed lumpens.

As armed regulars, the militariat should be distinguished from armed irregulars. Both share subaltern and lumpen attributes but irregulars lack proximity to the seats of power and usually take a longer time achieving political objectives, which may include the capture of state power. Armed regulars are members of permanent, standing armies that symbolize sovereignty and the continuity of states; armed irregulars, on the other hand, have a more ephemeral existence and are likely to disband at the end of hostilities or be incorporated into regular forces. Furthermore, in contrast to irregular forces, armed regulars are on the public payroll and are charged with safeguarding the population and protecting the territorial integrity of the state. Under normal circumstances, armed regulars, as extensions of the state, command greater legitimacy than irregular forces but in situations where the very legitimacy of the state is in question, irregular forces can possibly attract more support than armed regulars. This was the case in Somalia, Liberia, and the Democratic Republic of the Congo, where public support for rebel forces eased the removal of entrenched dictators.

There are growing signs of operational convergence between regular and irregular forces, as evidenced in Sierra Leone where the term *sobel* was coined to refer to renegade soldiers who colluded with rebels to extort, maim, and kill civilians. *Sobels* (armed regulars moonlighting as rebels) overthrew the democratically elected government of Sierra Leone in 1997 and invited rebels to join them in despoiling the country. This soldier–rebel alliance was made possible by the similar social background and political outlook of armed regulars and irregulars. Irregulars of the Revolutionary United Front (RUF) shared both the subaltern class location and lumpen culture of the militariat in Sierra Leone. Lumpen culture glamorizes violence and is the product of chronic deprivation and alienation. Regular or irregular, armed subalterns generally share a common repertoire of violence and a tendency, dating back to the colonial era, to extort, loot and maim. They betray a latent, and in some cases manifest, interest in disorder, which disconnects them from other subordinate strata.

This chapter explores the subaltern location and political agency of the militariat in West Africa. The militariat is shorthand for armed regulars (as distinct from armed irregulars) or the "other ranks" of military establishments, although it is not uncommon for the political leadership of this substratum to attract select junior officers. This conception of the militariat departs from Ali Mazrui's usage of the term "lumpen militariat." In describing the "lumpen militariat" as "that class of semi-organized, rugged, and semi-literate soldiery which has begun to claim a share of power and influence," Mazrui opined that "the emergence of the modern army in African countries has broken the correlation between political power and western education by interrupting the trend towards the dictatorship of the educated class in modern African history."[1] While the militariat's lumpen social origin constitutes a productive line of inquiry, it makes no sense to view an entire army as a social or political class. Failure to socially disaggregate the Ugandan soldiery limits the analytical value of Mazrui's "lumpen militariat." It is replaced in this study by a view of lumpen that, among other things, takes into account the distinction between structural and cultural lumpenization. While structural lumpenization has facilitated the popularization of lumpen culture and provided a backdrop for coups by the militariat, it is as a cultural construct that the lumpen category is most useful to the analysis of armed subalterns and state power in West Africa.

Subalternity of the Militariat

The term subaltern was used by Antonio Gramsci to describe a diverse social agglomeration that is marginal, subordinate, disunited, passive, spontaneous, and lacking autonomy. Subalterns, from this perspective, are said to share certain "negative" and "positive" traits. The "positive" attributes of subalternity include "elementary passions," common sense and spontaneity, which, according to Gramsci, can be "educated, directed, purged of extraneous contaminations" and transformed into a "living and historical force."[2]

Subaltern passions, energy, and spontaneity provide the raw materials for the development of class consciousness but "failing to give them a conscious leadership or to raise them to a higher plane by inserting them into politics may often have extremely serious consequences."[3] The "primitive and historical acquisition" that is common sense, or "the spontaneous philosophy of the multitude," can be minimally expressive of subaltern consciousness even as it serves to reproduce relations of domination in society.[4]

The "negative" markers of subalternity are passivity, disunity, spontaneity and the absence of collective consciousness.[5] Passivity as a negative subaltern attribute can be seen, for example, in the demobilized condition of West African peasants, who, despite their numerical preponderance, have the least voice in the politics of their states. Peasants may, as liberals and Marxists concur, wallow in rural idiocy or be superstitious in outlook but they are also quite capable of spontaneous outbursts of violence, not to mention covert or "everyday" forms of resistance. Peasant passivity can be misleading to the degree that it masks resentment of ruling sectors. Dissimulation, rumor, slander, footdragging, and withdrawal from exploitative relations with state and market forces have been among the forms of peasant resistance common to West Africa.

If peasants have been the most "passive" of subaltern groups, the same cannot be said for armed regulars who occupy a position in the class structure analogous to workers. The frequency of mutinies and coups by the "other ranks" in West Africa suggests that not all subaltern groups are submissive, at least not to the same degree. Inertia is not a function of political subjugation and while peasants may be disinclined to frontally resist exploitation and domination, this should not be taken to imply they would rather acquiesce than resist in ways that are best suited to their location in the class structure. Peasants cannot go on strike as workers, nor can they stage mutinies like armed regulars, but they can "exit" from relationships that are intolerably oppressive and exploitative.

Lack of cohesion is central to the problem of subaltern passivity and agency. Save for brief interludes, nowhere in West Africa have subalterns been able to consistently act with one voice. Workers may withhold their labor and peasants may smuggle their produce across porous borders in search of better prices but solidarity and collaboration among and between peasants and workers is seriously lacking. Factors that divide peasants include their subsistence mode of production, spatial deconcentration, cultural heterogeneity, and repression by the state. Diversity of social composition and political repression also stifle the political formation of workers. Even the militariat, the subaltern group most likely to usurp power, seldom acts as a group when some of its elements resolve to seize power. Conspiratorial groups, usually very small in number, are often the architects of subaltern coups, with the rest of the militariat bandwagoning along with the conspirators, assuming they succeed. But while the lack of cohesion among subaltern ranks may be temporarily submerged by the euphoria and lofty expectations that accompany a successful coup d'etat, the conditions and life chances of armed regulars have seldom improved under dictatorships of the militariat.

Linked to the problem of disunity is the absence of collective consciousness—another "negative" subaltern trait. Subaltern consciousness is, from a Gramscian perspective, inherently fragmentary and contradictory. Subalterns are said to have no "clear theoretical consciousness" of their practical activities as their consciousness can be in historical opposition to these activities. This poverty of historical perspective or contradictory mindset suggests

> . . . the social group in question may indeed have its own conception of the world, even if only embryonic; a conception which manifests itself in action, but occasionally and in flashes—when, that is, the group is acting as an organic totality. But this same group has, for reasons of submission and intellectual subordination, adopted a conception which is not its own but is borrowed from another group; and it affirms this conception verbally and believes itself to be following it, because this is the conception which it follows in 'normal times'—that is when its conduct is not independent and autonomous, but submissive and subordinate.[6]

At the most elementary level, subaltern consciousness is constituted by negation, solidarity, transmission and territoriality.[7] Negation is an inversive act of differentiation or otherization that defines subalterns in terms of what they are not (superiors); it represents the first step in the development of collective consciousness. Solidarity, which can find expression in hostility toward traitors, involves an articulation of class consciousness that competes with loyalties based on ethnicity, religion, and other affective ties. Transmission highlights the role of iconic signs and rumors in the propagation of subaltern insurgencies while territoriality underscores the significance of contiguity and consanguinity in the politicization of subaltern identities. The subaltern's negative assertion of identity and sense of solidarity represent one side of its dual or contradictory character while its consanguinity may express the other side. Another way of putting this is to say that the potential for subaltern solidarity is equaled, if not surpassed, by its tendency to disaggregate along parochial fault lines.

While there are many influences on subaltern consciousness—ethnic, religious, fetishtic, occupational, to name a few—that serve to perpetuate and reproduce subordination, deprivation, and exploitation, it is erroneous to assume that subalterns lack autonomy or are only capable of spontaneous political action. Subaltern historiography, which suggests otherwise, portrays subalterns as occupying an autonomous domain, albeit one that is infected by the interests and values of ruling sectors. James Scott and Goran Hyden, among others, have shown that peasants are not the passive objects of history they are often made out to be in liberal and Marxist analyses.[8] For Hyden, it is precisely the relative autonomy of peasants from state and market forces that allows them to exit from exploitative relations with these forces.

A related "negative" condition, which heightens the susceptibility of subaltern interests to distortion and misrepresentation, is the dialogic pattern of interest definition common to subordinate groups. Claus Offe and Helmut Wiesenthal have argued in another context that subordinate classes are permanently mired in disagreements over "real" interests because their dialogic pattern of interest definition, which is different from the monologic pattern of ruling sectors, is higly amenable to distortion. Based on different logics of collective action, the probability of interest distortion is greater for subordinate than for ruling classes.[9] Ambiguities and contradictions in subaltern interest definition suggest the absence of a common denominator or collective consciousness that can override dissonant loyalties and around which a common struggle and identity can be forged.

Disunity, passivity, spontaneity, and a contradictory, fragmented consciousness generally define subalternity but there are wide variations in the degree to which these traits are present among different substrata. The manner and degree of involvement with state and market forces differentiates subordinate categories, with peasants exhibiting greater autonomy from state and market forces than workers, lumpens, and armed regulars. The militariat is arguably the least passive of subaltern groups—whether it is enforcing the dominance of incumbents or dislodging them from power, subaltern ranks have been anything but bystanders in the politics of West African states. Proximity to the instruments of violence, combined with its protest repertoire, which includes mutinies and coups, separates the militariat from other subordinate strata.

There is considerable variability, therefore, in the propensity of different subaltern groups to engage in violence. Peasants mostly resort to violence as a last resort but violence for lumpens is a first option. As the most desocialized of subaltern strata, lumpens are highly prone to violence, lawlessness, banditry, and other forms of criminal behavior. Among subordinate groups, it is with lumpens that armed subalterns have the most in common. Not only are armed regulars disproportionately recruited from the ranks of *declasses*, their "public transcript" bears the imprint of a lumpen social background and cultural outlook. But who exactly are lumpens and what is lumpen about the militariat?

'Lumpenity' of the Militariat

Lumpens are portrayed in the writings of Karl Marx as the "social scum, offal, refuse of all classes." They are described as completely unreliable, "throroughly malleable" and "as capable of the most heroic deeds and the most exalted sacrifices as of the basest banditry and the foulest corruption."[10] Lumpens represent a mass rather than a class and they provide "a recruiting ground for thieves and criminals of all kinds, living on the crumbs of society . . . without a definite trade."[11] Friederich Engels regarded lumpens as "gutter proletarians," "low grade proletariat," "the worst of all possible allies" and a "rabble" that "is absolutely venal and absolutely brazen."[12] Lawlessness, meaninglessness, and an inordinate propensity to engage in crime and acts of mindless violence have historically defined the lumpen life world. Only in the musings of anarchists like Mikhail Bakunin—who consistently reinvented outlaws, criminals and bandits as revolutionary heroes—are lumpens viewed somewhat positively or favorably.[13]

Lumpens represent a motley amalgam of desocialized riff-raffs who are drawn from the "refuse of . . . social classes." While lumpenization can affect all social classes, subaltern youth tend to be the most susceptible. During periods of war and prolonged civil unrest, however, young and old alike are equally exposed to lumpenization. But unlike the young, who can readily take to a life of brigandage, older subalterns may find this option less practical or inviting. To the degree that armed regulars and irregulars are disproportionately drawn from the ranks of subaltern youth, it is the lumpenization of this segment of the population that is most critical to understanding the politics of the insurgent militariat.

Unlike peasants and workers, lumpens are commonly stereotyped as criminals and a potential threat to social peace.[14] They are seen as constituting the untamed and unrestrained social other, in opposition to which mainstream society defines itself. Consider, for example, this passage from an article on lumpen subalternity and politics in India:

> In the middle class imagination, the 'rowdy' inhabits the dark zone of the city, trafficking in illegal, immoral activities; a zone that is invariably in

> need of law and order, and always threatening to spread to the safer, cleaner habitat of the city. The term 'lumpenproletariat' (lumpen: shabby, paltry; rabble or riff-raff), used as a category in Marxian social theory, also situates them outside any social semiosis of class; a lumpen is precisely one whose relationship to money is unmediated by any value; any bonds of class solidarity or ties of community.[15]

It is this estrangement from society or social uprootedeness, as well as the predisposition to violence and criminality, that sets lumpens apart from other subaltern categories.

Closer to the African scene, Frantz Fanon described lumpens as a "horde of starving men uprooted from their tribe and from their clan" who are "one of the most spontaneous and the most radically revolutionary forces of the colonized people."[16] Lumpens, for Fanon, are "like a horde of rats; you may kick them and throw stones at them, but despite your efforts they'll go on gnawing at the root of the tree."[17] This romantic invention of lumpens as spontaneous but revolutionary was not shared by, among others, Amilcar Cabral, whose revolutionary experience led him to conclude that lumpens are "outrightly against our struggle, perhaps unconsciously so, but nonetheless against our struggle."[18] Cabral identified two categories of lumpens: the traditional *declasses* (petty criminals, jailbirds, prostitutes, beggars, pimps) and the modern *declasses* or "young people who are connected to petty bourgeois or workers' families, who have recently arrived from the rural areas and generally do not work."[19] Lumpens in the first category are desocialized and the least likely to support any socially emancipatory project; those in the second group "generally live at the expense of their families," and have not been completely alienated from familial moorings and social constraints, making them more likely than traditional *declasses* to "play a very important role" in social change.[20]

At the level of class structure, the lumpen category encompasses both *declasse* elements identified by Cabral. But although structural lumpenization has been progressing at an alarming rate throughout West Africa, it is as a cultural construct that the lumpen category is most useful to understanding the political outlook and role of the military underclass in West Africa. The militariat is, in many ways, lumpen in the cultural rather than structural sense. As salaried workers, the structural location of the militariat is not lumpen but working class. A disproportionate number of armed regulars were lumpen (urban riff-raffs, rural drifters) in the structural sense before finding employment in the armed forces but they never abandoned the consciousness and outlook of lumpenity. Others, like peasants and high school dropouts, who joined the military underclass were often more amenable to ruling class interests than lumpens recruited into armies. Irrespective of the social background of armed regulars, lumpen culture tends to be hegemonic within armed subaltern circles. This culture celebrates violence, thuggery, banditry, and myriad forms of criminal adventurism; it also often attracts mimicry by other strata, both subordinate and dominant. The slippage of lumpen locutions and behavioral propensities into elite and popular culture, and the valorization of some of the retrograde practices of this substratum, tend to enhance the explanatory value of cultural lumpenization in studies of subaltern coups, insurgencies, and dictatorships.

As a lumpen category in the cultural sense, the militariat is no less heterogeneous than other substrata. Ethnic differentiation, competing affective identities and patron–client networks tend to offset class-based solidarity. The extent to which subalterns develop a more powerful sense of ethnic, as opposed to class, solidarity may however depend on the substratum in question, since workers have generally shown greater class solidarity than their peasant and lumpen counterparts. Overall, however, subordinate groups in Africa have been politically cued less by class interests than by cultural ties and loyalties. Why this is so has to do with the politics of ruling class formation and subordinate class disarticulation.

Besides its cultural lumpenity, what fundamentally distinguishes the militariat from other subordinate strata is its coercive positionality. Access to and operation of the means of destruction in society translate into greater political voice for the militariat than for any other subordinate group. As constitutive element of the repressive apparatuses of the state, armed regulars, more than any other subordinate group, are strategically positioned to influence the course of political events in African states. Consciousness of this positional centrality, however, has seldom found expression in the pursuit of goals that can bring together all subordinate strata and make a difference in the lives of the majority of citizens.

Leaving aside the issue of proximity to the sites and instruments of power, some of the protest forms of armed regulars also set them apart from other subordinate groups. To the degree that social grievances are embedded in class structures, so are protest repertoires, which are also shaped by social location. It is, for example, as improbable for workers to stage coups as it for peasants to go on strike, but it is not uncommon for the militariat to engage in both forms of political action. Political action by the militariat tends to have a greater impact on politics and society than those of other subordinate groups. This is largely due to the coercive resources at its disposal and the centrality of its role in reproducing political domination. More than any other subordinate substratum, the militariat is the largest recipient of state subsidies and benefits and may, in a very real sense, constitute the new "labor aristocracy" in Africa.

In the final analysis, what distinguishes the militariat from other subaltern strata are its lumpen orientation and outlook, proximity to coercive instruments, and protest repertoire. Structurally working class but culturally lumpen, the militariat's subordinate location in the class structure is shared by other subalterns. This location is marked by chronic material destitution and lack of access to mobility opportunities in society. The positional centrality of the militariat derives from its role as enforcer of state power. This function has mostly precluded the formation of political alliances with other subordinate groups while the alternative role, as usurper of state power, has seldom brought subaltern ranks any closer politically to popular sectors or democratic forces.

Armed Subalterns as Political Force

In every society, writes James Scott, there are spaces occupied by subalterns that resist capitulation and silence. Given this objective reality, ". . . there is no reason to assume that the lower orders are so encompassed by an existing system of domination that they cannot either imagine its revolutionary negation or act on that negation."[21] Domination is always a work in progress and the degree to which ruling classes can effectively reproduce their dominance depends to a large extent on how successfully they accommodate and/or subvert the interests, loyalties and choices of subordinate classes. The space traversed by efforts of dominant classes to control subordinate classes is described by Robert Fatton as the "site of class disarticulation" or "the arena structuring the silence of class and feeding the cacophony of ethnic, linguistic, and religious particularisms." This arena, we are told, "emasculates subordinate classes by situating them in an ostensibly classless field of activities and struggles," thus "transforming them into rather powerless individual citizens" wedded to "the divisive solidarities of supraclass politics."[22]

But even when successful, subordinate class disarticulation can never "fully erase the realities of class exploitation, nor can it negate the shared experiences of common material deprivations."[23] Repression, exploitation, corruption, and social deprivation are likely to generate resistance, however muted or covert, among subordinate classes. Acts of defiance can raise the level of political consciousness among subordinate strata, helping them to "construct their own forms of mobilization and opposition" which, though not always class-based, are nonetheless constitutive of "an incipient class consciousness."[24]

Adapting Fatton's framework to an analysis of armed subalterns, the militariat can be seen as straddling the sites of subordinate class resistance and disarticulation. Like other substrata, the militariat is "inevitably exposed to the contradictory pulls of the sites of class disarticulation and subordinate class resistance."[25] Disarticulation is pursued through ethnoclientelist promotion and recruitment practices, preferential treatment for soldiers and the development of intelligence networks at all levels of armed forces. These safeguards, however, have not always prevented conspiratorial elements of the military underclass from capturing state power. While such actions are often motivated by opportunism and criminal adventurism, and could not therefore be interpreted as instances of subordinate class resistance, they are nonetheless embedded in the realities of class polarization within armies and in societies at large.

Class location, subaltern dialogic, cultural heterogeneity, and state repression combine to limit the organizational capacity of armed regulars. Commonality of deprivation has not evolved into solidarity of political outlook. Internally fissured by ethnicity, regionalism, and competing patron–client networks, the militariat's organizational potential is in large measure circumscribed by its social location. Political conspiracy and action seldom involve the entire substratum, not the least because of the manifest impossibility of horizontally mobilizing this disparate grouping into a unified political force. Thus, when the militariat seizes power, it is often a handful of some of its most adventurist and tenacious elements who initiate and benefit from such action.

The militariat's political enthronement underscores the bankruptcy of clientelism as reproductive mechanism or instrument of subordinate class disarticulation. This observation contradicts Nelson Kasfir's assertion that "patronage, particularly where access to state wealth is available, is a crucial instrument in creating class domination."[26] It also calls into question Fatton's contention that "by displacing subalterns from the site of subordinate class resistance to the site of class disarticulation, patron/client relationships strengthen the site of ruling class formation."[27] Kasfir obfuscates the distinction between class formation and class domination while Fatton offers no compelling reason why subaltern receipt of patronage should, *ipso facto*, strengthen the site of ruling class formation. If, as Fatton acknowledges, patron–client relations are motivated by personal interest rather than concerns for the collective good, it stands to reason that the reproductive potential of such relations would be quite limited. Like the state itself, patron–clientelism has been more effective as an avenue for class formation than as reproductive mechanism of domination.

The centrality of violence to political domination paved the way for the empowerment of armed subalterns. Political classes routinized and privatized violence in the pursuit and maintenance of power, and in the process carved out a major role for the military underclass as enforcer of state and class power. The establishment of paramilitary counterweights to national armies deepened the involvement of repressive apparatuses in politics and transformed security units into loci of political power. With their power dependent upon the capricious allegiance of armed regulars, especially those recruited from urban tenements, African leaders uniformly sought to politicize their armed forces and privatize their security arrangements. This diverted the loyalties of officers and the ranks away from the state and toward individual patrons, cliques, and organizations. But it is one thing to clientelize senior officers and quite another to satiate subaltern ranks, many of whom are not so blinded by ethnicity as to be oblivious to their depraved existence. While senior military officers and civilian incumbents may share a common ethnic bond and class position, ethnic loyalties do not offset or ameliorate the privations of subaltern existence. "Khranization" of the security forces of Liberia may have prolonged Samuel Doe's dictatorship but it could not prevent its downfall. In neighboring Sierra Leone, the fact that northerners dominated both the officer corps and ranks of the army under the All People's Congress (APC) did not prevent the 1992 NPRC coup.

The protest register of the militariat has often included pay strikes, insubordination, desertions, subversion, kidnappings, mutinies, coups and insurgencies. Although they have been known to graduate into mutinies, pay strikes tend to be less confrontational and easier to resolve. In terms of participation and given the minimal risks involved, pay strikes are more inclusive of the militariat as a substratum than coups and insurgencies. Pay strikes may help promote solidarity within the ranks but they do not incorporate the interests or attract the support of other subordinate strata. One reason for this is the exclusionary nature of the "corporate" demands of soldiers, the satisfaction of which always comes at the expense of the rest of society. Even under the best of circumstances, the corporate self-interest of the military, as Eric Nordlinger argued, can become a hindrance to economic and social change:

> . . . when the military are a more or less autonomous state within a state, without a constituency to which they are responsible or an executive to which they are subordinate, they are unlikely to be motivated by the goals of popular responsiveness, social and economic reforms, or economic development.[28]

Strikes by armed regulars are less likely to attract support from, and more likely to alienate, popular sectors.

Insubordination and outright refusal to carry out the orders of superiors—as happened in Burkina Faso in 1965, Ghana after the June 4 1979 coup, Liberia during the crisis leading to the 1980 coup and Sierra Leone for much of the 1990s—qualify as significant political action that can momentarily connect/disconnect the ranks with popular sectors.[29] When troops refuse to shoot at demonstrators, the days of the regime that ordered them to do so are predictably numbered. Such actions have the potential of improving the image of the military in the eyes of the public, especially if a populist posture is maintained and expanded to include other areas of grassroots solidarity. This, however, was not the case in Liberia and Sierra Leone where the military rapidly degenerated into rogue outfits at war with society.

Refusal to carry out orders point to the existence of cracks within armies that can endanger state security and personal safety. Widespread insubordination is a harbinger of mutinies and coups. When disquiet within the military is complemented by social unrest, the chances for subaltern coups multiply. But in the absence of popular support, subaltern coups are reversible, albeit at a very high cost in human lives and property. As the AFRC interregnum (1997–1998) in Sierra Leone demonstrates, subaltern coups can be very destabilizing especially when prompted by grievances that do not resonate with the rest of society.

Insubordination can sometimes dovetail into desertion among the ranks, particularly in crisis or emergency situations. If, as is so often the case, defection from national armies is preceded or followed by insurgent activity against the government (Liberia, Sierra Leone, and Ivory Coast come to mind), the very survival of the state may be in question. In Liberia, an estimated 50 percent desertion rate among armed regulars precipitated the collapse of the Doe dictatorship.[30] Some of these defectors first joined the failed 1985 insurgency led by Thomas Quiwonkpa before finding common cause with Charles Taylor's National Patriotic Front of Liberia (NPFL). Desertions from the Sierra Leone army under Joseph Momoh (1985–1992) and the NPRC (1992–1996) likewise impeded efforts by these governments to contain the RUF insurgency. As in Liberia, a significant number of defectors either joined the insurgency against the government in power or freelanced as *sobels* (renegade soldiers). A similar scenario unfolded in Ivory Coast where deserting northern soldiers swelled the ranks of the rebel movement that sought to unseat the government of Laurent Gbagbo in 2002–2003. As in Liberia, subaltern insurgents in Ivory Coast were motivated not by class but by ethnic, religious, and regional loyalties.

Subversion by rank and file soldiers represents a more sinister form of activity that frequently straddles the boundaries of protest and crime. Subversion can be motivated by political and/or personal considerations. In Uganda, Ali Mazrui observed that the sharp increase in "kondoism" (armed robbery) after the Amin coup was linked to efforts aimed at sabotaging the new government:

> Following the coup, in the wake of instability and uncertainty about the survival of legitimate authority, *kondoism* rose even more sharply. There . . . was suspicion that some members of the intelligence department of the Obote regime, stripped of power and disgraced following the coup, used the firearms they had acquired from the previous regime for new purposes. Old informers became new *kondos*, as they took to gangsterism and thuggery.[31]

Under similar circumstances, the 1992 ouster of the APC government in Sierra Leone sparked a dramatic upsurge in *sobel* activities among rank and file soldiers. Although much of the *sobel* action was for personal gain, there were APC loyalists among *sobels* who sought, through their actions, to destabilize the state and subvert the efforts of the NPRC leadership to restore peace and security.

Related to the above is the kidnapping of foreign aid workers, civilians and, occasionally, some of their own leaders by desperate elements of the militariat. This happened in Liberia under Doe and in Sierra Leone, where renegade soldiers resorted to hostage taking after maiming, amputating and dismembering thousands of their countrymen, women, and children. The demands of soldiers as terrorists can range from food and medicine to a share of ministerial positions and the spoils of office. There is no better illustration of this than the 1999 Lome Peace agreement signed between the Sierra Leone government and subaltern insurgents. This agreement ignored the horrific atrocities committed by rebels and renegade soldiers and instead rewarded their leaders with ministerial positions and sundry privileges. It was as if the chances for social mobility among elements of the militariat now depended on the degree to which they can brutalize and hold society to ransom. Terror, under these circumstances, is less an act of revenge against society than a calculated tactic on the part of armed subalterns to extract resources they can only access when disorder reigns.

Mutiny is another common form of protest action by the militariat that, unlike pay strikes, is unique to armed forces. Mutinies are by definition violent acts of defiance whose participants are drawn together as repressive functionaries with shared grievances. That mutinies can easily graduate into coups or lead to changes in governments further separates this protest form from those identified with other subordinate strata. As precursors of subaltern coups, mutinies attract higher levels of rank and file participation than coups, which are by their very nature more conspiratorial and exclusionary. Some of the mutinies in post-independence Africa that have had considerable political impact include the *Force Publique* mutiny in Congo-Kinshasa (1960), the East African mutinies (1964), the troop mutinies that culminated in the overthrow of Emperor Haile Selassie in Ethiopia (1975), the 1996 mutiny by the ranks of the Guinean army and the Ivorian mutiny that toppled the government of Henri Konan Bedie in 1999, to name just a few.

Insurgency and counterinsurgency also fall within the realm of political action by the militariat. Sierra Leone and Liberia again offer instructive examples of just how quickly a military force can cease being a counterinsurgency force and become an active insurgent force. After losing ground in the Liberian civil war, what remained of the Liberian army under Doe splintered into armed insurgent factions led by ethnic (Krahn and Mandingo) warlords. In Sierra Leone, the bulk of the army closed ranks with rebels in 1997 to overthrow the elected government of Ahmad Tejan Kabba. In the aftermath of their eviction from power by a Nigerian-led intervention force in 1998, remnants of the Sierra Leone army retreated to the countryside from whose redoubts they unleashed a vicious campaign of indiscriminate terror against the civilian population.

Coups are by far the most dramatic form of political action by the militariat. Subaltern coups express the social distance between senior officers and armed regulars and are often justified on populist grounds. They are generally characterized by hostility toward the status-quo, distrust of professional politicians, anti-intellectualism, anti-bureaucratism, and attempts to directly appeal to the people. In the case of Ghana, for example, the

> Concern for simple equity, respect and justice dominate the thinking of the insurgent ranks (even in the 'revolutionary' turmoil of the Rawlings coup it was the oft-repeated stories of the refusal of senior officers to offer drinking water to guards at their residences that most enraged the troops), and, while these may be dismissed as routine political values, in the circumstances of the military they proved nearly revolutionary.[32]

In most cases, however, the justifications for subaltern coups have not been vindicated by the performance of the regimes that are installed. False populism and the failure to translate populist coups into populist regimes disconnect subaltern coup leaders from popular forces. Populist regimes typically "attack established institutions and try to create new norms to govern political behavior;"[33] they seek to mobilize popular sectors, enhance state capacities, and construct new political institutions. In Africa, only two dictatorships of the militariat (led by petty bourgeois elements in Ghana and Burkina Faso) have contemplated such a transformative agenda. Yet, even these dictatorships ceased to be energized less by the ranks as they became more dependent on the charismatic appeal and moral exhortations of their leaders.

Conclusion

In the final analysis, it is more useful to view the militariat as a descriptive social category rather than an abstract construct, as a substratum rather than a class and as historical agent rather than passive enforcer of ruling class domination. As "weapon of the . . . neocolonial state" the militariat "is a beast . . . when unleashed against its . . . masters."[34] The alienation of the militariat from social and cultural moorings invites a more abusive, reckless and self-destructive dispensation of violence. In Basil Davidson's brilliant summation,

> Men like Doe are the children of their ancestral cultures. But they are also the product of an alienation which rejects those cultures, denies them moral force, and overrides their imperatives of custom and constraint. . . . They turn to the AK-47, and use it with the blindness of the damned, at which point their power rebounds upon itself and becomes a route to suicide. Such persons . . . are destined to a tragic fate, or would be if the squalors of their degradation deserved to be called tragic. They have demonstrated, time and again, just why it was that leaders of an entirely different mold and mentality, . . . such as Cabral in Guinea Bissau, so clearly warned that armed violence was a road to be entered with austere reluctance, and traveled with an ever present fear of its infections.[35]

CHAPTER 3

Historicizing the Militariat

The organizational structures, force doctrines, recruitment policies, and behavioral patterns of armed forces in Africa are deeply rooted in the colonial past. It is for this reason that any study of coercive apparatuses and processes in contemporary West Africa must begin with a brief consideration of how the colonial state pursued its security imperative and the impact this had on the postcolonial political landscape. Continuities in colonial and postcolonial state formation are not confined to the security realm but security provisioning is one of the areas where postcolonial arrangements most resemble their colonial antecedents. These legacies have shaped both the organization of military establishments and the relationship between armed regulars and mass publics.

A review of colonial military historiography in West Africa can help throw some light on the recruitment patterns, political agency and retrograde propensities of the militariat, as well as place the privatization of violence in in its proper historical context. Colonial administrations, after all, initially resembled armed regiments staffed mostly by military officers and the occasional psychopath. Africa at the turn of the nineteenth century was described by Ruth First as "a continent of bureaucratic rule, with armies behind the administrators ready to prove whenever necessary that *government existed by conquest.*"[1] Political developments since independence have merely served to accentuate and reinforce this primacy of violence and domination over consent and legitimation.

Armed Forces in Colonial West Africa

Compared to other regions of the world, the colonial conquest of Africa occurred at a time when European states, with professionalized bureaucracies and standing armies, were far more developed than when Christopher Columbus set sail for America in the fifteenth century. As Crawford Young put it,

> The European State about to explode into the African interior in the late nineteenth century was far more removed from the polity that began the imperial age five centuries before. The professionalization and specialization of its formal apparatus was far advanced. Uniformed forces included not just armies and navies but also gendarmes and police. Even as ideologically portrayed in Anglo-American liberal thought as the "night watchman," the nineteenth century state had a scope of action and capacity of control . . . which vastly exceeded that of its earlier imperial ancestor.[2]

The colonial conquest of Africa was also less protracted but more competitive than elsewhere. European diplomatic entanglements, growing industrial rivalry and Otto Von Bismarck's interest in Africa intensified competition for colonies among European states. Seven European states in all (Britain, France, Portugal, Belgium, Italy, Germany, and Spain) claimed colonies in Africa. By comparison, five European states (Spain, Portugal, Britain, France, Netherlands) colonized Latin America and the Caribbean, four (Britain, France, Netherlands, Portugal) held colonies in Asia and two (Britain and France) were colonial overlords in the Middle East. Both the large number of competitors and the need to prevent imperial rivalry from spiraling out of control led to the convening of the Berlin Conference of 1884. This conference, and the official partition of the continent that ensued, marked the transition from informal empires based on trade with coastal enclaves to formal empires based on military conquest.

Also differentiating the colonial project in Africa was the profoundly racist attitudes of Europeans toward Africans. Nowhere in the imperial domain was the "civilizing mission" refrain heard more loudly than with respect to Africa, especially among the French, Portuguese, and Belgian colonizers. Not only was the continent said to be "dark", its inhabitants were portrayed as "savages". whose "mental faculties were little superior to the ape's."[3] This dehumanization of Africans and their "objectification . . . as . . . 'barbarians' meant that the brutalities associated with" colonial conquest "rested lightly on the imperial consciousness."[4] These brutalities, needless to say, left an indelible mark on the postcolonial political landscape and consciousness of armed subalterns.

Pursuant to the colonial project, Africans were compelled to subsidize their own subjugation through taxation and service in colonial armies. Colonial motives for enlisting Africans in imperial and territorial armies included manpower requirements, strategic calculations that equated security with territorial expansion and the need to protect unimpeded access to Africa's raw materials and labor. Above all, and particularly in West and Central Africa, the high mortality rate among Europeans necessitated the recruitment of locals into colonial armies. As one commentator wrote,

> One of the great objects for which . . . Negro regiments were kept on foot was for the purpose of finding garrisons for our stations on the West Coast of Africa. The climate there is abominable and specially injurious to Europeans. We could not keep British soldiers there with safety for more than a few months at a time.[5]

Among colonial powers in Africa, Britain was initially the most reluctant to arm local Africans. With the West India Regiment (WIR) at its disposal, the British could suppress insurrections in Africa without having to rely on local troops. Goaded in their fears by the mutiny of the West African Regiment (WAR) in 1901, the British had every reason to be concerned about the reliability of African soldiers. Thus, despite the lobbying efforts of the War Office during World War I, it was not until World War II that soldiers from British West African colonies saw action in significant numbers outside the continent.

Restrictions on Africans serving in British colonial forces reflected the prevalent racism of the period. From the perspective of the Colonial Office, African soldiers lacked proper training, were unreliable, and could not survive in temperate conditions. But the primary reason for the Colonial Office's reluctance to enlist Africans to fight in European wars was the fear that armed Blacks could threaten colonial supremacy. Winston Churchill (at the time Secretary of War) was "strongly in favor of . . . beginning to employ African troops from West and East Africa, as well as from the Sudan, for imperial purposes outside the African continent," but this was not done until World War II.[6] As one colonial official who did "not want all the whites killed" remarked:

> Churchill backed up my efforts to get colored peoples recruited for the army . . . as concerns the colored army he was no doubt anxious for men, I for raising the status of the colored races; and we failed because the War Office thought it undesirable to put colored people on a par with white men. It might put ideas into their heads.[7]

Fears that the military training of Africans could endanger imperial domination partly explain the role of the WIR in the British conquest of Africa.

Before the introduction of this regiment to West Africa, the performance of British and local African soldiers had consistently fallen short of expectations. As Davidson Nicol (writing as Abioseh Nicol) recounts,

> The British soldiers sickened easily and also asked for the then excessive salary of a shilling a day. The African soldiers tended either not to obey orders at all, or to obey them too literally. On one occasion they locked up for a night in jail their commanding officer who returned to barracks after midnight, because they had been told to arrest anyone found loitering after that hour. It was not too surprising that the government began to look elsewhere for soldiers.[8]

One area the British turned to was the Caribbean, whose WIR was involved in virtually every British war of conquest in West Africa. Raised around the turn of the eighteenth century, the WIR served in wars against the French in Dominica, Martinique, and Guadeloupe. Initially, the backbone of the WIR consisted mainly of liberated slaves from Africa, with a recruiting company established as early as 1827 on Sierra Leone's Bunce Island.[9] Later, the WIR rank and file was dominated by soldiers from Jamaica (First WIR) and Barbados (Second WIR). Commenting on the differences between diaspora Africans and "liberated" Africans as WIR soldiers, Garnet Wolseley wrote:

> Our West Indian battalions retain many of their good old qualities, but they are no longer of the same use to us as formerly, when they were composed of liberated Africans. . . . The whole Negro race in these Islands is seriously infected with the diseases which have impaired the vitality of many European families. . . . The result is that only a small proportion of those who want to enlist can "pass the doctor." . . . The infusion of white blood into the West Indian Negro has certainly not improved his physical strength, whilst the education we have given him has as certainly injured his fighting qualities. He has lost the best qualities his forefathers possessed as savages, and he has failed to acquire those which belong to that civilization with which he is now more or less associated.[10]

Starting around the end of the nineteenth century, the WIR was augmented by the West African Regiment (WAR) and the Royal West African Frontier Force (RWAFF). The WAR, which was under the direct control of the War office until 1928, was supposed to be the West African version of the WIR.

Joseph Chamberlain, secretary of state for the colonies, ordered the establishment of the RWAFF in 1897 as a colonial expeditionary force to be used mainly in West Africa. Frederick Lugard, architect of British colonial policy in Africa, envisioned the RWAFF as a "homogeneous imperial force" that would be "available for all parts of Africa."[11] Three decades prior to the RWAFF's formal establishment, Sir John Glover, who later became Governor of Lagos, had organized Hausa and Yoruba freed slaves into a constabulary. Glover's so-called Hausa Constabulary, later renamed the Lagos constabulary, formed the nucleus of the RWAFF's Lagos battalion.[12] Other local constabularies were also absorbed into the RWAFF, including the Royal African Colonial Corps of Light Infantry in the Gold Coast, the Sierra Leone Frontier Police and the Royal African Colonial Corps Garrison of Gambia. The four territorial components of the RWAFF thus became the Nigeria Regiment, the Gold Coast Regiment, the Sierra Leone Battalion and the Gambia Company.

The "Indian model" informed the organization, structure, and composition of British colonial armies in West Africa. Experience in the Indian subcontinent had convinced the British they could raise local armies and place them under the command of European officers. This entailed the recruitment of rural men from "martial races" who possessed unique fighting abilities, as opposed to urbanites contaminated by the spread of nationalism and market forces. Rural dwellers were preferred because

> The wild tribes dependent upon hunting for their daily food possess a sort of intuitive knowledge of wild animals, of their ways and habits, which gives them in war an immense advantage over the ordinary town-bred soldier. The trapper's rude life of daily hardship and privation fits him physically for the ups and downs and rough usage which war brings with it. The hunter is already half a soldier, and not only accepts the miseries of war in an uncomplaining spirit, but regards them as the natural and ordinary incidents of everyday life.[13]

So-called martial races were identified throughout Africa, some of whom were privileged as recruits while others, like the Ashantis of Ghana, were shunned because they were considered to be dangerous. In the observation of one British colonial official, Europeans do not

> . . . learn drill as quickly as the Basuto or the Zulu. It is astonishing to see the zeal, the undisguised interest and application these savages bring to bear upon all military lessons given to them. There seems to be something in the disposition and genius of the common stock from which they come, some hereditary bias in their brain, in their very blood, which fits them for the easy acquisition of a soldier's duties.[14]

Soldiers in West Africa were disproportionately recruited from remote, peripheral areas, particularly from among those "identified in the minds of their officers as martial types."[15] Among the so-called martial *ethnies* were: the Hausa, Kanuri, Idoma, and Tiv of Nigeria; the Mossi, Grunshi, and Mamprussi of Ghana; the Mende, Temne, and Koranko of Sierra Leone: and the Wolof and Djola of the Gambia.

British recruitment practices in three (Nigeria, Ghana, and Sierra Leone) of its four West African colonies favored northerners who also happened to be predominantly Muslim. Muslims, the British reckoned, made better soldiers because the "Mohammedan Negro, even though few know much about their prophet or his teaching, . . . is a better fighting man than the idolater, or than the men of most of the tribes who have no religion at all."[16] The relative discipline and loyal disposition of Muslims were construed as positive traits upon which to build a docile soldiery.

In Nigeria, the local RWAFF evolved from the Lagos, Royal Niger, and Niger Coast Constabularies. The Lagos Constabulary became the Lagos Battalion of the RWAFF in 1901, the Royal Niger Constabulary was absorbed into the first and second battalions of the Northern Nigeria Regiment in 1900 and the Niger Coast Constabulary became the Southern Nigeria Regiment (3rd battalion) of the RWAFF in 1900. The rank and file of the Lagos Constabulary was at inception dominated by Hausas but this changed toward the end of the nineteenth century as more Yorubas and Igbos entered the force. Consequently, Yorubas and Igbos came to dominate the rank and file of the Southern Nigeria regiment while Hausas, Tivs, and Kanuris became preponderant in the Northern Nigeria regiment. With 5 battalions (3 in the north and 2 in the south—including the Lagos Battalion), 27 companies (8 each in the north and south), 4,153 regulars and 99 officers, the Nigeria Regiment in 1901 represented the largest African force in British colonial West Africa.[17]

The forerunner of the Gold Coast Regiment was the Royal African Colonial Corps of Light Infantry. Established by Sir Charles MacCarthy, this force was almost completely wiped out by the Ashantis at the Battle of Asamankow in which Sir Charles was beheaded. The British fought several wars against the Ashantis, one of which (1873) saw them siding with the Fantis against the Ashantis. Twelve thousand British troops, five to seven hundred soldiers from the WIR, few hundred members of the Lagos Constabulary and a force of soldiers from Sierra Leone fought on the British/Fanti side. After the campaign, about three hundred members of the Lagos Constabulary stayed behind to form the nucleus of the Gold Coast Constabulary, which was established in 1879 with 16 European officers and

1,203 Africans. This constabulary force was later incorporated into the RWAFF as the Gold Coast Regiment in 1901. Recruits for this regiment came mainly from the north and the Muslim "Zongos" (strangers quarters) of southern towns. With 12 Companies, 33 officers and 1,657 enlisted men, the Gold Coast Regiment was the second largest in the RWAFF.[18]

The precursors of the RWAFF in Sierra Leone were the Police Corps, incorporated in 1829, and the Sierra Leone Frontier Police, which was established by ordinance in 1890 to impose peace in the hinterland and halt French expansionism. Commonly referred to as the Frontiers, the frontier police was later incorporated into the RWAFF in 1901 as the Sierra Leone Battalion with 6 companies, 15 officers and 498 enlisted men.[19] While the rank and file of the Sierra Leone Police Corps in 1829 was dominated by Creoles, the ranks of the Sierra Leone battalion of the RWAFF at the turn of the nineteenth century consisted largely of Mendes and Temnes, with a strong preference for runaway slaves and rural drifters. This force, not unlike its counterparts in the continent, became notorious for its "wholesale oppression and ill-treatment of natives."[20]

Nearly a century before the establishment of the RWAFF's Gambia Company, Sir Charles MacCarthy (Governor of Sierra Leone and Gambia) created the Royal African Colonial Corps Garrison in 1816 for the ostensive purpose of suppressing the slave trade. By the second half of the nineteenth century, the main colonial armed force in the Gambia was a detachment of the WIR. To start the Gambia Company of the RWAFF in 1901, the British had to turn to soldiers from the Sierra Leone Battalion. Later, local recruits, mainly Mandinka and Wolof, came to dominate the ranks of the Gambia Company.

By 1930, there were an estimated 10,600 African men in the armed forces of British West Africa, including 5,323 in the RWAFF—3,513 in the Nigerian regiment, 1,273 in the Gold Coast regiment, 385 in the Sierra Leone battalion and 152 in the Gambia Company.[21] These forces experienced rapid expansion during World War II. From 1939 to 1945, for example, over a quarter million West Africans served in the armed forces of British West Africa.[22] To secure recruits, Chiefs were required to supply men based on a quota system and raids were conducted to round-up lumpen vagrants for military service. In one such exercise in the Gambia,

> All male Africans of military age found sleeping out were rounded up and herded into McCarthy Square. From there they were brought in lorries to the Denton Bridge camp, where, on ground across the road from the camp, a production line for large scale enlistment had been set

up. . . . This press gang may have cleared Bathurst of "corner boys," but it was not a great help to the Second Battalion.[23]

World War II witnessed a sharp increase in the use of African troops by the British outside the African continent. The Italian invasion of Ethiopia, Japan's entry into the war, and the fall of Singapore forced a change in the views of the Colonial Office regarding the deployment of African troops. From 1943 until the end of the war in Asia, over 120,000 African troops (basically Infantry and support units) served in Sri Lanka (formerly Ceylon), India and Myanmar (formerly Burma).

Africanization of the officer corps of military establishments became a pressing issue after World War II. The ranks of noncommissioned officers (NCOs) were the first to be Africanized and by the 1950s there were few if any British NCOs serving in West Africa. The first African officer, Seth Anthony of the Gold Coast, was commissioned during the war in 1942. But the pace of Africanization was so slow that only 10 percent (29 of 238) of officers in Ghana's military establishment in 1957 were Africans; the corresponding figure for Nigeria was 25 percent (82 of 325 officers were Africans).[24] In Sierra Leone, only three of the sixty officers serving in the army in 1958 were Africans.[25] Africanization, however, may have created more problems than it solved because of its ethnic selectivity and impact. Southerners in Nigeria (Yorubas and Igbos), Ghana (Ewes and Gas) and Sierra Leone (Mendes) dominated the ranks of NCOs and the Africanized officer corps of the armies of these states. In Ghana, for example, 92 percent of officers were from the coastal areas while 62 percent of the ranks were from the north.[26] A similar pattern of northern ranks commanded by southern officers unfolded in Nigeria and Sierra Leone. Thus, although West African armies were "bequeathed a 'national' personality as a result of the policy of territorialization of the RWAFF," these armies were anything but national in their composition and loyalties.[27]

France, unlike Britain, was far less reticent about enlisting Africans to fight in its numerous European wars. The French believed African soldiers posed less danger abroad than in their home territories. Imperial France recruited West Africans to fight wars in Europe, the Caribbean, Mexico, Indochina, and Algeria. Senegalese troops saw extensive action in the Napoleonic and Crimean wars, fifteen thousand African troops fought in the French war in Indochina and over thirty thousand were combatants in the Algerian war.[28] Roughly 175,000 African soldiers were recruited for World War I, many of whom served in Europe in combat and support roles.[29] Blaise Diagne, who at the time represented the four communes of Senegal in the French National Assembly and had been granted the title of "Commissioner of the Republic in West Africa," spearheaded the French recruitment drive in West Africa during World War I.

French West Africa was conquered by the *tirailleurs senegalais* (Senegalese Rifles).[30] As early as the 1850s, Louis Faidherbe (Governor of Senegal from 1854 to 1861 and from 1863 to 1865) began a process of French expansion into the African interior with the ultimate goal of subjugating the Islamic states of the Western Sudan (West Africa). With this objective in mind, Faidherbe reorganized the *tirailleurs senegalais* (first founded in 1829) into a battalion of four companies. Two more companies were added in 1860, bringing the total to six. This battalion was reduced from seven (another company was added after 1867) to five companies in 1873.[31] Altogether, there were 17,000 African troops serving imperial France at the start of the last decade of the nineteenth century.[32]

Recruitment into the *tirailleurs senagalais* was based on conscription. Voluntary enlistment was discarded after it became apparent that many locals would not enlist. A decree in 1912 stipulated that conscription would affect all males between the ages of twenty and twenty-eight. Exempted from conscription were Africans domiciled in Senegal's *quatre communes* (Dakar, Goree, Saint Louis, Rufisque) who also enjoyed electoral rights; a 1916 decree, however, required residents of these four communes to perform military service in separate units of the French *bataillon d'infanterie coloniale de l'A.O.F.*[33] Chiefs were instructed to furnish recruits and most of them sent former slaves, outcasts, and malingerers. The majority of the recruits were from Senegal, Ivory Coast, Burkina Faso, Sudan, Chad, and Guinea. Control over these forces was highly centralized in Dakar (capital of the French West African federation) and Brazzaville (capital of the federation of French Equatorial Africa), with sub-commands, in the case of West Africa, in Saint Louis, Bamako and Niamey. Headquartered in Saint Louis, the First Brigade was in charge of Senegal and Mauritania. The Second Brigade was responsible for Mali, Ivory Coast, and Guinea while the Third Brigade took care of Niger, Dahomey (now Benin), and Togo.

Although these units were identified with specific territories, their deployment was not determined by considerations of ethnic or national origin. As a general rule, soldiers were not assigned to their areas of origin but to territories with which they had the least familiarity. This, in addition to the role of the *gendamerie*, isolated French colonial armed forces from local communities. With the creation of the *gendamerie* to handle internal security problems, the armed forces were used only in extreme cases of "pacification."

The status of Africans in French colonial armies was determined by decrees passed in 1926, 1928, and 1930. Based on these edicts, no African could attain any rank above captain and African captains were to be appointed only under very special circumstances. African officers were never allowed to command whites or administrative units. The French, nonetheless, did more than the British to reward service in their armed forces. A 1917 decree provided a monthly allowance of 120 Francs to the families, widows and orphans of *tirailleurs* killed in action.[34] Loyalty to France, as demonstrated by service in the army and police, determined the appointment of Chiefs, with many ex-service men appointed to such positions. Jobs were reserved for veterans, the vote was extended to them as well as to their widows and men on active service, and they were also in some cases exempted from poll taxes. By 1954, one-fifth of job openings in local French colonial administrations were reserved for ex-service men and over half of the electorate in Benin (formerly Dahomey) in 1948 were veterans and soldiers.[35] The dependence of French colonies on France for veteran pensions and disability benefits, combined with the central role played by the military in colonial administration (especially in the person of the *commandante de cercle*), underscored the close identification of military and imperial power.

Events in Indochina (especially the French defeat at Dien Bien Phu) and the Algerian war of independence hastened the pace of decolonization in French West Africa. In the panic to avoid another Algeria, the French are said to have rapidly decolonized "at such a rate that they imposed independence on Houphouet-Boigny."[36] But Ivory Coast had no army to call its own at independence and had to create one a year later. De Gaulle's Community of African states (including Madagascar) was supposed to provide security for former French African colonies but with the disintegration of this scheme, the need for territorial armies was met by absorbing repatriated soldiers from French metropolitan and colonial armies into new territorial units. Africanization of the officer corps of these new regiments was aided by the post—World War II establishment of the *L'Ecole General Leclerc* in Chad to train officers.

The task of demobilizing the large armies raised by the French was daunting for many Francophone West African states. France extended the option of remaining in the French army, or serving in newly constituted territorial armies, to its African soldiers. About 283,000 men in all opted to return to their home territories and were "deposited . . . on small and struggling economies, and on new tiny armies;" Burkina Faso alone had to absorb 150,000 French army veterans.[37] Sylvanus Olympio of Togo saw these returnees as "mercenaries who were killing our Algerian friends when we were fighting for independence."[38] Olympio's refusal to absorb these "mercenaries" or repatriated soldiers into the new Togolese army cost him his job and his life.

In most cases, the transfer of troops was linked to the signing of defense agreements between France and its former colonies in Africa. Twelve African states (including five—Senegal, Ivory Coast, Benin, Niger, and Togo—in West Africa) signed bilateral and multilateral defense agreements with France during 1960–1961. Mali and Burkina Faso refused to sign any military agreement with France, with the latter demanding that the former colonial power dismantle its bases in Burkina Faso.[39] As part of these agreements, African officers who had served in the French army were appointed chiefs of staff or commanders in chief of the new armies. Men like General Christophe Soglo of Benin (who joined the French army at age twenty-one and fought in World War II and Indochina), Colonel Jean-Bedel Bokassa of the Central African Republic (who spent twenty-three years in the French army) and Colonel Etienne (now Gnassingbe) Eyadema of Togo (who joined the French army at sixteen and fought in Indochina and Algeria) are examples of former African soldiers in the French army who later commanded their own territorial armies before seizing power through coups.[40]

In general, the organization of French colonial forces was marked by: the absence of any clear-cut distinction between African forces and metropolitan armies; a centralized command structure; minimal territorialization; extensive involvement of the military in colonial administration; deployment of forces outside the subregion; preference for rural recruits from "martial tribes" and; recruitment through conscription. Given the centralized and integrated structure of French colonial armies, and the conflicting loyalties of its personnel, it is not surprising that African soldiers turned out, as the French had once feared, to be more dangerous in their home territories than abroad.

Subjugating Africans turned out to be a far more difficult undertaking for the Portuguese than for the British or French. The longer duration of conquest and pacification (1875–1924) mirrored Portugal's relative military and economic weakness. Guinea Bissau, where Portuguese imperial designs provoked stiff resistance from the Papel and Balanta, was not pacified until World War I. Few white regular troops, mostly *degregados* (convicts) required to perform service as punishment for their crime, served in the pacification campaigns of the Portuguese. African troops, such as those supplied by the Senegalese warlord Abdul N'jai, comprised the bulk of the rank and file of the Portuguese colonial army in Africa. Portuguese military officers dominated local colonial hierarchies, which provided avenues for professional advancement.

The Portuguese, like the French and British, exploited local rivalries in their recruitment policies. The focus of recruitment efforts was on groups whose contacts with "modernity" were comparatively recent. The Ngoni of northern Mozambique and the Fula of Guinea-Bissau were among those targeted for recruitment into Portuguese colonial armies. The Portuguese also employed the services of Boer irregulars in Angola who were allowed (as were Africans in the colonial army) to raid cattle and pillage whole communities. Describing a typical Portuguese pacification raid, Carlos Wiese wrote,

> In these bloody raids whole regions are devastated just as if a violent hurricane had passed over them . . . the men are killed or sold; all that cannot be eaten or taken away is destroyed and the villages are burnt. The women and children who escape death are exchanged with the Arabs for powder or trade goods, or go into productive slavery to cultivate the fields of the conqueror.[41]

At the height of its colonial wars against independence in Africa, Portugal had 150,000 troops in Angola, 40,000–60,000 in Mozambique and 30,000 in Guinea-Bissau.[42] Sixty percent of these troops were Africans.[43] As post-service rewards, the Portuguese provided loan subsidies and free plots of land (10–34 hectares) to those who enlisted in the counterinsurgency. For the insurgents, the process of anticolonial people's war led to the political mobilization of the countryside in Guinea Bissau and Mozambique but not in Angola where the base of support for the nationalist liberation movements was restricted to urban areas, especially Luanda.

To conclude this review of colonial military historiography in West Africa, the following points merit emphasis. First, colonial armies were by their very nature mercenary units that lacked legitimacy. Established to protect imperial interests, the mercenary character of colonial armies partly explains their historical estrangement from subjugated African societies. Second, colonial recruitment policies favored certain ethnic groups and classes (rural drifters, urban lumpens). This was to later create tensions and divisions within armies after independence. Third, colonial rule was itself based on the preeminence of force in subjugating Africans. In the words of a French colonial agent, "among the Malinke or at least among those I visited, any other sentiment other than respect for force is unknown; we are respected, we are considered as masters because we are strong and we have proved it."[44] The brutal manner in which this force was dispensed had a lasting impact on state—society relations and on the conduct of military personnel in Africa.

Specifically, the scorched earth brutality of colonial armies established a precedent and set the tone for armed subaltern violence. Consider, for example, Patrick Manning's description of how the French suppressed a peasant revolt in the Ivory Coast in 1910:

> The revolt was put down with pitiless severity. The government troops burned villages, executed prisoners, and displayed the heads of rebels on pikes at railway stations and in the villages. Thereafter tax payments were regular, and the villages provided the number of laborers demanded of them.[45]

Christopher Fyfe offers a similar account of a punitive expedition by the RWAFF in Sierra Leone:

> Fairtlough sent his Yoni allies to attack Bunjema; Fula Mansa was killed, but they took the town, returning triumphantly with Yayi's head, the only trophy the plundered prospectors could take home to Reading. . . . Later in the day the troops crossed over by canoe; as it was the Queen's birthday they held a ceremonial parade before burning the remaining towns.[46]

Given that arson and the wanton destruction of lives and property are staples of the militariat's repertoire of horrors, the colonial imprint on African armies cannot be overstated. Severed heads are still being displayed on pikes, not to mention penises that now adorn vehicles as war trophies.

Post-Colonial West African Armies

With the possible exception of few countries where independence was achieved through liberation struggle, armies in Africa have failed to cultivate a positive image and are mostly loathed by their publics. Speaking of his native Ghana, Colonel A.A. Afrifa acknowledged this negative public image of his country's soldiers:

> . . . people normally underrate the intelligence of the soldier. This has a long tradition. The British did not at first attract the most able of our men. To our people, therefore, it seemed that only the failures in our society joined the army.[47]

This sentiment is echoed by, among others, Ruth First:

> In countries as far afield as Nigeria and the Sudan, army service was considered a disreputable career for the sons of the educated and respectable. . . . In West Africa, particularly, the sons of the middle class or up-and-coming ranks of urban society set their sights on the elevated professions like law and medicine, or on government service. Those who

> joined the army, to rise through the ranks or, in the later period, to graduate from the military academies, tended to be the sons of minor officials, small farmers and petty traders. They were the sons of families in the rural areas and small towns, . . . sons of parents who could not afford to educate them.[48]

Civil–military relations and recruitment practices established during the colonial era carried over into the independence period. Hausas and other northern groups continue to dominate the ranks and, since 1966, the officer corps of the Nigerian army. In Sierra Leone, Africanization of the officer corps after independence created a southern, Mende-dominated army under Albert Margai (1965–1967) and a northern-dominated army under Siaka Stevens (1968–1985) and Joseph Momoh (1985–1992). A similar southern–northern divide has fractured armies in Benin, Togo, and Ghana. Eyadema's seizure of power in Togo and the 1967 coup in Benin respectively resulted in the displacement of senior Ewe and Fon officers from the Togolese and Beninois army. Sergeant Doe of Liberia also relied almost exclusively on ethnic Krahns for his protection. In most instances, the ethnic selectivity of army recruitment and the preference for peasants and rural lumpens continued into the postcolonial era.

One major change that came with independence was the emergence of the army as contending locus of political power. Military officers who were not clientelized by political incumbents often looked upon their political bosses with disdain and envy. Many African leaders continue to bend over backwards to accommodate the demands of not only officers but, where possible, the rank and file of their armies. Simon Baynham notes, for example, that senior military officers in Zambia and Kenya were the beneficiaries of land grants allocated by the state for commercial farming.[49] The problem with such "donatives," however, is that the more often they "are offered, the less effective each becomes in purchasing support; while, at the same time, it also becomes more necessary to offer them and the cumulative consequences become more unbearable for everyone."[50]

At latest count, there have been at least 80 successful coups, 108 failed coup attempts and 139 reported coup plots in sub-Saharan Africa since independence.[51] Almost half of the successful and failed coups have occured in West Africa. Among West African states, Nigeria, Benin, and Burkina Faso have recorded the most successful coups, with six each, followed closely by Ghana and Sierra Leone, with five each. In terms of the duration of military governments in office, Nigeria, Togo, Burkina Faso, Ghana, and Benin are ahead of the rest of the subregion. Where military disengagement from politics assumed the form of self-succession by military dictators (as in Liberia, Ghana, Togo, Burkina Faso, and Gambia), the reconstituted governments retained most of their military characteristics.

Eight of the eighteen sub-Saharan African states that have not experienced successful military takeovers are in Southern Africa (Angola, Botswana, Malawi, Mozambique, Namibia, South Africa, Swaziland, Zimbabwe), six are in East Africa (Djibouti, Eritrea, Kenya, Mauritius, Tanzania, Zambia), two are Central African nations (Gabon, Cameroon) and another two are in West Africa (Senegal, Cape Verde). No former British colony in West Africa has been able to avoid the coup virus, in contrast to East and Southern Africa where only two (Uganda and Lesotho) of the nine former British colonies have come under military dictatorships.

The only Francophone West African state (Senegal) to steer clear of military rule has had the luxury of neo-imperial protection. Existing defense agreements between France and Senegal have, in conjunction with the presence of French troops in Dakar, served to deter the army from staging coups. There are currently 8,650 French troops deployed in a select group of African states and, according to one estimate, the French army intervened thirty times in Africa between 1963 and 1993.[52] External security guarantees of the type enjoyed by Senegal are, however, rare and mostly limited to France's former prized possessions. Britain has no comparable military presence in Africa, although it intervened to suppress the East African Mutinies of 1964, restore the government of Gambia's Dauda Jawara in 1981 and prevent the government of Sierra Leone from falling into the hands of rebels and renegade soldiers in 2000. In the 1990s, the Economic Community of West Africa Monitoring Group (ECOMOG) had an easier time reversing a coup in Sierra Leone than restoring peace. Whether regional security arrangements can stem the tide of coups, especially those carried out against democratically elected governments, remains to be seen. Already, there are signs that Nigeria, whose troops often comprise the bulk of ECOMOG's forces, has grown weary of its role as a "shoestring" hegemon in the subregion.[53]

Chronology of Subaltern Coups

Any chronology of successful coups by armed subalterns in West Africa has to start with Togo where a group of veterans of the French army mutinied and overthrew the government of Sylvanus Olympio in 1963. Led by Emmanuel Bodjolle, a former Master Sergeant in the French army, the proximate cause of this mutiny-coup was the refusal of Olympio's government to absorb 626 ex-servicemen from the French army into the new Togolese army.

The army installed a civilian government led by Nicholas Grunitzky, a political opponent of Olympio, and Bodjolle promoted himself to the rank of colonel and commander of the Togolese army. Etienne Eyadema, another former sergeant in the French army, later wrested control of the army from Bodjolle and made himself colonel and commander of the Togolese army before eventually removing Grunitzky from power in 1967.

Following the events in Togo, the next successful coup by the militariat was in Benin, where junior officers from the north seized power from the Fon-dominated government of Christophe Soglo in 1967. The leaders of this coup were mostly captains, lieutenants and privates and one of the first actions they took after seizing power was to place all senior officers under house arrest. A Military Revolutionary Committee (CMR) consisting of three captains, eight lieutenants and three noncommissioned officers, was established to rule the country. The coup, however, was unpopular and despite attempts to purge the army of its southern Abomey clique, the Beninois army command remained "top-heavy with southerners" who resented the "meteoric rise" of upstart northern officers.[54]

Less than six months after the coup in Benin, noncommissioned officers in the Sierra Leone army captured state power from their senior military officers in 1968. Masterminded by northern ranks of the Sierra Leone army, this intervention targeted senior officers who had been ruling the country for almost a year. The coup leaders included two Sergeant Majors and four NCOs and Privates. Since the coup ousted a military government led by senior officers, one of the first actions taken by the coup leaders was to round-up and detain all senior military and police officers. In all, about ninety officers were stripped naked, beaten and detained by rebellious soldiers who also established an Anti Corruption Revolutionary Movement (ACRM) junta as a prelude to handing over power to the party that had been elected to office in the previous year.[55]

Mali also experienced a military takeover of its government by junior officers in November 1968. This coup overthrew the government of Modibo Keita and was led by a lieutenant, Moussa Traore, who pledged to end corruption, repression and statist economic policies. Traore had no intention of handing over power to an elected civilian government and instead established his own party, *Union democratique et populaire du Mali* (UDPM), which ruled Mali for two decades before it was overthrown in a coup d'etat in 1991. Traore's civilianization of his dictatorship began a trend that saw other military leaders in the subregion contesting elections and remaining in power.

The "First Coming" of Rawlings in Ghana (June 1979) heralded a dramatic shift in the objectives of subaltern coups. Inspired by Rawlings, armed subalterns in West Africa increasingly began to fancy themselves as leadership material. But what separated the Rawlings coup from prior and subsequent interventions by the militariat was the strong desire to right perceived wrongs and social injustices. Released from jail to lead the coup, Rawlings was dubbed "Junior Jesus" by his supporters and admirers. His Armed Forces Revolutionary Council (AFRC) embarked on a house-cleaning exercise designed to eradicate "corruption once and for all." The junta established revolutionary tribunals to prosecute military officers accused of corruption, and eight officers, including three former military heads of state, were summarily executed. Both the summary execution of senior officers and the relentless, albeit for the most part symbolic, war waged against corruption by the AFRC junta represented a significant change in the objectives, scope, and ramifications of subaltern military coups.

Less than a year after the Rawlings coup, the militariat struck in Liberia. At first a Rawlings wannabe, Liberia's Master Sergeant Samuel Doe followed the Rawlings script by summarily executing prominent leaders of the ousted True Whig Party (TWP) government of William Tolbert. Unlike Rawlings in 1979, however, Sergeant Doe had no intention of relinquishing power. After a turbulent nine-year stint at the helm, during which he eliminated most of the men with whom he staged the 1980 coup, Doe was himself brutally dismembered by an opposing warlord but not before destroying the Liberian state. Compared to previous dictatorships of the militariat in West Africa, Doe's regime in Liberia remains unrivaled in its protracted brutality and bestial inhumanity.

Two years after handing over power to the popularly elected government of Hilla Limann, Rawlings staged a comeback in 1981. Forced to retire from the army by the Limann government and alienated by what was shaping up as a corrupt, rudderless civilian government, Rawlings decided to oust the very government he had transferred power to in 1979. This time around, Rawlings had no intention of relinquishing power, calling instead for a holy, permanent war against corruption. He announced that he was "prepared . . . to face a firing squad if what I try to do for the second time in my life does not meet the approval of Ghanaians."[56] While Limann was spared the fate of General Fred Akuffo, the executed general who was in power at the time of the 1979 coup, gross human rights abuses nonetheless marked the early years of the People's National Defense Committee (PNDC) junta. Rawlings also softened his populist rhetoric to accommodate the International Monetary Fund and, confronted by pressures to democratize the political system, chose to civilianize his leadership by contesting elections in 1992. If the 1979 coup marked a turning point in political interventions by the militariat in West Africa, the "Second Coming" of Rawlings was the first successful coup by the militariat against a democratically elected government. Coups by the militariat against democratically elected governments were later repeated in The Gambia (1994) and Sierra Leone (1997).

Dubbed the "Robin Hood of the Sahel," Thomas Sankara was the most visionary leader of the militariat to emerge in Africa. He managed to capture the imagination and admiration not only of youths and subalterns in Burkina Faso but throughout the African continent. A dashing and charismatic figure, Sankara's eminent status in the pantheon of revolutionary leaders in independent Africa may have been assured by his untimely death at the hands of assassins. Despite his petty bourgeois background, Sankara was far more ideological in his political outlook than any other leader of the militariat. His abiding sense of mission, clarity of purpose, and sincerity of efforts to empower and uplift his country's peasants stand out as shining examples of an alternative possibility for the militariat.

Like most coups by the militariat, the 1992 coup in Sierra Leone was precipitated by acute social unrest. Marginalized elements opposed to the one-party dictatorship of the All People's Congress (APC) took up arms against the government in 1991. This insurgency, led by a group calling itself the Revolutionary United Front (RUF), severely weakened the APC government, whose response to the rebellion was to arm a demoralized army and increase recruitment into the army. After two decades of being disarmed, especially under Siaka Stevens (1968–1985), the militariat suddenly found itself in possession of combat weapons. The arms allotted for counterinsurgency were stockpiled and later used to topple the APC government in what is to date the most popular coup in Sierra Leone's history.

Like Sierra Leone, Gambia before the 1994 coup was ruled by an oligarchy that had been in power for too long. The first serious challenge to the dominance of the People's Progressive Party (PPP) came in July 1981 when a group of civilian radicals, led by Kukoi Samba Sanyang and Koro Sallah, attempted to overthrow the government. Although Jawara, with the help of Britain and Senegal, was able to foil the so-called Taxi Drivers Coup and reestablish his authority, he failed to tackle the gnawing problems of corruption, cronyism, endemic poverty, and mounting public discontent. Rather than view the failed coup of 1981 as a wake-up call to reform the political system and restore probity to public institutions, Jawara continued to surround himself with sycophants and opportunists whose abuses damaged the credibility of his government. It was against this backdrop of a complacent and floundering leadership that four lieutenants in the Gambia National Army seized power in 1994. Not unlike other military leaders in the subregion, Yayah Jammeh, the leader of the 1994 coup, has since civilianized his personalist dictatorship.

The 1997 coup in Sierra Leone was, for all intents and purposes, an attempt to sequelize the NPRC dictatorship. The leaders of this usurpation had either served on the NPRC junta or were former security guards and sidekicks of prominent NPRC chieftains. Both officers and the ranks of the Sierra Leone army had made no secret of their opposition to the 1996 elections, which formally ended NPRC rule. Also opposed to these elections was the RUF, the rebel movement that fought successive governments from 1991 to 2001. That armed regulars of the Sierra Leone army joined forces with rebels to overthrow the democratically elected government underscored the degree to which the Sierra Leone army had become a rogue outfit. The violence and destruction that followed this coup is to date unprecedented in the annals of coupmaking in Africa. Prolonged domestic resistance to the coup in the form of civil disobedience and armed resistance by civil defense militias, were also without precedence in the subregion. ECOMOG managed to put a temporary end to the misery of Sierra Leoneans by routing the junta from power in February 1998. This represented the second time in West Africa (the first time was the 1981 Gambia coup) that an external military force reversed a coup with the objective of reinstating a democratically elected government.

Conclusion

In summary, the recruitment patterns and political role of armed forces in West Africa bear a striking resemblance to their colonial antecedents. Alienation from popular sectors, clientelization of military officers, ethnicization of the ranks, and the propensity for soldiers to engage in arson, pillage, and wanton destruction of life and property are partly vestiges from the colonial past. Postcolonial changes in military establishments did little to alter the perennial antagonism between armed forces and popular sectors in the sub-region. While the rhetorical populism of subaltern coups held out hope for a restructuring of civilian—military relations, most of these interventions turned out to be unmitigated disasters.

CHAPTER 4

Ghana: Mainstreaming "Junior Jesus"

On June 4, 1979, Flight Lieutenant Jerry Rawlings was sprung from his sweltering jail cell to lead a coup by the other ranks of the Ghanaian army. This coup turned out to be a pacesetter event that reverberated throughout West Africa, with many Rawlings wannabes attempting to topple predatory oligarchies. Along the way, the farcical spectacle of generals saluting corporals in Ghana degenerated into the tragedies of Liberia and Sierra Leone, where armed subalterns waged brutal criminal campaigns against innocent civilians.

Armed regulars were the driving force behind the 1979 coup that brought the Armed Forces Revolutionary Council (AFRC) to power. By contrast, the 1981 coup—otherwise known as the "Second Coming" of Rawlings—did not originate from within the militariat; rather, it was the product of the conspiratorial scheming of populist/leftist radicals, many of whom belonged to the June Fourth Movement (JFM), the People's Revolutionary League of Ghana (PRLG) and the Pan African Youth Movement (PANYMO). With the exception of a handful of militant soldiers, the members of these organizations did not belong to the military underclass but were rather petty-bourgeois elements who sought to use their organizations as springboards to power.

Despite its petty-bourgeois origins and leadership, the Provisional National Defense Council (PNDC) represented an attempt, however controversial and unsuccessful, to resurrect the revolutionary fervor and populist thrust of the AFRC interregnum. Both the AFRC and PNDC sought to cultivate the support of popular sectors and were not simply concerned with the corporate interests of the army or rank and file soldiers. To fully comprehend the emergence, character, and performance of the AFRC and PNDC, it is first necessary to provide a brief overview of military interventions in Ghana.

NLC, NRC and SMC Antecedents

Ghana had an army of 600 officers and 14,000 regulars at the time of its first successful coup in 1966.[1] The ranks consisted mainly of northerners, with officers coming from coastal areas. As a counterweight to the army, Kwame Nkrumah (first prime minister and president of Ghana) established the President's Own Guard Regiment (POGR). This regiment was assembled with help from the Soviet Union and was supposed to protect the president and keep the regular military forces at bay. First established in 1960 as the Guard Company and attached to the regular army, it was renamed POGR in 1961 and gradually detached from the army. As one of the architects of the 1966 coup explained,

> While the regular army could not get replacement for the smallest article without fighting for it, the Guard regiment had everything they required; worse still, much of the little that was obtained for the regular army was siphoned back to the Guard Regiment.[2]

It was not surprising, therefore, that the fiercest resistance to the 1966 coup came from this private security regiment.

Led by colonels, the February 1966 coup was triggered by Nkrumah's attempts to politicize the army and encroach on its privileges. One commentator blamed the 1966 coup on "a combination of fear and resentment."[3] Anxiety that the POGR would displace the army as recipient of state patronage and resentment at Nkrumah's meddling in military affairs—especially in the area of promotions, retirements, officer assignments, and troop deployment—were considered key factors behind the coup.[4] Beyond these proximate irritants were the economic and political contexts of the coup. Ghana's economy in 1966 was in the doldrums, with foreign reserves totaling a paltry 3.5 million pounds (Sterling). The economy grew by only 0.2 percent in 1965 and there were acute shortages of consumer goods throughout the country. Export prices for cocoa had plummeted, inflation and unemployment rates soared to new heights and the balance of payments deficit and debt burden of the state grew exponentially.[5] Politically, Ghana under Nkrumah was a repressive, personalist, one-party state in which all forms of political opposition were banned. Since "there were no constitutional means of getting rid of" Nkrumah, the 1966 coup was, according to one of its leaders, "necessary to save our country and our people."[6]

The National Liberation Council (NLC), which replaced the Convention People's Party (CPP) government of Nkrumah, initially consisted of seven men, three of whom (J.W.K. Harley, B.A. Yakubu, J.E.O. Nunoo) were from the police force. Another police officer, A.K. Deku, was later added to the list of council members, bringing the total to eight. The four other members—J.A. Ankrah, E.K. Kotoka, A.A. Afrifa, and A.K. Ocran—of the council were from the armed forces. Ankrah, who had been forcibly retired from the army by Nkrumah but had played no role in the planning and execution of the coup, was asked to head the new junta after Colonel Kotoka declined to do so. Although there were attempts to interpret the coup as an "Ashanti coup," only one member (Afrifa) of the NLC junta was Ahsanti. Kotoka, Harley, and Deku were Ewes; Ankrah and Nunoo were Gas; and Ocran and Yakubu were Fanti and Northerner respectively.

The NLC set out to reverse the statist course of the previous government and was quick to accept the prescriptions of the International Monetary Fund (IMF). Parliament was dissolved, the CPP and its affiliates were banned, strikes were outlawed (although this did not prevent an estimated two hundred strikes in the first year of NLC rule), and Soviet and Chinese technical advisers were expelled from the country. The junta went out of its way to win the support of civil servants by appointing some of them to replace politicians at regional and district levels. The NLC also replaced or demoted chiefs appointed by Nkrumah and reinstated previous incumbents. The junta practically joined forces with Nkrumah's civilian opponents, thereby internalizing broader political conflicts. Most of the members on the Political Committee (an advisory body to the junta), the Constitutional Commission, the Electoral Commission, and the National Advisory Council (which later replaced the Political Committee) were dominated by Nkrumah's opponents, most notably the former United Party leader Kofi Busia. Busia wrote the preface to Afrifa's autobiographical account of the 1966 coup and was declared the winner of the 1969 transfer elections organized by the NLC.

Kofi Busia continued the monetarist and anti-deflationary policies of the NLC junta. The 1971 budget banned a wide range of imports, abolished certain allowances for civil servants and army officers, and reduced expenditure on the armed forces. These policies alienated potential supporters in the civil service, judiciary, trade unions, universities, army, and among cocoa farmers and market traders. Falling cocoa prices, escalating short-term debts, and a massive (44 percent) devaluation of the Cedi worsened an already intolerable economic situation. The impact of Busia's austerity measures on the military, his discrimination against Ewe military officers or 'Akanization' of the officer corps, and the personal ambition of a group of young officers whose career progress had stalled under the NLC combined to set the stage for the 1972 coup. As Simon Baynham surmised, ". . . personal career and political considerations . . . meshed with corporate military concerns" as "the essential ingredients leading up to the 'officers amenities coup' on 13 January 1972."[7]

In his first broadcast to the nation, Colonel Ignatius Kutu Acheampong recited a litany of grievances against the Busia government. These included the dismissal of army and police officers, political interference in promotions and officer assignments, curtailment of benefits, and the lowering of morale. One of the first actions taken by the coup leaders was to arrest some senior officers, especially those who had been promoted on account of their loyalty to the Busia government. These arrests decimated an already inexperienced command structure that had been weakened by earlier waves of retirement—the retirement of Nkrumah loyalists in 1966, the semi-retirement of officers whose loyalties were considered questionable after the 1967 aborted coup, and the departure from the army of all the military officers on the NLC junta in 1969. According to one count, half of the officers holding the rank of Lieutenant Colonel and above in 1966 had left the army by 1970.[8]

With the exception of Acheampong who was a colonel, the rest of the core group of coup plotters held the rank of major. Two of these majors (K.G. Agbo, A. Selormey) were Ewes while another (K. Baah) was Brong. Acheampong, who was Ashanti,

> . . . belonged to a class of officers whose careers had suffered because they were not affiliated with the group that brought off the 1966 coup against Nkrumah. As he plaintively explained, Afrifa had been a Company Commander under him, and was now a retired Lt. General.[9]

Upon seizing power, the coup leaders established a National Redemption Council (NRC) under the chairmanship of Acheampong. In contrast to the NLC, which was "subserviently pro-west and hostile to the East,"[10] the NRC was initially anti-imperialist, reformist, and Pan-Africanist. But unlike the first coup which was followed by military disengagement, albeit three years later, the NRC showed no signs and made no commitment to withdraw from the political scene. Rather, Acheampong insisted that "the NRC will only hand over power when we are satisfied that a firm foundation has been laid both economically and socially."[11]

The statist economic policies of the NRC evoked memories of the Nkrumah years in much the same way that Busia's economic liberalism represented a carry-over from the NLC. Although the NRC was to later seek the assistance of the IMF, its initial posture vis-à-vis global financial institutions was one of defiance. The NRC revalued the Cedi, *welshed* on some of the country's debts, expanded the state sector (especially in mining, banking and insurance), lifted the ban on the Trade Union Congress (TUC), restored workers' rights, and promoted a program of self reliance. The NRC also resumed diplomatic relations with the People's Republic of China and in general pursued a more radical foreign policy than the NLC or Busia government. Economic conditions, which were favorable in the first two years of NRC rule, began to deteriorate after 1975, leading to the introduction of import controls, which were grossly mismanaged. Budget deficits were financed by printing money even as adverse economic conditions multiplied opportunities for corruption. A major development under NRC rule was the "emergence of a comprador or *Kalabule* stratum, closely connected to the regime and parastatal managers, and deriving massive rents from the exploitation of state controls and critical resource shortages."[12]

The reconstitution of the NRC into the Supreme Military Council (SMC) in 1975 relegated NRC junta members to the administrative branch of the regime. This arrangement did nothing to resolve the problem of low morale in the army or stem the tide of officers seeking appointments in parastatals and other revenue-generating agencies of the state. The 1975–1979 period became notorious for widespread *kalabule* (corruption) practices and networks that involved senior military officers, bureaucrats, and civilians. As an alternative to military disengagement and in a bid to protect senior military officers from prosecution, Acheampong organized a referendum on a proposal to share power with civilians. Known as "UNIGOV" (United Government—comprising the army, police, and politicians), this quasi-corporate proposal was conceived and promoted even as opposition to the regime mounted. It was against this background of growing public unrest that Acheampong was removed from office in a 1978 palace coup and replaced by General Fred Akuffo.

Departing from previous coups that toppled civilian governments, the 1978 palace coup was the first successful coup against a military government in Ghana. The coup leaders reconfigured the SMC into what became known as SMC II. The SMC under General Fred Akuffo devalued the Cedi by 50 percent, reduced government spending, tightened the supply of money and phased-out price controls. The combined effect of these measures plunged the country into the worst crisis period of its brief history as workers downed tools and began spending more time picketing. The spate of strikes involving workers, students, civil servants and professionals ventilated mounting popular opposition to the IMF formulated policies of SMC II. Although the regime lifted the ban on politics in December 1978 and announced a date for multiparty elections in 1979, it declined to take any action against the legion of military officers implicated in *kalabule* practices. Not only did Akuffo's SMC II refuse to investigate senior military officers for corruption and mismanagement of the economy, it sought to indemnify them from prosecution. These moves enraged an already alienated public, setting the stage for the second coup against a military government in Ghana. As Rawlings was to complain, "after seven years in office, the army was going back to barracks without any steps having been taken to punish those who had tarnished the name of the armed forces."[13]

The AFRC Coup and Interregnum

The first attempt by Flight Lt. Jerry Rawlings and fifteen airmen to overthrow Akuffo's SMC II failed. Despite this setback, Rawlings was able to transform his subsequent court martial appearances into a platform from which he lashed out against a corrupt and discredited military hierarchy that, in his words, had "made deals with the politicians to protect their class and sectional interests, leaving the corporate interests of the army and the interests of the men of the ranks unattended to."[14] Three weeks after this unsuccesful coup attempt, Rawlings was liberated from his prison cell and asked to lead the June 4, 1979 coup after Lt. Agyeman Bio, who is said to have been the original coup leader, was killed by forces loyal to the SMC II.

The reasons advanced for the June 4 coup were a rehash of the injustices articulated by Rawlings during his trial, especially the depraved condition of the average Ghanaian and the need to bring those who had plundered the country to justice. The coup leaders, especially Rawlings, presented themselves as moral crusaders whose intent was to rid Ghana of corrupt and oppressive military officers and restore "integrity, accountability and . . . honesty" to the armed forces.[15] Although sergeants, corporals, and a handful of junior officers initiated the coup, students, workers, and other popular sectors rallied in fervent support. Commenting on the domestic popularity of the June 4 coup, Naomi Chazan wrote that although the AFRC was "drawn almost exclusively from the enlisted ranks," it nonetheless "succeeded in molding the have-nots of Ghanaian society into a potent political force by capitalizing on their discontent and speaking on their behalf."[16]

The main agenda of the AFRC was punitive rather than transformative. In the view of Dennis Herbstein, the June 4 coup was not a revolution "but a law enforcement operation within existing structures."[17] Disruptive but not transformative, the AFRC was preoccupied with personalities rather than the system of corruption. According to Rawlings at the time, "it is not a question of systems but of personalities"—what was important was "to find the right people in the right places to do the correct thing."[18] This emphasis on personalities may reflect the fact that the AFRC had only four months to clean house, a time frame that did not allow for systemic overhauls.

The original ten-member Armed Forces Revolutionary Council (AFRC) included a Flight Lt. (Rawlings), one Captain (Djan), two Majors (Opoku and Gbedemah), a Lt. Commander (Barnor), one Sergeant (Adjei), a Lance Corporal (Gatsiko), Warrant Officer (Obeng), and a Private (Addo). The junta's membership, which was later expanded to fourteen, was dominated by members of the Young Officers' Club, also known as the Free Africa Movement. Captain Boakye Djan, a university graduate and self-professed socialist, had formed this club in the 1970s with the aim of using it as a catalyst for revolution in Ghana.[19] The AFRC retained most of the civilian commissioners inherited from SMC II, including Dr. J.L.S. Abbey (Economic planning), Gloria Nikoi (Foreign Affairs), Kwame Afreh (Information), Justice Kingsley Nyinah (Electoral Commissioner), and A. Amissah (Attorney General).

The internal popularity of the AFRC coup contrasted sharply with the external hostility that greeted Rawlings and his men.[20] The leaders of Nigeria, Ivory Coast, Togo, and Burkina Faso were incensed by events in Ghana, with Nigeria expressing its displeasure by tightening conditions for supplying oil to Ghana. What rankled external actors were the executions and the fact that the coup took place a few weeks before the date scheduled for transfer elections. Akuffo, after all, was seen as poised to hand over power, hence there was no need for a coup in the eyes of some critics. But what this reasoning failed to grasp is the primacy of justice, however crudely conceived and brutally pursued, over democracy in the politics of armed subalterns. As a punitive intervention designed to bring those who had ruined Ghana to justice, the June 4 coup was about eradicating corruption rather than restoring democracy. As far as the AFRC was concerned, democracy could only have a chance and prove meaningful to the masses if it is preceded and accompanied by sustained efforts to curb official corruption.

Corruption

In its fervor to cleanse Ghana of corruption, the AFRC first targeted senior military officers, eight of whom (including three former heads of state and the former naval and air force commanders) were executed for "crimes against the state."[21] Many other senior officers who happened to be unpopular with the ranks were humiliated, severely beaten, and detained. Scores of senior civil servants were dismissed from their positions and many had their assets frozen or seized. Private businessmen, among them Lebanese and Indians, were also subjected to investigation, dispossession and, in some cases, deportation. Revolutionary tribunals handed down long prison sentences in cases of individuals summarily adjudged to be guilty of corruption and crimes against the state. The main Accra market was demolished in the belief that this would loosen "the grip held by the market women on trade for all these years" and end hoarding "once and for all."[22] In yet another symbolic act, soldiers razed the Kumasi money market to the ground so as to stop black-market currency dealings.[23]

The AFRC was extremely ruthless and arbitrary in the discharge of its self-appointed task of "house-cleaning" Ghana. According to section 3 of the decree establishing the People's Revolutionary Courts, "any person found guilty . . . of any of the offenses specified shall be liable on conviction to suffer death by firing squad or to imprisonment with penal labor for a term of not less than three years and the confiscation to the state of any assets found by the court to have been illegally acquired by such a person."[24] Executions sanctioned by these parallel courts were, in the words of Rawlings, necessary to "satisfy the wishes of both military and civilians" and to "serve as a warning to any future government."[25] In a more expansive mood, Rawlings explained his position on executions as follows:

> I don't believe in taking a man's life because I can't make one, but if shedding blood is the only thing that will make the Ghanaian change his greedy character, then I will do it. You smugglers, embezzlers, profiteers and wicked people should know that by taking bread out of the mouth of the ordinary man, you are killing him. . . . We will be totally ruthless with the exploiters.[26]

But even if one were to accept the argument that executions were necessary to deter others from "chopping Ghana small," the AFRC executions and the *Kangaroo* trials that preceded them represented a travesty of justice. Elizabeth Ohene, writing in the *Daily Graphic*, warned the AFRC against resorting to the death penalty as a weapon in the fight against corruption:

> It is all very well cleaning up your house for as long as there is a house left at the end of the exercise. If everybody who has used his position to amass wealth in Ghana is to be killed we shall have a veritable blood bath in this

> country, and mighty few will be left . . . the executions will not solve the problems that we have, the anger that we all feel will not even be expurgated after the killings because we shall still be hungry after they have all been shot.[27]

Indeed, the average Ghanaian was in no better shape at the end than at the beginning of the AFRC interregnum. People were still hungry after the generals were shot, their properties confiscated and their associates "house-cleaned."

In addition to the executions, the revolutionary courts also imposed long prison sentences on individuals judged to be guilty of corruption. Leading members of the NRC and SMC were among those given long prison sentences. The assets of former senior army and police officers, as well as those of their wives and children, were either frozen or seized.[28] An Assets Committee was set up to supervise and coordinate the disposal of six categories of confiscated assets: motorized, housing, finance and banking, land, business, and miscellaneous property.[29] All senior officers, executive chairmen, managing directors, managers, accountants, secretaries of boards and corporations, judges, and procurement officers of state corporations and enterprises, were required to declare their assets. Individuals instructed to declare their assets were limited to withdrawals of no more than 500 cedis per month from their private bank accounts.[30] In the case of market women, many had their stores routinely emptied in what one observer described as a campaign of "looting populism."[31]

Commissions of inquiry were instituted to probe corporations, financial institutions, the civil service, private commercial houses, motor firms, universities, and schools. Most of these probes continued after the AFRC relinquished power but the Limann government never acted upon their reports. The failure to follow up on these probes, coupled with attempts by Limann to rescind some of the sentences of the revolutionary courts, created a pretext for Rawlings and his supporters to stage a political comeback on New Year's eve of 1981.

Human Rights

The AFRC coup remains the bloodiest and most disruptive in Ghana's post-independence history. Hundreds died during the first few weeks of the coup and there was massive looting by soldiers. For the first time in Ghana, three former heads of state (all military men) were executed. There were also executions of individuals charged with embezzlement of public funds, hoarding, smuggling, profiteering, looting, and other "anti-state" crimes. Scores of market women were publicly flogged, stripped naked, and molested for alleged price gouging and hoarding of commodities. Senior officers had their heads shaven with broken bottles and forced to carry placards denouncing themselves. This vengeful usurpation by the ranks, and the need to contain its anarchic potential, became a major preoccupation of the AFRC leadership during its brief tenure in office.

The executions of eight military officers stand out among the prominent atrocities of this period. Prior to these executions, a list of 207 senior officers earmarked for execution had been compiled and reportedly circulated by the ranks. While Rawlings and his second-in-command, Captain Boakye Djan, preferred long sentences for corrupt officials, the ranks would settle for nothing less than the execution of their corrupt officers. Even before the military courts began sitting, soldiers had already mounted execution stakes at the Teshie Firing Range (near Accra) in anticipation of executions.[32] At issue was not whether there would be executions but how many would be executed. Joining the ranks in calling for the execution of corrupt officials were students and workers who organized demonstrations in which they carried placards that read: "Finish Them All," "Let The Blood Flow," and "For Heaven's Sake, Kill."[33] Thus, although Rawlings was inclined to delay the execution of Afrifa, Akuffo, and four other senior officers, he was in the end "compelled" to sign their death warrants "knowing that if he failed to do so he would lose control of the situation and then things would really fall apart."[34]

The executions were "in grim contrast to the 18 June election," with the two events representing "both sides of Ghanaian fortune—one a dark bloody scene of tribunals and summary justice, the other the hope of peaceful change through democratic elections."[35] External condemnation of the AFRC executions forced Rawlings to respond by pointing out that his critics were oblivious to the suffering of the average Ghanaian:

> The unfortunate thing is that they are living outside Ghana. They are not in a position to know how a worker or soldier feels, and he has held his resentment and bitterness for so long. I mean, if only they would realize what an uprising is.[36]

External pressures, however, were critical in putting a stop to more executions. The International Commission of Jurists, as did many donor and neigboring countries, appealed to the AFRC to uphold the rule of law. Locally, the Bar Association joined political parties in calling for an end to secret trials, summary executions, and the flogging of citizens for unproven allegations of hoarding and profiteering.[37]

Although senior military officers bore the brunt of AFRC atrocities and human rights abuses, market women were also frequent targets of abuses and all sorts of indignities. The myth that market women are wealthy and powerful was based on the assumption that most of them were involved in hoarding and smuggling activities. Yet most market women are poor and the few "Commodity Queens" that are relatively affluent were seldom the victims of attacks by the government. Scapegoating market women for the country's economic problems was, however, a common feature of the AFRC dictatorship. Plundering the stalls and wares of market women in a bid to curb hoarding and profiteering was, however, counterproductive. Makola market, for example, was bulldozed but only "after . . . soldiers had plundered money and goods from the stalls."[38] In Claire Robertson's gendered misreading of this episode,

> . . . the attack on Makola can be seen as an effort by the men to destroy one of the last realms of influence left to women. . . . But this war on women has resulted in a pyrrhic victory for men: an even worse economy, that all the beatings, killings, and bulldozings in the world will not improve. Nothing has replaced the valuable functions of traders for Ghana. . . . Far from being exploiters, most traders are victims, who, moreover bear the blame for an exploitative system not of their own making. They are exploited by the big firms . . . they are exploited by the socio-economic system. The plan to replace the Makola market with a car park was a fitting symbol for the triumph of privilege.[39]

Far from being an attack on women, the demolition of Makola market by AFRC operatives represented a symbolic, albeit ineffective, assault on some of the sources of ill-gotten wealth.

Democratization

The AFRC leadership maintained from the outset that it had no intention of holding on to power. The junta did not outlaw political parties or ban political activities. Rather, the limited objective of the junta was to "complete its house-cleaning exercise within the armed forces before the next civilian government takes office."[40] Thus, although elections were held on May 18, six weeks after the AFRC coup, the date for handing over power to a civilian government was postponed from July 1 to October 1 so as to allow the junta more time to clean house. In opting to go ahead with multi-party elections, the AFRC was

> . . . caught between two opposed forces, one being the other ranks whose power was at first concretized in the AFRC, and the other being the entrenched forces in Ghanaian society, those political and spiritual leaders whose representativity can often be . . . questioned.[41]

The decision to proceed with the elections was in the end "crucial in consolidating civilian support for . . . a brief period of house-cleaning under the aegis of the AFRC."[42]

The 1979 presidential and parliamentary elections were the country's first in ten years. They featured the same institutional contestants, albeit under different names, as in previous elections. No party was allowed to adopt the name of any party that had participated in previous Ghanaian elections. Thus, even though the People's National Party (PNP) and Popular Front Party (PFP) leaders spent much of their time respectively touting the legacies of Nkrumah's CPP and Busia's PP, they were not supposed to portray themselves as heirs to these competing traditions. Individuals found guilty of corruption by commissions of inquiry during the period 1966–1979 were banned from contesting the elections or holding any official party post. In all, seven parties were registered for the 1979 elections. These were the People's National Party (PNP), the Popular Front party (PFP), the United National Convention (UNC), the Action Congress Party (ACP), the Third Force Party (TFP), the Social Democratic Front (SDF), and the Vanguard Party (VP). The Vanguard Party of Blay Miezah, a wealthy businessman, withdrew from the race after its leader was jailed on charges of corruption.

Of the six parties that contested the elections, four were serious contenders while the other two were also-rans. The PNP claimed mantleship of Nkrumah's CPP legacy while the PFP saw itself as logical successor to Busia's PP. The PNP had a broader political base than the PFP, which was widely viewed as an Ashanti party. With the selection of Hilla Limann, a northerner, as its presidential candidate, the PNP hoped to reverse the gains made by the PP in the north during the 1969 elections. By reaching out to northerners, "the CPP of the south in 1951–1954—the party of mobility opportunities for the young common men—finally arrived in the north in 1979" in the guise of the PNP.[43]

The PFP, as aforementioned, grew out of an attempt to revive Busia's PP. Led by Victor Owusu, the party could not rid itself of its Ashanti stigma. Although many PFP leaders had been prominent in the Popular Movement for Freedom and Justice (PMFJ), they balked at the prospect of forming a more inclusive party based on the PMFJ alliance, which had earlier brought together leadership elements of the former PP, the National Alliance of Liberals (NAL), and Afrifa's NLC. The failure to form a political party based on the PMFJ alliance led to the formation of an Ashanti-based PFP and a Ga and Ewe-based UNC. Led by William Ofori-Atta, the UNC was widely believed to have taken more votes away from the PFP than from the PNP. The ACP sought to ride the reputation of its leader, Colonel Frank Bernasko, to power but the party's support base was limited to urban Fantis. The TFP of Dr. John Bilson was a personalist outfit that splintered from the PFP while the SDP, whose presidential candidate was Dr. Ibrahim Mahama, was supposed to be a worker's party.

Generally, "the pattern of voting in the 1979 elections . . . was arguably determined . . . by communal identifications rather than broad ideological differences."[44] Results from the parliamentary elections gave Limann's PNP a razor-thin majority (71 of 140 seats) in the National Assembly. In the first round of balloting for president, Limann received 630,034 votes (35.51 percent), compared to 520,249 for Owusu (29.66 percent), 309,756 for Ofori-Atta (17.46 percent), and 167,742 for Bernasko (9.45 percent).[45] Limann and the PNP did well in every part of the country except in the Ashanti and Brong Ahafo regions. Owusu and the PFP's best showing was in Ashanti and Brong Ahafo while the UNC and ACP garnered most of their support from the Eastern and Central region respectively. In the presidential run-off, Limann bested Owusu with 61.98 percent of the popular vote.[46] A Sissala from the north, Limann was the first northerner to become head of state in Ghana.

After the elections, Rawlings reiterated the AFRC's commitment "to cooperate with all parties and to be loyal to any popularly elected government."[47] But even as he was preparing to transfer power to the democratically elected government of Hilla Limann, Rawlings warned that he could "see waves of revolution worse than what is happening in the country right now should the incoming administration undermine the revolutionary intelligence of the Ghanaian and take him for a ride."[48] It came as no surprise, therefore, that two years into Ghana's third republic, another coup by Rawlings ousted the Limann government.

Economic Performance

The AFRC did not pretend to have the solutions to Ghana's economic problems, nor did it have the time to devise any credible strategy for reversing the country's economic woes. At the time the AFRC seized power, *kalabule* trading was rampant, as was administrative corruption, cocoa smuggling and hyperinflation, all of which devastated the Ghanaian economy. In the summation of Richard Jeffries,

> Acheampong and his henchmen encouraged smuggling by fairly openly engaging in it themselves. They not only condoned but actually ordered the allocation of import licences and scarce foreign exchange to girl friends and cronies intent either on making monopoly profits in the domestic black market or else on diverting already scarce imported items into neighboring territories.[49]

The average annual decline in Ghana's GDP per capita during 1970–1979 was 3 percent. The inflation rate was 116 percent in 1977, 74 percent in 1978 and 54 percent in 1979. Huge balance of payments and budget deficits (the Government's budget deficit as a percentage of revenue was 136 percent in 1977–1978) and a sharp decline in the production of major exports (cocoa, gold, diamonds and timber) contributed to Ghana's economic problems. Cocoa farmers in 1979 were paid 49 percent of what they received in 1963, a development that encouraged the smuggling of cocoa and other items to neighboring countries.[50] Richard Jeffries blames most of Ghana's economic problems at the time on the statist policies of Nkrumah and Acheampong whose

> . . . coup of January 1972 can be seen to have been in itself a major and fairly direct cause of the economic catastrophe of 1975–79 in the sense that it reversed an initiative which might well have provided a way out of the disaster-inducing logic of Nkrumahist policies.[51]

The initiative referred to by Jeffries was Busia's 1971 devaluation and efforts to liberalize the economy. Ironically, it was some of these policies that Rawlings later embraced after the "thermidorization" of his "Second Coming."

Other than instituting price controls for basic items like petrol, bread, and meat, and nationalizing certain industries, the junta did not embark on any significant economic policy that could have started the process of turning Ghana's economy around. Petrol was rationed after Nigeria's military government shortened Ghana's supply credit from ninety to thirty days and requested that existing arrears be paid in full. Students responded by denouncing Nigeria (telling its leaders to "eat its oil") for what was perceived as an attempt at sabotaging the AFRC junta.[52] Libya and Algeria came to the rescue by supplying huge quantities of oil. There were also a few nationalizations, the most notable being the takeover of the Tata Brewery by the government after the company failed to pay a 30 million cedi tax evasion penalty imposed by the junta. About seven companies in all were nationalized, including those belonging to Alfred Aschkar, a Lebanese businessman deported by the junta. Restrictions were also imposed on the issuance of foreign exchange permits; such approvals were suspended for holiday travel and unauthorized trips.[53]

Among the important economic decisions taken by the AFRC were the abolition of the Cocoa Marketing Board (CMB), which was replaced by a Cocoa Council, and the revocation of all cocoa buying licenses. The AFRC also announced that no landlord should evict tenants without its approval and that all tenants occupying State Housing Corporation (SHC) and Tema Development Corporation (TDC) units should stop paying rent until further notice. These changes and symbolic gestures, when combined with the increase in the producer price for cocoa, won kudos for the junta among peasants and chiefs. Taken together, however, these redistributive measures fell short of what was required to improve economic conditions in the country. As Rawlings himself remarked, "no matter the quantity of money that's going to be pumped into this country or systems devised, the success or failure of this system will depend on one thing—integrity, accountability, a certain degree of honesty."[54]

In the final analysis, the significance of the June 4 coup for Ghana is that "it constituted a prelude to a more permanent populist takeover" two years later.[55] AFRC rule had a direct bearing on the survival of the third republic under President Hilla Limman. The June 4 coup decimated the senior ranks of the Ghanaian army, weakened the authority of the remaining (mostly newly appointed) officers, radicalized junior officers and gave rise to perceptions of Ewe domination within the army.[56] Since Ewe officers have been perennial architects of coups in Ghana (Kotoka in 1969, Agbo and Selormey in 1972, Rawlings in 1979), it was not difficult to see how the AFRC coup could be perceived, rightly or wrongly, as an Ewe-inspired plot to establish hegemony in the institutions of state power. As it turned out, none of the eight senior officers executed by the junta was Ewe. Having said that, however, there is nothing to suggest that the June 4 coup was motivated by ethnic considerations rather than deep-seated social grievances.

The PNDC Coup and Dictatorship

Prolonged economic recession, unbridled corruption, and the disintegration of the army and police threatened the viability of Ghana's third republic. To make matters worse, the Limann government's attempt to reorganize the army and police created more problems than it solved. The two top-ranking officers of the armed forces, Brigadiers J. Nunoo-Mensah (chief of defense staff) and

A. Quainoo (army commander), were unceremoniously sacked. After failing to cajole Rawlings into leaving the country, Limann ordered the retirement of the former AFRC chairman from the armed forces on November 27, 1979. This forced retirement, according to President Limann, was prompted by the need to "simply . . . correct an anomalous and untenable situation in which a former Head of State was continuing to serve in a very junior position."[57]

The rustication of Rawlings from the army freed the former AFRC leader to pursue his resolve to protect the "gains of the AFRC revolution" through the June Fourth Movement—a radical amalgam of students, soldiers, and workers committed to maintaining the corrective momentum of the June 4 coup. In addition to his removal from the army, the Special Branch and Military Intelligence orchestrated a sustained disinformation campaign whose sole purpose was to discredit Rawlings and the AFRC. The final straw that broke the back of Limann's government was the attempt to undo sentences handed down by the AFRC in 1979 and revisit the issue of indemnity for AFRC members. Boakye Djan, Rawlings' number two in the AFRC, was flown in from London by the government to hold a press conference where he joined calls for a public probe of the AFRC. These developments clearly violated the pact between the AFRC and PNP, which had enshrined AFRC indemnities in the constitution. Given these developments, Rawlings in the end felt it necessary to once again move against the government in a relatively bloodless coup on New Year's Eve, 1981.

Rawlings described his "second coming" as an attempt to "stem the rapid national decline that was upon us." He went on to explain that "the 31st December action . . . was a joint officer-ranks action" that targeted "officers who feel they can simply use their rank to exploit other ranks."[58] Rawlings dismissed the Limann government as "the most disgraceful government in the history of the country," accusing it of turning "our hospitals into graveyards and our clinics into death transit camps where men, women and children die daily because of lack of drugs and basic equipment."[59]

One of the main differences between this coup and the 1979 usurpation is the fact that it was masterminded by a conspiratorial group of populists and radicals who were linked to two civilian groups with contradictory persuasions and motives—the June Fourth Movement (JFM) and the *Dzulekofe Mafia.* Radical students, workers, intellectuals, and community activists formed the JFM in July 1979. The goal of the movement was, in the words of one of its founding members, "to build a revolutionary organization capable of organizing and leading the workers to capture political power by revolutionary means and to continue the social process began on June 4 1979."[60] In the wake of his forced retirement, Rawlings used the JFM platform to attack the deviationism and corruption of the Limann government. Members of this movement played a prominent role in the December 1981 coup and were appointed to key positions in the Provisional National Defense Council (PNDC) government that was installed immediately after the coup.

In contrast to the JFM whose members were brought together by class ideology, the *Dzulekofe Mafia* was an ethnic cabal comprising prominent Ewe intellectuals, soldiers, businessmen, and cultural entrepreneurs from the Volta region of Ghana. Notable among the members of this shadow group were individuals who later held key positions in the PNDC government—Tsatsu Tsikata, Kojo Tsikata, Kofi Awoonor, Mawuse Dake, Dr. K. Agama, and Brigadier A.K. Katta. According to Zaya Yeebo, a former JFM stalwart and one-time member of Rawlings' cabinet, the *Dzulekofe Mafia* provided critical financial backing for the December 1981 coup.[61]

The original PNDC junta consisted of seven members—Rawlings, Brigadier Nunoo Mensah, Rev. Damuah, Warrant Officer Adjei Boadi, Amartey Kwei (a trade unionist and JFM member), Sgt. Aloga Akata-Pore and Chris Atim (JFM Secretary-General). Akata-Pore, Atim, Kwei, and Boadi constituted the radical bloc within the PNDC while Mensah, Damuah and Rawlings were considered relatively moderate or conservative.[62] The PNDC cabinet or Committee of PNDC Secretaries, as it was called, was also split along ideological lines. Among the "progressives" were Zaya Yeebo, Ama Ata Aidoo, Johnny Hansen, and Ato Austin while the conservative wing included Rawlings and *Dzelukofe Mafiosos.*

In contrast to the 1979 coup, there was hardly any organized resistance to the 1981 intervention. The 1981 coup also went far beyond the 1979 usurpation in redefining "the political and ideological character of militarism in Ghana."[63] The key elements of this new militarism, as outlined by Eboe Hutchful, were: the emergence of the militariat as an autonomous political force; the radicalization of the ranks; the attempt to forge alliances between the militariat and popular forces, especially workers and students; and the demands for sweeping reforms.[64] In short, the December 1981 intervention was, from the standpoint of its architects, not a coup but a revolution whose primary task was to wage a "holy war" on corruption.

The social forces behind the 1981 coup and the extensive participation of elements outside the army in its planning and execution made it less of a coup by the militariat, in comparison to the June 4 intervention. Northern soldiers, radical intellectuals, Ewe cultural entrepreneurs, and a sprinkling of workers and students were among the wide array of forces that sought to influence the coup and its outcome. Most of these elements were by no means subaltern, although many saw themselves as ideologically aligned with the oppressed, exploited, and downtrodden. The *Dzelukofe Mafia*, on the other hand, brought to the PNDC class interests and ethnic concerns that were at variance with those of the insurgent militariat and subordinate classes in general. The prodding of this informal but influential group was later credited for the exodus of radical elements from the PNDC and for the conservative reorientation of the junta after 1983.

The first two years of PNDC rule were marked by tension within the junta between leftist radicals and moderate populists. Some PNDC policies and actions, such as the attacks on elite privilege, reflected the views and policy preferences of the socialist or leftist faction of the junta. Other initiatives like the emphasis on popular empowerment and the establishment of People's Defense Committees (PDC) and Workers Defense Committees (WDC) emanated from the populist wing of the junta. But even on the issue of the role of these popular organizations, leftist radicals had serious disagreements with Rawlings and other moderate members of the junta.

The decision by the PNDC to attack privileged elements of society had a devastating impact on public institutions and the economy. Wealth, for the most part, was equated with corruption and those targeted had to prove their wealth was not illgotten. Attacks on the state bureaucracy decimated its ranks as many top bureaucrats were shown the door or thrown in jail. Within a short period,

> . . . the Rawlings government systematically undermined already weakened state agencies. In its attempt to rid the formal apparatus of corrupt elements, the PNDC divested these institutions of almost all of their skilled personnel. . . . By opening up the bureaucracy and the parastatal sector to popular participation, Rawlings and his associates not only exposed the state as an institution to a broad spectrum of demands, but they also provided some of the tools for the realization of those demands. The populist notion of the desirability of the people capturing the state and transforming it was effectively disproven and wholesale and unregulated access effectively stripped the state of any semblance of structural independence. By the beginning of 1983, the Ghanaian state had become effectively delegitimated and incapacitated.[65]

How the PNDC went about the task of fighting corruption and popularizing the exercise of political power, as well as its human rights and economic record, are taken up in the remainder of this chapter.

Corruption

After declaring a "holy war" on corruption, the PNDC took drastic measures to tackle this problem. Public Tribunals (or People's Revolutionary Courts) and Citizens Vetting Committees (CVC) were the main instruments of the PNDC's anticorruption crusade. Established in September 1982, public tribunals were supposed to be operationally unfettered "by technical rules which in the past . . . perverted the course of justice and allowed criminals to go free."[66] The tribunals handled only criminal cases but the definition of what was criminal ran the gamut from petty theft to political subversion.

The establishment of a parallel legal authority by the PNDC was denounced by the Bar Association as a "misguided attempt to supplant the machinery of the ordinary criminal courts in Ghana."[67] To register their opposition to these tribunals, members of the Bar Association resolved to boycott all of their proceedings. This, however, did not halt the proliferation of the tribunals, a development that effectively undermined the regular courts. The tribunals began to lose their appeal by the mid-1980s as they "turned their attention to petty crimes like pick-pocketing and armed robbery, while a blind eye was turned on more serious crimes by government officials."[68] Most damaging to the tribunals was the perception that they were tools of PNDC repression rather than mechanisms for fighting corruption. This perception overlooked the growing "conflicts between the PNDC and the officials of the public tribunals," especially after 1983 when the government launched its IMF-inspired Economic Recovery Program (ERP).[69] As Roger Gocking wrote,

> From being upholders of the 'revolutionary' goals of the 'Holy War', the tribunals had become obstacles on the road to the new order. Few people were willing to defend them from the charge that they had 'tended to subvert the course of justice.' . . . The memory of their faults, and the scandals in which their personnel had been involved far outweighed whatever their contribution might have been.[70]

The tribunals were later integrated into the regular court system after it became clear that they had become a political liability to the government.

The Citizens Vetting Committees (CVC) were empowered to probe cases of alleged tax evasion, the finances and assets of individuals charged with corruption and the accounts of anyone with 50,000 Cedis (roughly 16,000 U.S. dollars at the official rate of exchange in 1983) or more in their bank account. Working alongside the CVCs was the National Investigations Commission (NIC), which had the authority to freeze assets and detain individuals on suspicion of corruption. A major problem that dogged the CVCs was the contradiction between its objectives and membership. According to one early PNDC supporter and official, "the composition of the CVC did not reflect the class character necessary for its functions."[71] Membership was restricted to middle-level military officers and lawyers, some of whom were later found guilty of crimes similar to those they had been investigating. The 1984 trial of Major Kwabena Adutu, former Chairman of the CVC, for alleged fraud is a case in point. Initially effective in cases involving tax evasion, invoicing scams, currency trafficking, and bank fraud, CVCs later became discredited for some of the same reasons as the public tribunals. The power to investigate bank accounts created a disincentive to save and this contributed to the collapse of the banking system. In the end, the CVCs failed because of corruption by "leading members of the PNDC" who "were busy trying to reconcile their position with members of the old ruling class who were supposed to be investigated by the CVC."[72]

By the mid 1980s, the war on corruption had lost its steam as "embezzlement reached unprecedented levels in some key public institutions." Although "the government . . . stayed above such base practices, its inability to eliminate them in the public sector . . . cast doubt over the effectiveness of its many exhortations, and . . . weakened the people's responsiveness to the on-going revolution."[73] Rawlings, meanwhile, continued to insist that he was incorruptible. According to him, "all that I have done is to offer leadership and integrity—I'm incorruptible."[74]

Human Rights

The human rights record of the PNDC was no less appalling than the AFRC's. The main targets of human rights abuses under the PNDC were coup plotters, "subversives," market women, traders, armed robbers, and the thousands of Ghanaians forced to flee the country out of fear for their personal safety.[75] The rate of executions and murders skyrocketed under the PNDC, as did incidents of harassment and molestation of civilians by soldiers and vigilante groups. According to one account, twenty-three coup plotters and nine armed robbers were executed in 1983 by the PNDC. In the following year, another twenty-five coup plotters but no armed robbers were executed. There were no executions in 1985, but seven more coup plotters were executed in 1986 and fourteen in 1989.[76] Many alleged coup plotters were reclassified as armed robbers and shot. These executions, however, do not even begin to capture the severity of the human rights abuses in Ghana during the first half of the 1980s. In the summation of a Catholic Bishop's Communique of July 10, 1982,

> . . . inhumanities of epidemic proportions have been committed with impunity. Villagers and the marginalized of our society are terrorized and intimidated . . . Humble men, women and children have been and are being molested, maimed, killed or otherwise repressed without cause . . . The powerless of our nation have been rendered more helpless through the indiscipline and arbitrary action of people who have constituted themselves into demi-gods . . . In the face of the present moral, legal, political and social disorder, the insidious lack of economic accountability of the past pales into insignificance.[77]

Murders were as much a staple of the PNDC's violent repertoire as were executions. A case in point was the gruesome murder of three judges (Cecilia Koranteng-Addow, K.A. Agyepong, F.P. Sarkodee) and a former parastatal manager (Major Sam Acquah) by PNDC operatives in June 1982. Besides their profession, what the dismembered judges had in common was their activism in overturning sentences handed down by the AFRC dictatorship in 1979. Rawlings initially blamed the murders on "enemies" of the revolution but the Special Investigations Board (SIB) appointed by the PNDC to probe this horrendous act recommended the arrest and prosecution of Kojo Tsikata (Special Security Advisor to the PNDC). This recommendation, however, was never acted upon. Instead, four individuals, including two former PNDC members (Amartey Kwei and Aloga Akata-Pore) confessed to the crime and were subsequently executed. These executions, however, did nothing to quell rumors that top PNDC leaders, especially Kojo Tsikata, were behind the murders.

The brutal elimination of these judges was consistent with PNDC antagonism toward the regular courts. Prior to these murders, the lawyer-dominated Association of Recognized Professional Bodies (ARPB) had published a list of 180 victims alleged to have been murdered during the PNDC's first seven months in power. As Kevin Shillington observed,

> Within a matter of weeks, power to the people became power to the brutal and the violent in society, especially those with guns. Arbitrary assaults and even killings were carried out in the name of the revolution, many of them by armed police, border guards and soldiers. There were . . . significantly few public condemnations of the armed forces who seem to have been responsible for most of the killings.[78]

An elite squad known as "the Panthers" was believed to have carried out most of the murders and disappearances that occurred under the PNDC's watch.[79]

In addition to murders and executions, there were also attacks on religious organizations and the independent press. The Castle Information Bureau (CIB) was formed in 1983 to monitor local and international media reports on events and developments in Ghana. The Newspaper Licensing Decree (PNDC Law 211) empowered the government to pick and choose the media outlets that would be allowed to operate. PNDC Supporters torched the premises of the *Echo* newspaper in 1983 and several newspapers (including the *Catholic Standard* and the *Free Press*) were shut down for criticizing the government. Journalists were routinely arrested and thrown in jail for opposing PNDC policies. Apostle Barnabas, editor of *The Believer* and an implacable opponent of the government, died under mysterious circumstances.

Churches, Mosques, Masonic Lodges, and religious organizations were not spared the wrath of the PNDC. In one incident, soldiers demolished a mosque in Accra in 1986 because it was allegedly used for currency racketeering. The PNDC banned two indigenous religious sects—Jesus Church at Dzorwulu in Accra and Nyame Sompa Ye Church at Ekwamkrom in the Central region. The Mormon Church and Jehovah's Witnesses were also banned and their assets frozen. PNDC Law 221 (The Registration of Religious Bodies Law) stipulated that "every religious body in existence in Ghana shall be registered under this law and no religious body in existence in Ghana shall after three months from the commencement of the Law operate as such unless it is registered under this law."[80] Registration requirements included a written constitution, a financial statement and a registration fee of 50,000 Cedis (100 U.S. dollars at the time). Major churches (Catholic, Anglican, Methodist, and Presbyterian) refused to register because, in the opinion of church leaders, PNDC Law 221 infringed upon their fundamental right to worship.

By far the most repressive arm of the PNDC was the Bureau of National Investigations (BNI), an offshoot of the Special Branch of the Police Force. Established in 1983 and under the direction of Kojo Tsikata, the BNI operated independently of the police force and enjoyed wide powers of arrest, detention, and, in some cases, execution. Preventive Custody Law allowed the BNI and other affiliates to detain individuals without charge or trial as long as they were deemed to constitute a threat to national security.

The involvement of Public Tribunals and PDCs (later renamed CDRs) in human rights abuses led many Ghanaians, some of whom (especially students) were initially sympathetic to the PNDC cause, to withdraw from politics. As Bafour Agyeman-Duah recounts,

> . . . the PDCs/WDCs initiated a reign of terror reminiscent of the Red Guards in China during Mao's cultural revolution. People with private

> cars were ridiculed as exploiters, and many Ghanaians of high social or business standing were removed from their posts without any evidence of malpractice. Armed soldiers, in some cases, collaborated with the Defence Committees, but frequently acted on their own to terrorize civilians, with whom they repeatedly clashed.[81]

The PNDC track record on human and political rights was not significantly different from the AFRC's (see Table 4.1). AFRC atrocities were intense, concentrated and limited in duration while those of the PNDC were protracted. PNDC abuses tapered and did not grow in intensity and scope, as was the case in Liberia, after the first few years in office. Political violence and human rights violations by the AFRC and PNDC were neither byproducts of a predatory agenda (as in Liberia and Sierra Leone) nor did they facilitate the compradorization of its leadership elements. Subaltern violence, in other words, was less indiscriminate and less connected to accumulation by insurgents in Ghana than, say, in Liberia (1980–89) and Sierra Leone (1992–1996, 1997–1998).

Democratization

Having ousted a democratically elected government, the PNDC came to office with no intention of holding elections and returning the country to constitutional democratic rule. As Rawlings himself maintained,

> Democracy does not just mean paper guarantees of abstract liberties; it involves, above all, food, clothing and shelter, in the absence of which life is not worth living.[82]

One of the first steps taken by the PNDC leadership after seizing power was to suspend the constitution and ban all political parties and activities. This ban on political organization and activity, which lasted for all but three

Table 4.1 Index of civil and political liberty under AFRC/PNDC rule

Regime	*1979/80*	*82/83*	*83/84*	*84/85*	*85/86*	*86/87*	*88/89*	*89/90*	*90/91*
AFRC	P4/C4								
PNDC		P6/C6	P6/C5	P7/C6	P7/C6	P7/C6	P7/C6	P6/C6	P6/C5

Source: Freedom House: Country Ratings at http://www.freedomhouse.org.
P = Political Rights; C = Civil Rights; 1 = Most Free; 7 = Least Free.

months of the PNDC's eleven years in power, did not prevent the emergence of social clubs that were linked to competing political traditions and personalities.

The PNDC's conception of democracy was clearly at odds with liberal orthodoxy. Rawlings detested politicians whom he believed were corrupt, elitist, and out of touch with the masses. He and his PNDC colleagues promoted a participatory and social conception of democracy that emphasized accountability, transparency, grassroots empowerment, and basic need satisfaction. Incorporating popular sectors into the process of governing was held up as more important than multi-party elections.

The main avenue for citizen participation in governance was supposed to be the People's Defense Committees (PDC), later renamed Committees for the Defense of the Revolution (CDR). The origins of these "revolutionary" committees can be traced back to the Police Junior Ranks Association (PJRA) and the JFM. The need to form "committees of ordinary people" was first articulated in the *Workers Banner*, the official organ of the JFM. In one of its editorials, the *Workers Banner* hailed these committees as "the highest form of democracy (grassroots democracy) because through them all the people will participate in taking vital decisions and in running the country."[83] Rawlings later presented this rationale for the establishment of PDCs in a statement to the press in which he declared:

> Ordinary people everywhere—workers, farmers, fishermen, soldiers, policemen, all hitherto oppressed people—have the right to form their own PDCs without waiting for instructions from anyone, just as senior staff and other top officials have their own associations . . . These committees are expected to defend the rights of ordinary people, expose any deal with corruption and other counter-revolutionary activities at the various work places or their communities, to maintain collective national discipline and supervision over national resources and to afford everyone the opportunity to participate in the decision making process in the country.[84]

Rawlings went on to point out that the revolution was

> meant to transfer power from this small group of greedy, avaricious bandits to where power really belongs—the farmers, workers and ordinary people of this country. The transfer of power is achieved by the people organizing themselves into their PDCs to expose the faceless power brokers and their nefarious activities, stamp out corruption and organize themselves into productive units.[85]

Despite these lofty goals, the operations of revolutionary committees were stymied by the PNDC's ambivalence on the issue of revolutionary reform. Disagreement within the PNDC over the character and pace of reform became more apparent as the regime sought to consolidate power. Tensions between Rawlings and the civilian and military left led to the suppression of the JFM after 1982. In Eboe Hutchful's assessment, ". . . as the PNDC attempted to consolidate its control, the defense committees, in theory the mass base of the regime, . . . [became] the major source of resistance."[86] Reports abounded of

> discredited elements . . . taking advantage of the totally spontaneous character of the PDCs and WDCs to form or hijack them for their own purposes. . . . In some factories and work places, managers formed WDCs and appointed themselves as chairmen. . . . In some rural areas, chiefs and landlords rushed to form defence committees and to use them to settle long-standing family feuds or land disputes in their favor or for ejecting tenants.[87]

In the end, CDRs were subverted in their mission by both the tension between the need to consolidate power and involve the masses in governance and by the abuses of the system. These committees also fell far short of satisfying popular demands for multiparty elections.

Demands for multi-party elections gained momentum toward the end of the 1980s. Leading the internal agitation for democratic change was the Movement for Freedom and Justice (MFJ), an agglomeration of politicians and activists from the first, second, and third republics. Among MFJ demands were the unbanning of political parties, the release of all political prisoners, and the announcement by the government of a timetable for democratic elections. In addition to local pressures from both the left and right of Ghana's political spectrum, other factors such as the liberation of Eastern Europe, the end of the cold war and the adoption of political liberalization by the World Bank and the IMF as a conditionality for financial assistance, had a positive impact on processes of democratization in Ghana.

The initial response of the PNDC to growing demands for some kind of representative system was to establish District Assemblies in each of the country's 120 districts in 1988. Two-thirds of the members of these assemblies were elected by popular vote while a third was appointed by the PNDC. But even at this stage, Rawlings continued to express a preference for a no-party government in which each of the district assemblies would elect two representatives to a national assembly whose membership would also include representatives of the military, trade unions, farmers, and other special interest groups. However, any talk of such quasi-corporatist arrangement only resurrected the ghost of Acheampong's disastrous "Unigov" proposals.

The issue of what type of democratic system is most suitable for Ghana dominated political debate in the late 1980s. The PNDC leadership remained opposed to party politics although, as events were to later prove, "Rawlings was shrewd enough . . . to ensure that the growing tide of popular opinion in favor of multipartyism did not . . . flow against him personally."[88] The MFJ declared its preference for a multi-party system of government and dismissed as a "fraud and an imposition" the notion that district assemblies can be the basis for the formation of a national assembly.[89] Taking the position that "multi-party democracy has not been given the chance to thrive in Ghana by populist military takeovers," the National Union of Ghana Students (NUGS) issued a statement aligning itself with the forces calling for a speedy return to constitutional democracy.[90] The Ghana Bar Association (GBA), the Christian Council, and the Catholic Church also joined those demanding a return to pluralist democracy.

The National Commission for Democracy (NCD) took the first step on the road to constitutional rule. Established in 1982 to serve as an Electoral Commission and an agency for promoting democracy, the NCD organized seminars and held deliberations on the form of government Ghanaians would prefer to adopt. The government in March 1991 accepted the NCD's recommendation that some form of multi-party system should be adopted as this was the preference of a plurality of Ghanaians. Ignoring the preference of the MFJ and the Bar Association for a constituent assembly, the PNDC opted for a consultative assembly, which was convened in August 1991. Membership of this assembly included representatives of district assemblies (117), corporate groups (121) and government appointees (22).[91] The main task of the consultative assembly was to approve a new constitution that had been drafted by a committee of constitutional experts. A draft constitution similar to the 1979 document was approved by 92 percent of voters in a referendum in which only 43.7 percent of the electorate bothered to vote.[92]

Whether Rawlings would contest the presidential election, and if so under which party, remained unresolved as the transition process got underway. Rawlings himself kept many people guessing and it was not until September 30, 1992 (the official date for nominations) that he declared his candidacy. Rawlings decided to succeed himself for a number of reasons, not the least of which were fears of reprisals and a very good chance of winning the presidential contest. After deciding to throw his hat in the electoral ring, Rawlings was confronted with the choice of either forming his own party or joining one of the Nkrumahist parties already in existence.[93] In the end

Rawlings decided to form his own political party, which he named the National Democratic Congress (NDC).

In addition to the NDC, four other political parties took part in the 1992 elections. These were: the New Patriotic Party (NPP), which was led by Adu Boahen (a retired history professor and leader of the MFJ) and strongly linked to the Danquah/Busia wing of Ghanaian politics; the People's National Convention (PNC) led by Hilla Limann (president of the third republic); the National Independence Party (NIP) of Kwabena Darko (a wealthy businessman and evangelist) who was closely tied to CPP old guard politicians like Kojo Botsio; and the People's Heritage Party (PHP) of Emmanuel Erskine (a professional soldier), which was home to many young Nkrumahists. There were also two other parties—the National Convention Party (NCP) and the Every Ghanaian Living Everywhere (EGLE) party—closely aligned with Rawlings; both parties endorsed Rawlings as their presidential candidate after failing to convince him to be their leader.

Although there were some stark differences among the parties with respect to political agenda, leadership style, and support base, all were without exception personalist vehicles. The election focused almost exclusively on the personalities of Rawlings and the men who wanted to replace him. In the presidential balloting, Rawlings polled 58 percent of the popular vote, compared to 30 percent for the NPP's Adu Boahen. What was striking about these results was the fact that Rawlings received at least 50 percent of the popular vote in all regions except Ashanti—home region of Boahen. The main opposition parties cried foul and boycotted the parliamentary election in protest over alleged rigging of results by Rawlings and his supporters.[94] As a result of this boycott, Rawlings and his allies ended up with 198 of the 200 seats in the fourth republican parliament.

The electoral victory of Rawlings in the 1992 elections can be attributed to several factors. One was the way in which "the government began to openly manipulate economic policy to achieve political purposes as soon as Ghana's political opening began in earnest, in 1990."[95] The PNDC/NDC electoral strategy focused on winning the rural vote. To win over the peasantry, the prices of food and cocoa were raised, which benefited rural inhabitants. The PNDC also embarked on projects that specifically targeted rural areas and inhabitants. These included a national electrification scheme, a rural water works project, a rural feeder road project, and the construction of rural schools and clinics. In addition to these rural initiatives, the Rawlings government directed the COCOBOD agency to pay all property taxes to the District Assemblies instead of the Central Government. A District Assembly Common Fund, which was to allocate 5 percent of Ghana's total revenue to the District Assemblies for development, was also established.[96] Sensitivity and responsiveness to the needs and concerns of rural dwellers certainly aided Rawlings' victory in the presidential election.

Other factors that contributed to Rawlings's electoral triumph in 1992 were dissension within the ranks of the opposition, the apparent overconfidence of some NPP party leaders and the extensive use of government resources in the NDC campaign. Jeff Haynes observed how the coalition represented by the MFJ splintered immediately after Rawlings announced that multi-party elections would be held in 1992.[97] Bolstered by the support of business people and the professional class, NPP leaders believed, rather erroneously, that it would be impossible for Rawlings to win a free and fair presidential election. What these leaders failed to discern was that public loathing of PNDC secretaries did not extend to Rawlings, who continued to be popular among subordinate classes. This popularity, which was not unrelated to government spending in the rural areas, contributed to Rawlings victory in the 1992 elections.

In contrast to the populist style and posturing of Rawlings, NPP leaders were condescending, elitist, and out of touch with the masses. As E. Gyimah-Boadi wrote, Ghana "has always had middle and professional classes . . . but the course of post-colonial events" and "the prevalence of opportunism among the middle classes makes them a poor candidate to fill the role of democracy's champion." In general terms,

> . . . the social base of the prodemocracy movement has remained quite narrow: primarily the elite and middle class professionals, intellectuals, large traders, and large farmers. It has been unable to attract peasants, urban workers, students, and other popular elements to its ranks. Thus liberal democracy and its advocates remain vulnerable to the charge that they represent a mere bourgeois irrelevancy.[98]

It was precisely this disconnection between the political class and popular sectors that created an opening for Rawlings to win the 1992 presidential election.

Ghana's 1992 transition to constitutional democratic rule did not, however, result in significant changes in the composition or policy direction of the government. Besides Rawlings, who continued to serve as head of state, the former deputy chairman of the PNDC was named Speaker of the Fourth Republican parliament. Most of the ministers in Rawlings's postelection cabinet were holdovers from the PNDC dictatorship. This, however, was not unexpected since Rawlings promised continuity rather than a departure from past policies.

Economic Performance

The Ghanaian economy was on virtual life support when Rawlings and his co-conspirators seized power on December 31, 1981. Per capita GDP had fallen steadily at an annual rate of 3.2 percent during the 1970s. Exports (cocoa, gold, diamonds, and timber) were down by almost 50 percent and chronic scarcities of basic consumer items made life intolerable for the average Ghanaian. The persistence of structural imbalances, the overvaluation of the local currency, hyperinflation, and the failure to tackle corruption and smuggling typified economic conditions under Limann's PNP government. An overvalued Cedi encouraged smuggling, as did the government's refusal to increase the price paid to farmers for cocoa even though farmers were receiving (in real terms) a meager 14 percent of what they were paid in 1963.[99] Limann's initial attempt to flood the market with consumer goods did not provide a temporary respite as the government clearly lacked the resources to continue importing what the average Ghanaian could no longer afford. Allegations of malfeasance and corruption scandals involving "old guard" politicians in the PNP further tarnished the public image of the Limann government.

Reversing Ghana's economic downslide was a top priority of the PNDC. During its first fifteen months in office, the PNDC pursued a populist economic policy that emphasized popular mobilization and self-reliance. The focus during this period was on smuggling, which the regime identified as one of the main economic problems facing the country. As Rawlings pointed out at the time,

> Smuggling has become the number one enemy of our country. Cocoa is smuggled. Rice is smuggled. Maize is smuggled. Imported tractors and bicycles are smuggled. The smuggling does not only reduce our foreign exchange earning, but also increases our import bill. . . . And unless we put a decisive stop to it, our efforts at national reconstruction and transformation of the economy will be seriously undermined.[100]

The targets of the government's anti-smuggling campaign included large-scale farmers, wealthy traders, transport owners, bureaucrats, and politicians. In a desperate effort to curb smuggling, the government closed its land borders for much of 1982, and imposed stiff penalties (including forfeiture of property and execution) on smugglers.

It was clear from the outset that the PNDC's anti-smuggling campaign was not working because it addressed the symptoms rather than the underlying causes of the problem. As Paul Nugent observed,

> . . . very little was done during 1982 to ameliorate the conditions that encouraged smuggling. Nothing could be done to rein in the black market as long as the PNDC was unwilling to grasp the nettle of the overvalued currency. . . . Without a devaluation, it was not possible for the government to raise producer prices, since the tripling of prices by the Limann regime in 1981 had placed the Cocoa Marketing Board in deficit.[101]

It was not until later in 1983, when the government embarked on its Economic Recovery Program (ERP), that the focus of its anti-smuggling effort began to shift away from interdiction and punishment to an emphasis on addressing the structural causes of the problem. This policy journey from radical populism to liberal economic orthodoxy alienated the support base of the PNDC, although this did not hinder the government's ability to implement its IMF adjustment programs.

Launched in April 1983, the goal of the Economic Recovery Program (ERP) was to reverse Ghana's economic decline and build the foundations for sustainable economic growth and development. The ERP was implemented in two phases: the first (stabilization) phase covered the period 1983–1986; the second (adjustment and development) phase lasted from 1986–1989. The objectives of the PNDC during the first phase were to restore the productive capacity of the economy (especially in agriculture), control inflation, expand exports, rehabilitate infrastructure, and improve the standard of living of the average Ghanaian. Second phase goals included maintaining an annual economic growth of 5–5.5 percent, increasing the level of public investment from 10 to 25 percent of national income by the end of the 1990s and improving public sector management.[102]

The objectives of both phases of the ERP were pursued through a combination of fiscal, monetary, labor, and liberalization policies. Fiscal measures were aimed at lowering the budget deficit, reducing income and corporate taxes, ending government subsidies for basic items, broadening the tax base, and improving tax administration. In the area of monetary policy, all restrictions on borrowing and lending were lifted and interest rate policy was liberalized. Liberalization measures led to the privatization of public enterprises and the lifting of price controls. Of an estimated one hundred state-owned enterprises, seventy-eight were privatized. These included the State Fishing Corporation, State Farms Corporation, Food Production

Corporation, Achimota Brewery Company (confiscated by the AFRC in 1979), Tema Textile Printing Company, Metalico Ghana, and DL Steel Ghana. Most of these companies were either operating at a loss or were among companies confiscated by previous military governments.

On balance, the results of the PNDC's structural adjustment policies were mixed. On the one hand, the macro-economic targets of the ERP were largely met. The economy was stabilized, inflation was brought under control, the budget deficit was erased, and there were significant increases in exports and imports, the latter financed primarily by the IMF, World Bank, and donor agencies. Annual growth in real GDP was over 6 percent from 1984–1986; growth rates in the last three years of the 1980s hovered around 5–6 percent. Significant improvements were recorded in gross national savings and domestic investment (see Table 4.2). Exports rose by an average of 18 percent from 1984 to 1987 but plummeted in 1989 as a result of falling cocoa prices. Cocoa, gold, timber, and electricity contributed 87.5 percent ($722.1 million) of total exports in 1990, compared to 93.2 percent ($409.2 million) in 1983.[103] With the exception of the 1987–1989 period, exports generally outpaced imports in annual growth rates. A general decline in rural poverty from 41.9 percent of the rural population in 1987–1988 to 33.9 in 1991–1992 suggests that the gains of the ERP were not hopelessly skewed in favor of the wealthy.[104]

Macroeconomic indicators of Ghana's economic performance under the PNDC can, however, be misleading. As Jon Kraus argued,

> . . . comparing Ghana's growth during 1984–1989 with baselines of 1982 and 1983 is not useful or honest, since Ghana's economy was devastated

Table 4.2 Ghana: Selected economic indicators

Indicator	*1980*	*1990*
Real GDP (US $)	4.6 bn.	5.7 bn.
Exports (US $)	1.26 bn.	897 m.
Imports (US $)	1.1bn.	$1.2bn.
Intl. Reserves (US $)	199m.	$282 m.
Total External Debt (US $)	1.4bn.	$3.85 bn.
Total Debt Service (US $)	108 m.	$193 m.
Govt. Revenue (% of GDP)	24.1	13.2
Govt. Expenditure (% of GDP)	38.9	13.0
Gross Nat. Savings (% of GDP)	4.5	10.7
Domestic Investment (% of GDP)	5.6	14.4

Source: *African Development Report 1997*.

> by the worst droughts in fifty years, bushfires that destroyed crops, post-war low cocoa prices, and, consequently, plummeting imports. In some senses Ghana's economic recovery has been slow and anemic. Output continues to be relatively low in cocoa, timber, mining, and industry in comparison with 1970 production levels, and this is also true for consumption, minimum wages, and access to social services.[105]

Trevor Parfitt echoed this view in the case of manufacturing output, which in 1989 amounted to only 63 percent of its 1977 level; in addition, the contribution of Ghana's manufacturing sector to GDP was the same (10 percent) in 1989 as in 1960.[106] And although the government's budget deficit as a percentage of GDP dropped from 4.7 percent in 1982 to 0.3 percent by 1987, this was primarily the result of the government's dwindling capacity to provide health, education and transport services, as well as rehabilitate the country's dilapidated infrastructure.

Conclusion

Ghana under Rawlings remains the only country in sub-Saharan Africa where the militariat under the leadership of petty-bourgeois populists was able to reverse processes of state decomposition. Although this turnaround occurred under conditions of extreme repression and human rights abuses, it is doubtful whether economic achievements under Rawlings would have been possible under more liberal political circumstances and in the absence of massive infusions of funds from the IMF and other international financial institutions. While some of the human rights abuses committed by AFRC and PNDC operatives were horrendous and indefensible, they nonetheless pale in comparison to the massive crimes against humanity committed by armed subalterns in Liberia and Sierra Leone. The mainstreaming of Rawlings produced not only a macro-economic turnaround; it also coincided with the abatement in human rights abuses and the beginning of a process of genuine democratic change and consolidation.

CHAPTER 5

Liberia: "No Doe, No Liberia"

Both the timing of the April 1980 coup in Liberia and the inaugural populism of its lumpen leadership were influenced by the 1979 coup and AFRC interregnum in Ghana. Not unlike its Ghanaian antecedent, the Liberian usurpation was instigated by armed subalterns and immediately followed by the execution of key officials from the ousted regime. But the combustible interplay of class and ethnicity that made the Liberian situation so explosive was absent in the Ghanaian case. Moreover, where Ghana's AFRC dictatorship kept its promise to hand over power to a democratically elected civilian government, Liberia's People's Redemption Council (PRC) rapidly degenerated into a personal dictatorship. As it turned out, Samuel Doe and his coterie of lumpen upstarts were perfectly content to destroy Liberia if they could no longer access and control its public offices and resources.

Doe's dictatorship offers some useful insights into the degenerate propensities of armed subalterns. Where Rawlings popularized the phenomenon of *coups from below*, Doe epitomized the horrors associated with subaltern military rule in West Africa. His dictatorship devoured the Liberian state, plunged society into armed conflict, and showcased the retrograde predilections of armed subalterns. It is for this reason, among others, that a study of Liberia under Doe is relevant to mapping the pathologies of subaltern rule in West Africa.

Political History

The dominant political and social group in Liberia prior to the 1980 coup was the minority Americo-Liberian community, a settler group descended mainly from freed American slaves who resettled in Africa during the first half of the nineteenth century. The leadership of this relatively privileged community broke away from the American Colonization Society (ACS) and declared Liberia independent in 1847. Thereafter, for 133 years, this settler minority, which comprised no more than 3 percent of the Liberian population, monopolized political power and disenfranchized the majority of Liberians. The main political instrument of Americo-Liberian domination was the True Whig Party (TWP), a *de facto* one party machine that dominated Liberian politics for almost a century (1884–1980).

Denigrated as "heathen savages" by the settler minority, the majority of Liberians remained isolated from the mainstream of political and social life for the better part of the twentieth century. It was not until the presidency of William Tubman (1944–1971) that the TWP leadership began to take steps to rectify some of the inequities and discriminatory practices that defined relations between Americo-Liberians and indigenous Liberians. Two reforms in particular, the Open Door Policy and the Unification Scheme, initiated a process of opening the hinterland to economic development, which in turn increased interactions between the Americo-Liberian ethnoclass and indigenous Liberians.

The Open Door Policy facilitated the exploitation of mineral resources and the spread of rubber cultivation. The massive exploitation of mineral resources, especially iron ore, fueled Liberia's economic boom from the 1950s to the 1970s. Export earnings, for example, grew from $30 million (U.S. dollars) in 1953 to an average of $505 million during the last five years (1975–1980) of the first republic.[1] Under the unification scheme, Tubman attempted to eliminate some but not all of the legal and other distinctions separating the settler minority from indigenous Liberians. This scheme modified the property requirements for voting and extended parliamentary representation to the people of the hinterland.

Tubman's patronizing style and cosmetic moves to unify the people of Liberia could not, however, obscure the realities of a deeply polarized society. During the final years of his presidency, a number of coup attempts against the TWP oligarchy were reported. One such effort involved General George Toe Johnson while another implicated Henry Fahnbulleh Sr., who was at the time Liberia's ambassador to Tanzania and Kenya. There was also a noticeable upsurge in student activism, which the President blamed on students who were not breast-fed by their mothers when they were babies. According to the president,

> Mothers these days have stopped breast-feeding their babies. They begin feeding babies with cow's milk as soon as they are born. Thus, they develop a cow's instinct.[2]

The armed forces in the last decade of the Tubman presidency consisted of the National Guard, a small Coast Guard and a militia (an organization of 20,000 men). The Liberian National Guard (LNG), a force estimated at 3,000–4,000 men in 1971, was used mainly to suppress internal disturbances (Monrovia strike of 1961, and the Firestone, Goodrich, and LAMCO strikes of 1966 serve as examples). The ranks of the LNG comprised mainly of indigenous Liberians, mostly from the Loma, Bassa, Kpelle, and Kru ethnic groups. Although the officer corp opened its ranks to indigenous Liberians in the 1960s, it continued to be dominated by Americo-Liberians and the clients of TWP oligarchs. In many ways, this division between the officer corps and the ranks of the LNG mirrored the settler—native cleavage in society.

William Tubman died in office in 1971 and was replaced by his vice President, William Tolbert. The grandson of Daniel Frank Tolbert, a former South Carolina slave who migrated to Liberia in 1880 and settled in Bensonville, Tolbert had served as Vice President under Tubman for nineteen years (1952–1971) before inheriting the presidency. The TWP under Tolbert continued to embody and promote the interests of the Americo-Liberian ethnoclass and foreign capital. Although a few educated leaders from the hinterland (Edward Kesselly and Jackson Doe come to mind) were co-opted into the TWP leadership, "there was no channel through which independent interests, organizations or political perspectives, could be incorporated into government."[3] Furthermore, sloganized responses to festering problems, such as Tolbert's "Rallytime," "Higher Heights" and "Mats to Mattresses" campaigns, did nothing to ameliorate the social deprivation and political marginalization of the vast majority of Liberians.

Tolbert's promise of an open society and his efforts to liberalize the political system were tempered by the fact that the president was committed to "an open society as long as his own actions and those of his relatives were not subject to close scrutiny."[4] Thus even as he reduced the voting age to eighteen, appointed indigenous Liberians to important government positions and allowed political parties to register, the president did not shrink from banning independent news outlets and imprisoning editors for criticizing his brother who happened to be the finance minister at the time. Steven Tolbert, the president's brother and one-time finance minister, held monopoly interests in rice importation, fishing (Mesurado Fisheries), automobile sales and service, poultry, and the distribution of textbooks and uniforms.[5] Having his father-in-law as head of the Supreme Court further strengthened the hand of Steven Tolbert in his numerous business ventures.[6]

Unrestrained by conflict of interest considerations, the activities of the president's family members underscored the corruption and nepotism of the Tolbert era (1971–1980). Tolbert himself was reported to have owned seventy-one houses while the former TWP secretary general, Clarence Simpson, owned forty-two houses.[7] The President "would frequently have junior officials of government charged and prosecuted for embezzlement and malfeasance while using human and material resources of government ministries to construct buildings . . . and undertake millions of dollars of other improvements on his personal property in his hometown."[8] In his last months in office, Tolbert was both conciliatory and repressive—he allowed opposition parties to register and announced a date for multi-party elections in 1983 but these concessions were overshadowed by the president's decision to close universities, jail political opponents and use the army to quell labor and popular unrest. Tolbert's vacillation between reform and repression was in part due to pressures from TWP barons and leaders of the Masonic order to slow down the pace of liberal reforms and crack down on the political opposition before it was too late.

The last two years of the Tolbert presidency were marked by rising urban political activism. Led by radical intellectuals and students, opposition to the TWP oligarchy coalesced around two main organizations, the Movement for Justice in Africa (MOJA) and the Progressive Alliance of Liberia (PAL). In contrast to the elitist and conservative TWP, these organizations, particularly MOJA, were inclusionary and mass-based. MOJA was established in 1973 by a group of radical professors and students at the University of Liberia. Originally conceived as a pan-Aficanist support group for liberation movements in Lusophone and Southern Africa, MOJA later became involved in local issues concerning civil liberties, urban and rural poverty, and social justice. MOJA was an active force in the student movement and was closely aligned with the Student Unification Party (SUP), the dominant student party at the University of Liberia in the late 1970s and early 1980s.[9] The decision by Amos Sawyer, one of the movement's leaders, to contest the 1978 Monrovia mayoral election galvanized the political opposition and provided a test for a floundering TWP machine. As the "Sawyer-for-Mayor" campaign gained momentum, and faced with the prospect of losing the mayoralty of Monrovia to someone outside the TWP circle, the Tolbert administration abruptly postponed the elections. This action incensed the opposition and fodderized the confrontation between the government and urban civil society.

The most adventurist and irrepressible of the urban political movements that emerged in the waning years of the Tolbert administration was PAL. Founded in 1975, PAL was the brainchild of Liberian students in the United States whose aim was to transform their pressure group into a political party and challenge the TWP at the polls. More demagogic than MOJA, PAL appealed to and attracted the support of *declasse* elements, especially urban lumpens. The movement was involved in organizing the 1979 demonstration against the planned increase in the price of rice, an event that marked the beginning of the end of TWP domination. Later, the movement became the first legal opposition party to be registered in Liberia in twenty-five years, after which it changed its name to the Progressive People's Party (PPP). Led by Gabriel Bachus Mathews, the PPP leadership was not prepared to wait for scheduled elections in 1983, prefering instead to mount a campaign to oust the government through public protests. As part of this campaign, Mathews in March 1980 called for a general strike whose stated goal was to bring down the government.

Tolbert responded to the PPP's call for a mass uprising against his government by banning the party and arresting most of its leaders on treason charges. In an address to the Liberian legislature, the President accused the PPP leadership of inciting an armed insurrection:

> Despite our pronouncements, and in brazen defiance of our laws . . . members of a recently organized political party . . . led by Gabriel Baccus Mathews, conspired to overthrow the legally constituted government, . . . enthrone anarchy and deprive the sovereign people of Liberia of their inalienable rights and cherished tradition of choosing their leaders through the electoral process.[10]

MOJA distanced itself from PAL, describing the latter's actions as "infantile" and "ridiculous." In the assessment of a prominent MOJA leader, the PPP's "constituency, its lack of objectives other than to contest for power, and constant subjugation to security harassment" made it impossible for the movement to "rise above anomic outbursts."[11] Many PPP leaders were in jail awaiting trial on treason charges at the time of the April 1980 coup.

A major turning-point in the confrontation between the Tolbert government and an increasingly emboldened political opposition came in April 1979 when Tolbert announced a 50 percent increase in the price of rice, the country's staple food. The fact that members of the president's family stood to benefit directly from this price hike was not lost on the general public. Announcement of the price increase triggered a mass demonstration in the capital city of Monrovia, which left over a hundred civilians dead—mostly the victims of police brutality since soldiers refused to shoot at demonstrators. In a move that betrayed the government's dwindling confidence in its own army, Guinean troops were brought in to restore calm but not even this external intervention could save the Tolbert administration.

From the time of the rice riots in 1979 to the coup that toppled the TWP oligarchy in 1980, Liberia was rife with rumors of a right-wing palace coup orchestrated by TWP barons. TWP oligarchs like Richard Henries (speaker of the house), James Pierre (chief justice), Joseph Chesson (justice minister) and Reginald Townsend (TWP national chairman) campaigned for the death penalty to be imposed on PPP leaders on trial for treason. The "Dead or Alive" posters put out by the Justice ministry for fugitive PPP leaders betrayed growing anxiety, fear, and desperation within ruling circles. Many in the TWP blamed Tolbert for starting a process of political reform that was inimical to their interests. Assuming there were TWP elements planning to oust the president, their task was not made easier by the widespread arrest of officers and enlisted men in March 1980. The rank and file of the army had, after all, refused to shoot at demonstrators during the rice riots of 1979 and there was every reason to believe that they would have resisted a right-wing coup. Rather than a right-wing coup to protect ruling class privileges, all it took was a small group of armed subalterns to shatter the crumbling TWP edifice.

The PRC Coup

The coup of April 12, 1980 brought a violent end to settler hegemony in Liberian politics. The ease with which lumpen upstarts captured state power reflected the fragility of settler domination in Liberia. It only took seventeen noncommissioned officers and privates (none Americo-Liberian) to oust the Tolbert regime. The majority of the coup makers were from southeastern and north-central Liberia—mainly from the Krahn, Dan, and Kru ethnic groups. All of these men, without exception, "partook of the subculture of the urban unemployed and reflected the characteristic suspicion and opportunism typical of that group, tempered by the harshness of urban poverty and neglect."[12] In a very real sense, the coup of 1980, as George Kieh observed, "was propelled by the inequities and the attendant injustices that were inherent in Liberia's lopsided class structure."[13]

According to Master-Sergeant Samuel Doe, he and his co-conspirators "had no alternative but to overthrow the government" because of its "continued failure . . . to handle effectively the affairs of the Liberian people."[14] The new leaders pledged to liberate indigenous masses from the domination of a tiny minority, ensure a more equitable distribution of the nation's wealth, and return the country to civilian rule as soon as corruption was eradicated. The constitution was suspended, the executive and legislative branches of government dissolved, political parties and activities banned, and martial law imposed. A Provisional Ruling Council (PRC), composed of the seventeen coup makers and chaired by Doe, was established as the new governing body.

Given the overlapping ethnic and class divisions in Liberian society, it was not surprising that internal reactions to the PRC coup were overwhelmingly positive. Many welcomed the change in government but the euphoria that greeted the 1980 coup had more to do with the demise of a loathed government than optimism regarding the new leadership. External reactions to the coup, on the other hand, were mixed. Libya, Ethiopia, and Cuba initially welcomed the coup but Sierra Leone, Ivory Coast, Guinea, Nigeria, and Burkina Faso expressed strong reservations. In the view of Sangoule Lamizana, then President of Burkina Faso, "Everybody can change their regime but the methods used in Liberia are a dishonor to Africa."[15] The Presidents of Sierra Leone and Ivory Coast (two of Liberia's three neighbors) were particularly shocked by events in Liberia. Siaka Stevens of Sierra Leone was a close friend of Tolbert and the latter's son, A.B. Tolbert, was married to the niece of the Ivorian president, thus making the demise of the Tolbert presidency unsettling for both Stevens and Felix Hophuet-Boigny, the Ivorian leader. In an attempt to diplomatically ostracize the new Liberian leadership, Liberia was not allowed to take its seat at the May 1980 Economic Community of West African States (ECOWAS) summit in Lome, Togo. The plane carrying Bachus Mathews (the PRC's first foreign minister) to a planned ministerial meeting of ECOWAS ministers was not permitted to land in Lagos. The PRC's response to the hostility of other governments in the subregion was to recall its ambassadors to Sierra Leone, Ivory Coast, ECOWAS and the Mano River Union. Liberia closed its diplomatic mission in Nigeria after the latter shut down its embassy in Monrovia.

The PRC milked the cold war for all it was worth by posing as anticommunist zealots. Although Cuba was among the first countries to welcome the change of government in Liberia, the PRC was quick to distance itself from America's enemies, especially Cuba and Libya. In a baffling gesture to the Reagan administration, Doe ordered all Cuban technical and military advisers to leave Liberia but was reminded by *Prensa Latina*, the Cuban news agency, that "such an expulsion would be difficult to carry out because there have never been any Cuban advisers in Liberia."[16] Later, the government went out of its way to sack schoolteachers with alleged socialist sympathies and vowed to hold schools and universities responsible for "harboring individuals who attempt to teach socialsm in whatever form."[17]

Given Doe's antisocialist posturing, it was not surprising that the United States was the PRC's principal external patron. Other than expressing displeasure at the murder of Tolbert and the executions of April 1980, it was business as usual between the United States and Liberia. In the words of Blaine Harden,

> After a few wobbly months in office, with investors fleeing the country and his fellow coup-makers fleecing local businessmen, Doe turned to the U.S embassy in Monrovia for guidance. . . . He obliged the anti-communism of the early Reagan years by booting Soviet diplomats out of the country. He ordered the creation of a constitutional commission (funded by U.S money) and promised that he would be stepping down when a civilian president was elected. Believing his promises, the U.S government showered Doe with money, subsidizing one-third of his government's spending between 1980 and 1985.[18]

Doe and the PRC in Power

Upon assuming the reins of government, the PRC appointed a largely civilian cabinet that included four PPP leaders (Bachus Mathews, Gabriel Nimley, Oscar Quiah, George Boley), two MOJA leaders (Boima Fahnbulleh, Togba-Nah Tipoteh), and three holdovers from the Tolbert administration (Kate Bryant, Gabriel Tucker, Lansana Dunzo). The ministries of finance, commerce, and postal affairs were assigned to military officers—Major Perry Zulu, Major Joseph Douglas, and Colonel Emmanuel Tweby respectively. The tenure of most of the civilians in the PRC's first cabinet was, however, short-lived. Gabriel Tucker (Public Works) Lansana Dunzo (Action for Progress and Development), and Togba-Nah Tipoteh (Economic Affairs and Planning) failed to return from trips abroad. Bachus Mathews was dismissed for not working "in the interest of the government" and by the end of the PRC's first two years in office, hardly any of its original civilian ministers remained in office.

As was the case in Ghana, the 1980 coup in Liberia represented a dual usurpation of governmental authority and military hierarchy. The PRC purged the Liberian army of most of its senior officers and reconstituted it along ethnic lines. The first, second, fourth, and sixth battalions were placed under the command of Krahn officers. The first infantry battalion at Camp Sheiffelin, the largest (2,000 strong) in the country, was commanded by Colonel Moses Wright, Doe's brother-in-law and ethnic compatriot. The fourth battalion (based in Zwedru, Grand Gedeh County) was later implicated in widespread atrocities committed against Gio, Mano, and Grebo civilians in Grand Gedeh. The Executive Mansion Guard (EMG), whose primary function was to protect Doe, was also a Krahn outfit, as were the Special Anti-Terrorist Unit (SATU), the National Security Agency (NSA) and the G-2 or military intelligence wing of the army. The NSA functioned as a secret police under Doe while the first battalion and EMG played leading roles in suppressing the Quiwonkpa coup of 1985.

Retribalization of state—society relations, personalization of power and privatization of violence were hallmarks of Doe's dictatorship. Compared to Rawlings in Ghana, who was articulate and petty-bourgeois, Doe was unschooled and lumpen to the core. He had no genuine interest in a populist transformation of society and the PRC mantra—"In the cause of the people, the struggle continues"—became just another hollow refrain devoid of any liberating or progressive meaning. Rather than struggle with the people to achieve what had been denied them for over a century, Doe's PRC unleashed the power of the state against the very masses that supported the 1980 coup. As Thomas Quiwonkpa, one of the leaders of the PRC coup, was to later complain,

> I thought I staged the 1980 coup to free the people of Liberia from 133 years of oppression, but now Doe has declared war on our people again. I have no other choice but to join my people in their struggle for . . . freedom.[19]

Corruption

As part of a short-lived attempt to pass themselves off as revolutionaries, PRC leaders lavishly appropriated populist slogans and symbols during their first few months in power. The public was deluged with official salutations touting the centrality of popular struggles. The "cause of the people" was rhetorically elevated into a sacred undertaking that justified the execution of former public officials and the confiscation of their properties. An end to corruption, according to Doe, was to be the main preoccupation of the PRC junta and a precondition for its return to the barracks.

The PRC chose to fight corruption in its first month in office by executing key members of the ousted TWP oligarchy. These officials were said to be guilty of "high treason, rampant corruption, and gross violations of human rights."[20] All but one of the executed men, Cyril Bright, was Americo-Liberian. Among those shot by firing squad were the murdered president's elder brother (Frank Tolbert), the former finance minister (James Phillips), foreign minister (Cecil Dennis), justice minister (Joseph Chesson), speaker of the house of representatives (Richard Henries), chairman of the True Whig Party (Reginald Townsend), and chief justice of the supreme court (James Pierre). The official reasons given for these executions involved an *ex post facto* reclassification of corruption as treasonable offense, an interpretation that allowed the PRC leadership to set about eliminating the entrenched political power of the Americo-Liberian ruling class.

Besides these executions, over 400 leading officials of the deposed government were arrested and detained on charges of corruption and treason. The PRC announced that corrupt government officials were not only to be dismissed from office and denied "employment anywhere in the country as long as the PRC is in power" but, as Doe warned, "when you are grabbed . . . hey . . . you may not live to tell the story."[21] In a revealing statement that underscored the false populism of the PRC, Doe promised Liberians that "we will all enjoy like the corrupt Tolbert government enjoyed."[22]

The anticorruption stance of the PRC was from the very beginning a publicity stunt that quickly unraveled in the face of glaring inconsistencies and contradictions. The refusal of PRC leaders to declare their own assets called into question the sincerity of their anticorruption grandstanding. As Bachus Mathews complained in an appearance before his PRC bosses to answer questions about his assets:

> I am appearing in protest before you because you should have declared your assets before requiring the ministers appointed to declare theirs. However, in due respect for you, I am happy to appear in the cause of the people.[23]

Boima Fahnbulleh, the PRC's first minister of education, voiced similar outrage at the lifestyles of PRC members; "how can you ride," he asked, "in the same cars, sleep in the same houses and adopt the same values as those of your predecessors if the revolution is to succeed?"[24]

In his description of corruption under Doe, Stephen Ellis noted that "since the state had historically been used as a means of personal enrichment, it was not illogical for Doe to use it for the same purpose."[25] It is estimated that Doe and his associates embezzled over $300 million during the 1980s; Doe himself was said to have at least $5.6 million stashed away in a Bank of Credit and Commerce International (BCCI) account.[26] The proliferation of banks in Liberia, even as the formal economy was collapsing, mirrored the involvement of Doe and his associates in money laundering. Both ". . . the speed with which" Doe "and his military supporters acquired wealth and the brutality which they employed were of a different order from what had gone before."[27] Thus, in little less than a year "Doe was rapidly metamorphosed from a gaunt and hungry-looking sergeant in ill-fitting battle fatigues, into a plump, immaculately suited figure," albeit with tacky Jerry curls.[28]

Human Rights

Liberia under Doe was the scene of some of the worst human rights atrocities in Africa during the 1980s. After eliminating the top hierarchy of the TWP, the PRC turned on itself with unrelenting ferocity. Most of the PRC executions targeted former associates of Doe. First from within the PRC to be executed for allegedly plotting to overthrow Doe was General Thomas Weh Syen, Lt. Col. Nelson Toe, and Harris Johnson. Many others were to follow later, including Thomas Quiwonkpa who was killed during an attempt to overthrow his erstwhile comrade-in-arms, and Moses Flanzamaton (deputy commander of Doe's Executive Mansion battalion) who was executed without trial after a bizarre plot to implicate civilian politicians in an alleged coup was exposed.[29] Within five years, only five of the original seventeen coup makers were still members of the PRC. Six were executed, one fled for his life and four were retired from the army after their release from prison on treason charges.

Amos Sawyer has described the first six years of PRC rule as "years of rape and plunder by armed marauders whose ideology is to search for cash and whose ambition is to retain power to accumulate and protect wealth."[30] This assessment is echoed by Max Sesay:

> The Doe era (1980–1989) was characterized by sustained levels of brutality, dramatic economic decline, political immobilization, and purges of real or imagined enemies. The regime's brutality was markedly represented by the haste with which those allegedly implicated in plots to overthrow the government were summarily executed.[31]

Human rights abuses by the PRC took a turn for the worse after Doe civilianized his dictatorship in 1985 and as opposition to his rule mounted. Threatened by an armed rebellion that enjoyed the support of neighboring Ivory Coast, and relying exclusively on armed elements from his Krahn ethnic group, Doe unleashed waves of violence against ethnic groups (Gio and Mano) accused of supporting his rivals.

A key legal instrument of PRC repression was Decree 88A, which empowered the government to detain anyone believed to be spreading "rumors, lies and disinformation" about the PRC and its leaders. Under the provisions of this decree, Liberians were routinely detained for all sorts of reasons, including the casual discussion of Doe's educational credentials or lack thereof. Many critics of the government were arrested and detained without trial for not working in the "interests of our revolution and party." This forced what remained of the political opposition, especially the followers of Quiwonkpa in Nimba County, to go underground only to reappear a few years later as the National Patriotic Front of Liberia (NPFL).

The summary execution and mutilation of political opponents was a signature occurrence under the PRC. In one of their first gruesome acts, soldiers disemboweled Tolbert and gouged out his eyes before dumping his mutilated body at the John F. Kennedy hospital morgue; his remains were later hurled into a mass grave. A.B. Tolbert, the former president's son, also met a similar fate at the hands of Doe and Thomas Weh Syen. According to Quiwonkpa's account of what happened,

> Doe sent Weh Syen at about midnight to get A.B from the Post Stockade . . . It made me sick when I was told how A.B was killed. They said after he was shot, A.B was still moaning when they buried him.[32]

Weh Syen was himself executed the following year for his alleged involvement in a coup plot to overthrow Doe.

Summary executions escalated into mass killings after the Quiwonkpa-led abortive coup of November 12, 1985. Hundreds of soldiers were mutilated and dismembered in the days and weeks following the coup. The main victims of these killings were Gio and Mano soldiers believed to have sided with Quiwonkpa. Krahn and Loma (Liberia's version of martial *ethnies*) soldiers carried out most of the atrocities against fellow soldiers and civilians. Civilians who had openly but prematurely celebrated the downfall of Doe were dragged from their homes, shot and buried in mass graves. The mindless brutality of this period was captured by the eyewitness account of a soldier:

> They identified this one as one of the enemies. Even though he was already dead, they were cutting his body part. They took the bayonet and opened his stomach, and cut his testicles off. They were cutting out people's eyes, even though they were already dead. These were the things I really saw.[33]

Most of these atrocities were committed at the Executive Mansion and the Post Stockade Prison, sometimes in full view of civilian onlookers.

More revolting than the executions was the consumption of the body parts of some of Doe's opponents. According to a civilian detained at the Executive Mansion after Quiwonkpa's failed coup,

> This is how it was done. They took fifteen at a time. After shooting the people, they would cut off parts of their bodies. Then they would force

> the people inside, the prisoners, to eat it. Some of the people refused. The soldiers forced them to eat the flesh. I saw one of them shove the head into a prisoner's mouth. They broke his teeth. In one case, they opened up the stomach of a corpse.[34]

Quiwonkpa was himself castrated and dismembered at the Post Stockade on November 15, 1985. One eyewitness described the scene at the time as follows:

> . . . Krahn soldiers verging on hysteria kicked and pummeled Quiwonkpa's body beyond recognition. The body was transported to Barclay Training Center in downtown Monrovia, directly across the street from a large outdoor market filled with shoppers and market women. There, as hundreds looked on, the rebel leader was castrated, dismembered and consumed.[35]

Tunde Agbabiaka, a Nigerian journalist in Liberia at the time, offered this explanation for the consumption of Quiwonkpa's remains by Doe loyalists:

> At the Barclay training ground, before hundreds of spectators, Quiwonkpa's body was chopped up into bits in a macabre cannibalistic ritual by some of Doe's soldiers who astonishingly . . . still believe that by eating bits of a great warrior's body, some of that greatness would come to them. The heart, of course, was the prize delicacy . . . traditionally shared on a hierarchical basis.[36]

Cannibalism among armed subalterns was unheard of in Rawlings's Ghana and Sankara's Burkina Faso but not in Liberia and Sierra Leone, where some of the worst human rights violations by armed subalterns were committed.

Doe's point man in carrying out the summary executions of suspected Quiwonkpa supporters was Colonel Harrison Penue, a Krahn from Doe's village of Tuzon in Grand Gedeh County. Penue, who claimed to have personally disemboweled former president Tolbert in 1980, ordered and organized many of the summary executions and mutilations at the Post Stockade and Executive Mansion. Pennue reportedly compiled a "death list" of all suspected sympathizers of Quiwonkpa's failed attempt to seize power. Besides Pennue, Charles Julu, another Krahn and close associate of Doe, was involved in directing summary killings and other atrocities in Nimba County.

Nimba County, home of the Gios and the slain Quiwonkpa, was the scene of horrific abuses during the Doe period. Thousands of Gios and

Manos were slaughtered and buried in mass graves in the aftermath of Quiwonkpa's failed coup. Most of the atrocities in Nimba took place in the mining town of Yekepa, where Charles Julu doubled as local Chairman of Joint Security for the County and Director of Liberia-American-Swedish Minerals Company (LAMCO) security division, otherwise known as the Plant Protection Force (PPF).[37] Relying on both regular soldiers and PPF personnel, Julu spearheaded a campaign of reprisal against Gios and Manos. He single-handedly transformed the PPF headquarters into a detention center and used company facilities and vehicles to carry out revenge killings. Given the suffering of ordinary Gios and Manos at the hands of Doe's private army and militias, it was not surprising that support for the insurrection, which finally drove Doe from power, was strongest in Nimba County.

In Grand Gedeh County, home of Sergeant Doe, extortion and summary killings by Krahn soldiers and their machete-wielding civilian compatriots was the order of the day, especially during tense periods. The role of Krahn civilians in these atrocities distinguished events in Grand Gedeh from other parts of the country. According to a local resident,

> If the soldiers were the only ones causing the pain, I probably would have accepted it easier (as orders from the top). However, the Krahn in town were just as ruthless. Some Krahn men had gathered their hunting guns and formed a posse. They searched the bush area each day for "enemies" of the state. . . . Other Krahn involved in violence against the innocent were my own students. They went on a rampage, looting homes and beating various individuals.[38]

The involvement of Krahn civilians in ethnic reprisals ultimately endangered all Krahns as forces opposed to Doe sought to exact revenge against the entire ethnic group.

Compounding the aforementioned abuses, Doe banned all political activities and student organizations, clamped down on newspapers and imprisoned journalists at will. Ironically, the University of Liberia, whose students had been generally supportive of the PRC coup, became the target of sustained repression under the PRC dictatorship. PRC Decree 2A of 1982 banned all academic activities which "directly or indirectly impinge, interfere with or cast aspersion upon the activities, programs or policies of the People's Redemption Council."[39] Tensions between the PRC and the academic community came to a head on August 22, 1984 when soldiers from Doe's Executive Mansion Guard unit tried to suppress a student demonstration on the campus of the University of Liberia (UL). Students were protesting the arrest of Amos Sawyer and George Kieh, both Political Science professors at the University, on suspicion of plotting a coup against the government. In the melee that followed the armed invasion of the University campus, a few students were killed, many were severely beaten, and some were stripped naked and raped by soldiers.

Following this confrontation, Doe dismissed key members of the University administration. Among those given the axe were Mary Sherman (university president), Philip Banks (dean of the law school), Amos Sawyer (dean of the political science department), Patrick Seyon (administrative VP of the University), and J. Teah Tarpeh (VP for Academic Affairs). These dismissals were preceded and followed by a series of faculty detentions. In 1980, Dr. J. Teah Tarpeh and Prof. H.B. Yaidoo were detained at Post Stockade on suspicion of engaging in subversive activities. Patrick Seyon was jailed for two weeks, along with other civilians and soldiers, on suspicion of plotting to overthrow the government. Seyon was later tried and found not guilty by a military tribunal, after which he was released. Although Amos Sawyer and George Kieh were later "pardoned" by Doe after their arrest sparked student demonstrations, they, like many others, were never charged. In November 1985, Mary Sherman (dismissed president of the university) was arrested and detained at the Post Stockade for her alleged involvement in a coup plot.

The detention of students by the Doe government predated the 1984 disturbances on the campus of the University of Liberia. Comany Wisseh, a student leader, was arrested for "anti-revolutionary activities" in June 1981. Other student leaders were soon to follow, most notably the leadership (Ezekiel Pajibo, Siaffa Blackie, Klon Brownwell, James Kwiah, Alaric Tokpa, Kpedee Worwor) of the Liberian National Students Union (LINSU). These students were tried by a military tribunal, sentenced to death and later "pardoned" and released in response to mounting international criticisms and pressures. In December 1984, six student leaders (Pajibo, Tokpa, Lucia Massally, James Fromoyen, Dempster Yellah, Christian Herbert) were held for over a month at the National Security Agency before being transferred to Belle Yella prison. After nine months of incarceration, they were released without ever having being charged.[40]

Journalists did not fare any better than students and academics under Doe. Charles Gbenyon, editor-in-chief of the Liberian Broadcasting Service (LBS), was murdered at the Executive Mansion in November 1985. Gbenyon's apparent offense was the airing of scenes of civilians rejoicing at the premature news of Doe's ouster by forces loyal to Quiwonkpa. Doe interpreted Gbenyon's professional decision to broadcast public reactions to the coup as an act of support for the coup makers. Less than twenty-four hours after the broadcast, Gbenyon was apprehended, beaten, handcuffed, and taken to the Executive Mansion where he was reportedly murdered. Doe later claimed that Gbenyon accidentally shot himself at the Mansion, even though he was taken there in handcuffs.[41]

Independent journalists were constantly harassed, threatened and detained by PRC operatives. The detention of journalists without charge and the closure of independent newspapers by the government had a chilling effect on independent news outlets. Doe threatened Rufus Darpoh, editor of the *Sun Times*, with death before shutting down his paper; the *Daily Observer* and *Footprints* were also effectively muzzled by death threats and arson.[42] Kenneth Best, founder and editor of the *Daily Observer*, was detained on at least two occasions before his paper was shut down in January 1985. When he tried to resume publication of his newspaper in 1986, the premises of his paper were fire bombed by Doe operatives.

By the time Doe was murdered by forces loyal to Prince Yormi Johnson, violence and terror had already assumed a terrifying ethnic dimension and trajectory. Forces loyal to Doe and those opposed to him committed massive atrocities against innocent civilians. Responsibility for Liberia's descent into terror, however, primarily lay with Doe. In the summation of one study,

> President Doe . . . sanctioned an undercurrent of lawlessness and random brutality among soldiers of the Liberian Armed Forces. Looting, arson, extortion, arbitrary beatings and persistent reports of rape have all been attributed on a wide scale to government soldiers. Almost no one has been held accountable for these crimes. The government's consistent failure to investigate or prosecute abuses of human rights . . . reinforced the widely held view that the soldiers remain a law unto themselves.[43]

Democratization

Liberia was experiencing a partial democratic opening at the time of the 1980 coup. Political parties had been allowed to register even though one of them (PPP) was later banned. The announcement that multi-party elections for the legislature and the presidency would be respectively held in 1981 and 1983 provided further hope for democratic forces. But even as Tolbert appeared to accept the need for some kind of liberalization of the political system, questions remained as to how far the president was willing to go with his reformist posturing. After all, Sawyer's attempt to contest the Monrovia mayoral election of 1979 had been thwarted by the TWP after it became clear Sawyer would win. This event, and the banning of the PPP in 1980, raised serious doubts about Tolbert's commitment to democratization.

Based on some of the statements made by PRC leaders, it was quite evident from the outset that the PRC was not interested in beating a hasty retreat to the barracks. Henry Zuo (PRC member) could not, for instance, understand "why people" were "concerned about the government returning to civilian rule so soon."[44] When Quiwonkpa suggested to Doe that they should relinquish power and further their education, the PRC chairman's response was that "the late President Tubman never graduated from high school . . . so why should he (Doe) worry about school."[45]

Lacking any desire to relinquish power but under pressure from the United States to at least hold multi-party elections, Doe lifted the ban on political parties, formed his own party and announced a date for multi-party elections in 1985. A new constitution was promulgated in 1984 and a Special Electoral Commission was established. Doe also appointed an Interim National Assembly dominated by military personnel. To clear the way for his presidential bid, he overturned a constitutional provision excluding military and police personnel from participating in the electoral process. Doe also padded his age by a few years to become eligible as a candidate in the presidential election.

Over ten political parties announced their intention to participate in the elections after the ban on political activities was lifted in 1985. Most of these parties, however, faced a myriad of legal and procedural obstacles that prevented them from registering and taking part in the elections. Several party leaders were either detained or banned from politics. Decree 88A, which allowed the government to detain individuals spreading "rumors, lies and disinformation" that undermined state security, made it virtually impossible to hold free and fair elections. It was under the provisions of this decree, for example, that Ellen Johnson-Sirleaf, a prominent opposition figure, was arrested and tried for criminal sedition and libel after she gave a speech in the United States in which she referred to government officials as idiots. Others detained under this decree included Bachus Mathews, Amos Sawyer, Dusty Wolokolie, John Karweaye, and the entire leadership of the Liberian People's Party (LPP).

Arguably, the two most popular political parties in Liberia at the time were banned from contesting the 1985 elections. The United People's Party (UPP) of Bachus Matthews and the Liberian People's Party (LPP) of Amos Sawyer were excluded from the electoral process. The UPP was denied registration because its leader was demonized as a socialist by the government even though the UPP denied any committment to a specific ideology. According to Doe's Justice minister, Jenkins Scott:

> Bachus Mathews is an avowed socialist. What are his sources of support? When an individual living in a capitalist society tells us he is an avowed

> socialist, and we're capitalists, should he be permitted to run? He has a degree of support but what kind? Car washers? The unemployed. The hard core unemployable who don't want to work. A lot of the people who follow his organization are hoodlums. Is this the man one wants to see as head of the government?[46]

Disenfranchising so-called socialists not only removed some of the main obstacles to Doe's bid at self-succession, it also received the blessing of a Reagan administration that was more interested in ensuring that Liberia was not run by so-called socialists than in free and fair elections.

With a truncated field of presidential candidates, the following parties actually contested the 1985 elections—Doe's National Democratic Party of Liberia (NDPL); the Liberian Action Party (LAP) led by Jackson Doe; the Unity Party (UP) of Dr. Edward Kesselly; and Gabriel Kpolleh's Liberian Unification Party (LUP). The LAP, which included some former MOJA leaders, was dominated by the "liberal reformist wing of the True Whig Party," which had "actually challenged Tolbert publicly on some of his principal policies and programs."[47] In choosing Jackson Doe, a Gio from Nimba County as its presidential candidate, the LAP sought to project itself as the party of national reconciliation. Jackson Doe grew up as a ward of Louis Grimes (former chief justice of the supreme court) and had represented Nimba County in the House of Representatives (1967–1972) and the Senate (1975–1980) before his appointment as vice national chairman of the TWP during the last year of Tolbert's presidency. Sharing identical goals with the LAP, the UP of Edward Kesselly (a Loma from Lofa County) favored privatization of state corporations. Like the LAP flag-bearer, Kesselly had also served in various cabinet positions under the TWP.

Doe's NDPL faced stiff competition from the LAP, whose leader is widely believed to have actually won the 1985 presidential contest. The electoral campaign was itself marred by widespread intimidation and thuggery, with the NDPL "task Force" orchestrating a systematic campaign of intimidation directed at LAP and UP leaders. The closure of the *Daily Observer* in January 1985 and the *Sun Times* in August 1985, deprived the electorate of its most reliable and independent sources of information and journalistic analysis. By outlawing parties, politicians and newspapers, Doe and his NDPL made it virtually impossible for anyone else to win the elections.

With initial tallies showing Doe doing poorly in all but Grand Gedeh County, the Chairman of SECOM, Emmet Harmon, arbitrarily appointed a fifty-member committee to recount the ballots because of what the Chairman alleged were "irregularities." Doe supporters dominated the

Committee, with nineteen members coming from his Krahn ethnic group.[48] Thus, although the original count had Jackson Doe winning the presidential election by 60 percent, the results of the recount showed Doe winning the election with 50.9 percent of the vote. This contrived turnaround was rendered more incredulous by the results of the parliamentary election, which gave the NDPL a majority in ten of the thirteen counties, including Nimba—a hotbed of political opposition to Doe. Doe's NDPL claimed to have won twenty-one of twenty-six senate seats and fifty-one of the sixty-four seats in the House of Representatives.

While the outcome of these elections, especially the fact that they were held, may have satisfied United States policy makers (Doe's primary target audience), they did not further the cause of democracy in Liberia (see Table 5.1).[49] Both the LAP and LUP denounced the results and refused to participate in the new parliament. Five years after these elections, Doe was murdered and Liberia is farther away from democracy as a consequence of Doe's rule than at any other time in the country's modern history.

Economic Performance

The economic problems inherited by the PRC were the product of both the recession of the 1970s and corruption within the ruling oligarchy. The quadrupling of oil prices in the 1970s, the sharp reduction in the price of iron ore (Liberia's main export at the time) and the global recession of the 1970s led to stagnation and decline of the Liberian economy. The high growth rates recorded from the 1950s through the early 1970s all but disappeared by the time Tolbert was overthrown.

The 1980 coup triggered capital flight and a domestic liquidity crisis in the first few months of PRC rule. Over 20 percent of deposits in the commercial banking sector was transferred abroad and less than two years after the PRC coup, private sector liquidity fell from $175.5 m. to $102.6 m. The volume of United States currency in circulation dropped from $10.5 m. in 1980 to $4.2 m. in 1984 while Liberian coins (Doe dollars, as they were

Table 5.1 Index of civil and political liberty in Doe's Liberia

1980/81	*81/82*	*82/83*	*83/84*	*84/85*	*85/86*	*86/87*	*87/88*	*88/89*
P6/C6	*P6/C6*	*P6/C6*	*P5/C5*	*P6/C5*	*P5/C5*	*P5/C5*	*P5/C5*	*P5/C5*

Source: Freedom House Country Rankings at http://www.freedomhouse.org
P = Political Rights; C = Civil Rights; 1 = Most Free; 7 = Least Free.

called) in circulation increased from 11.6 m. to 31 million Liberian dollars.[50] The total foreign debt of the Liberian state quadrupled from $750 m. in 1980 to $4.0 bn. in 1990. While government expenditure was subsidized by aid from the United States—which increased from $10 m. a year before the PRC coup to over $80 m. a year after the coup—the unbridled corruption of Doe and his cronies hastened the demise of the Liberian economy.[51]

Economic devastation was particularly evident in the extractive sectors of the economy. Since Monrovia was later cut off from "Greater Liberia" by the civil war, the Doe government lost substantial revenue from iron ore, diamonds, timber, and agricultural products. The abandoned Bong Iron Ore Mining Company was plundered and its machinery sold overseas by Charles Taylor. LAMCO, another iron ore multinational, had to work out an arrangement with NPFL forces to continue using port facilities at Buchanan. Since Taylor's forces controlled much of Liberia outside the capital of Monrovia, the Doe government lost access to critical resources needed for regime survival. This in turn fostered the state's allocative enfeeblement.

From the standpoint of economic performance, aggregate indicators show a general decline in virtually all sectors of the Liberian economy under Doe (see Table 5.2). Although the United States gave more money to Liberia during the Doe era than at any other time in the country's history (Liberia was the largest per capita recipient of U.S. aid in sub-Saharan Africa in the 1980s), there was nothing to show for it. There was a general downturn in economic activity that affected both the Agricultural and industrial sectors (see Table 5.3) and

Table 5.2 Liberia: Basic economic indicators

Econ. indicators	*1980*	*1981*	*1982*	*1983*	*1984*	*1985*
Population			1.98	2.04	2.11	2.19
GDP ($m)			899.5	834.6	835.4	811.2
GDP Growth (%)			−2.2	−3.3	−3.0	−0.9
Exports ($m)			477	428	452	436
Imports ($m)			428	412	363	284
Intl Resv. ($m)			6.5	20.4	2.11	2.19
Ext. Debt ($m)			658	740	810	912
Debt Serv. Ratio			6.7	6.5	4.5	3.9
Ore Prod. (000t)			18.0	15.6	14.9	14.4
Rubbr Prod. (000t)			68	76	86	84
Current Act ($M)			2	−84	13	75

Source: Economist Intelligence Unit, *World Outlook, 1989*.

average growth rates in agriculture, industry and exports were consistently negative.

The high revenue and expenditure growth rates under Doe reflected the massive infusion of aid money from the United States, the bulk of which was spent on the construction of housing for the military while the remainder was illegally diverted into private bank accounts by Doe and his associates.

Under pressure from the United States, and in a partial abdication of sovereignty, Doe placed the Liberian ministry of finance under the supervision of U.S. financial advisers in 1987, but not even this act of desperation could reverse the downward spiral of the Liberian economy. Liberia's international reserve was a paltry $1m. in 1987 and, with a high external debt burden, the Liberian economy was in a virtual free fall as the Doe years came to a close. Growth rates were consistently negative and the effects of official corruption diminished the state's capacity to provide basic social amenities. No significant development project was undertaken during the Doe years and the average Liberian was in every sense worse off at the end than at the beginning of Doe's dictatorship.

Doe blamed the revenue shortfalls of his government on "evil forces" bent on destroying the Liberian state. As he put it,

> We have had to expend valuable resources and energy against evil forces which have been tirelessly at work to destroy our country, discredit every legitimate effort we have made, and offer the most negative impressions of our country to the outside world. The disruptive forces of coup attempts have contributed to our economic difficulties and the crisis of confidence in the country.[52]

Table 5.3 Liberia: Average growth rates (1980–1990)

Indicator	*1980–85*	*1986–90*
GDP	−2.4	0.9
Inflation	5.2	15.7
Agriculture	−1.3	0.1
Industry	−5.0	−6.1
Exports	−3.1	−3.7
Imports	−8.6	−4.0
Govt. Revenue	23.6	22.2
Govt. Expenditure	33.4	39.3
External Debt	13.1	8.6

Source: African Development Report, 1997.

Doe also blamed the hosting of the 1979 OAU summit for Liberia'e economic difficulties. According to him, "our obligation for that event has been the single heaviest burden this government and its citizens are bearing."[53] While some of these factors, especially hosting the O.A.U. conference, contributed to Liberia's economic woes, it is unlikely that a more favorable inheritance could have made any difference. Plunder by Doe and his coterie of Krahn loyalists could not be reconciled with maintaining Liberia's economic viability even under the best of circumstances. It, therefore, came as no surprise that the Liberian economy and state tumbled in tandem after the United States withdrew support for the Doe government in 1988/89.

Conclusion

More than any other subaltern dictatorship to emerge in West Africa, Doe's personal rule was a harbinger of some of the worst abuses associated with subaltern military regimes in Africa. That Doe stayed in power for as long as he did was due mainly to U.S. financial and diplomatic support. A beneficairy of the cold war, Doe was to later become a victim of the cold war's end after the United States terminated its financial assistance in 1989. With America no longer willing to prop up its former despotic allies (Doe, Barre of Somalia, Mobutu of Zaire) in Africa, Doe, according to Tunji Lardner, became a victim of "imperial euthanasia"—he "died because his treatment was withheld by the United States and his life-support system shut off."[54] Stated differently, American policy was to help "create the mess, then stand back and watch the slaughter."[55]

CHAPTER 6

Burkina Faso: "Robin Hood of the Sahel"

Armed Subalterns did not initiate the August 1983 coup in Burkina Faso but they were the driving force behind the regime that was installed in the aftermath of this intervention. The leaders of the 1983 coup were highly trained young military officers who did not share the lumpen social background and class location of the PRC coup leadership in Liberia. What these leaders had in common with other armed subaltern dictatorships was hostility toward senior officers and the usual populist rhetoric. Under the leadership of Thomas Sankara, the *Conseil National de la Revolution* (CNR) pursued the most radical transformative project attempted by a military regime in the subregion. In contrast to most other military dictatorships, including those examined in this study, the CNR leadership cultivated its social base among the peasantry. Politically seeking to align the Burkinabe militariat with the peasantry distinguished the CNR from other military dictatorships in Africa.

As a vanguardist dictatorship, the CNR came to office determined to mobilize the Burkinabe population for a "genuine popular revolution." Guiding this revolution was a populist-socialist ideology that identified the peasantry as the new social base of the regime and the primary focus of development efforts. Compared to other dictatorships of the militariat in Africa, the CNR was the most ideologically motivated and committed. As Thomas Sankara was quick to point out, "there is no politics without ideology;" "ideologies provide a beacon, tools of analysis which enable us to better understand our social reality."[1]

Just as the Doe coup in Liberia was influenced by the "first coming" of Rawlings in 1979, the Burkina Faso coup of 1983 was also shaped by events in Ghana, particularly Rawlings's "second coming" (1981). According to Sankara, it was the populism of Rawlings that most appealed to him and other CNR leaders:

> If Rawlings has admirers in Upper Volta, whose fault is that? It is imperialism's fault. . . . Ghana can impose nothing on us nor we on it. Rawlings can't give us lessons nor we him. However, when he says "No way for *Kalabule*"—no to corruption—he says something that is in the interest of the people of Ghana and of all other peoples. The Voltaic people, too, are against corruption.[2]

This solidarity of populist outlook nothwitstanding, the contrastive fortunes of Sankara and Rawlings suggest that even when its leadership is in touch with mass aspirations, the performance of dictatorships of the militariat are often ambiguous, contradictory, and sometimes tragic.

Coups in Burkina Faso

Burkina Faso was granted flag independence by France on August 5, 1960. Maurice Yameogo, the country's first president, installed a one-party political system without amending the constitution, which called for a multi-party system. Those opposed to Yameogo's power grab were arrested and jailed, with some finding their way back into the government upon their release. The elimination of the political opposition cleared the way for the subordination of state institutions to Yameogo's *Rassemblement Democratique Africain* (RDA). It was, however, easier subverting the state and personalizing power than coopting and/or repressing the labor movement and professional organizations. A standoff between striking workers and the Yameogo government precipitated the latter's ouster in January 1966. As Claude Welch observed at the time, it was the president's "illusions of strength and support" that "contributed to the initial armed Forces seizure of power, a reluctant act taken in the face of major urban unrest."[3]

Colonel Sangoule Lamizana, the country's army commander, led the coup that toppled Yameogo's government. Lamizana belonged to the old school of military officers in Francophone Africa who gained their spurs in French colonial armies. He had served in the French armed forces from 1936 to 1961 and was a veteran of World War II and French military campaigns in Indochina and Algeria.[4] He seized power in the midst of escalating political tensions that stemmed from Yameogo's proposal to slash the wages of civil servants by 20 percent. The declaration of a state of emergency to deal with a January 1966 strike backfired as troops refused to shoot at strikers who were openly clamoring for the army to intervene.

Upon seizing power, Lamizana dissolved the National Assembly, suspended the constitution, and announced the formation of the Superior Council of the Armed Forces (headed by himself) and a Consultative Committee as the supreme ruling organs of the state. The Superior Council included all senior officers and over half of Lamizana's cabinet ministers were soldiers. Of the forty-six Cosultative Committee members, ten were military officers, five represented trade unions and four were representatives of political parties; other members included religious leaders, traditional authorities, and representatives of professional organizations. Both Council and Committee members were appointed by the military.

Lamizana formally terminated military rule in 1969, announced the resumption of political activities and established a committee to draft a new constitution. The new constitution was approved in a referendum on June 14, 1970 by 98.41 percent of voters.[5] This document allowed Lamizana to remain in office as head of state for another four-year term and although the new National Assembly could withdraw confidence in the government, the prime minister was still appointed by the president. Legislative elections held in 1970 saw the RDA winning thirty-seven of fifty-seven seats, followed by the *Parti du Regroupment Africain* (PRA) with twelve seats. Lamizana appointed Gerard Ouedraogo of the RDA as prime minister and the latter assembled a cabinet composed of eight RDA members, five military officers and two PRA members. This second republican experiment, however, ran into trouble in 1973 after strikes by teachers and labor unions prompted a showdown between the prime minister and the speaker of the National Assembly, Joseph Ouedraogo. The latter's attempt to force the prime minister from office through a vote of censure brought the government to a standstill. Responding to this political deadlock, Lamizana once again suspended the constitution in 1974, dissolved the National Assembly, banned all political parties, dismissed the Ouedraogo government and appointed a new government of "National Renewal" (*renouveau national*).

Lamizana's attempt to institutionalize his idea of national renewal through the agency of a single-party system was vehemently opposed by the unions who had grown increasingly assertive and combative in the absence of political parties. Facing opposition from the unions, Lamizana gave up on his idea of establishing a new political party—*Mouvement National pour le Renouveau* (MNR)—, choosing instead to settle for a new constitution that allowed limited competition. This new constitution was approved by 92.7 percent of voters on November 27, 1977.[6]

The third republic (1978–1980) was ushered in by multi-party elections, which, in the view of Richard Vengroff, were "one of the most open, democratic elections ever witnessed in Sub-Saharan Africa."[7] Four candidates—Macaire Ouedraogo of the *Union Nationale pour la defense de la Democratie* (UNDD), Joseph ki-Zerbo of the *Union Progressiste Voltaique* (UPV), Joseph Ouedraogo of the *Front du Refus* (FDR) and Lamizana, who did not belong to a political party but was supported by the RDA, PRA and the *Union National des Independants* (UNI)—were on the first ballot of presidential polling on May 14, 1978. With over 60 percent of registered voters abstaining from the elections, Lamizana failed to secure an absolute majority in the first round; in the ensuing run-off, he won 56.2 percent of the popular vote, compared to 43.8 percent for the UNDD's Ouedraogo.[8]

Assembling a new government was one of the unenviable tasks confronting President Lamizana after the 1978 elections. Joseph Conombo, the President's choice as prime minister, failed in his effort to form a government of national unity; his overtures to the UPV and FDR were rebuffed. As a result, Conombo's cabinet was reduced to a mere RDA/PRA coalition, with the RDA filling eleven ministerial positions and the PRA four. In a replay of events in the second republic, the "feuding Ouedraogos" (Joseph and Gerard) paralyzed the National Assembly. Joseph Ouedraogo, whose FDR had closed ranks with the UPV to form the *Front Progressiste Voltaique* (FPV), made no secret of his desire to oust Gerard Ouedraogo (Lamizana's second republic prime minister) from the speakership of the national Assembly. A Strike by primary school teachers and their union, *Syndicat National des Enseignants Africains de Haute-Volta* (SNEAHV) was joined by the *Confederation Syndicale Voltaique*(CSV) whose leader, Soumane Toure, was a member of the communist *Ligue Patriotique pour le Developpement* (LIPAD). Taken together, these strikes and the squabbling in the national assembly severely weakened the Conombo government and hastened the demise of the third republic.

A coup on November 25 1980 finally brought an end to the Lamizana era in Voltaic politics. Soldiers from the *Regiment Inter-Armes d'Appui* (RIA), under the command of Colonel Saye Zerbo, overran the capital of Ouagadougou, declared a state of emergency, suspended the constitution, banned political parties, and took over the reins of government in what was, for all intents and purposes, a popular coup. Support for the coup came mainly from marginalized sectors in the third republic. These included

> All those who had stood to lose or who felt sidelined by the civilian Lamizana regime—SNEAHV and the FPV, the Mossi (Lamizana was

> Bissa), the Catholics (Lamizana was Muslim), the UNDD—cheered the new government (although the new president, Saye Zerbo, was also a Muslim Bissa). The Unions' backing (another pattern reminiscent of 1966) was expressed on 1 December by the SNEAHV and the SUVESS, which declared themselves ready to take part in the 'drive for recovery'.[9]

Zerbo announced the formation of the *Comite Militaire pour le Redressement et le Progres National* (CMRPN) whose membership, in addition to the core group of twenty-five officers, included officers below the rank of Captain, five noncommissioned officers and one private. A cabinet of nine civilians, none of whom had served in the third republic, and eight military officers was entrusted with the everyday running of the government. Under Zerbo, the CMRPN implemented austerity measures that enraged the unions whose right to strike was proscribed in November 1981. But while the CMRPN managed to hold the unions in check, it could neither prevent nor resolve the growing factionalism within the CMRPN and the military as a whole.

Factionalism within the CMRPN and the military pitted senior officers and veterans of World War II against junior officers and graduates of military academies. As products of military academies, junior officers were younger and more inclined to be radical than their senior counterparts, many of whom had been involved in the politics of the postindependence era. The fact that the CMRPN excluded radicals and conservatives from the government provided a unique opportunity for leftist organizations to forge political alliances with radical junior officers in the army. Thomas Sankara's resignation from the junta in April 1982 was immediately followed by his arrest and detention at Dedougou. Also arrested and detained after resigning from the CMRPN were Blaise Compaore and Henri Zongo, the principal architects of the August 4, 1983 coup.

Having alienated both conservative and radical factions of the military and political establishment, the ouster of the CMRPN on November 7, 1982 did not surprise anyone. Led by Colonel Gabriel Yorian Some, leader of the Military's conservative faction, the 1982 coup removed Zerbo from office and established a *Conseil de Salut du Peuple* (CSP) with Commmander Jean-Baptiste Quedraogo (a military physician) as president. Although Yorian Some belonged to the conservative faction of the army, army radicals, most notably Sankara and Compaore, supported the coup. The CSP had 120 members (forty officers, forty noncommissioned officers and forty privates) representing a multiplicity of contending factions and political persuasions, and it did not take very long for the junta to be torn apart by tensions and acrimony from within.

The conservative leadership of the CSP was soon to clash with its radical elements led by Thomas Sankara. Sankara used his position as prime minister in the CSP government to advance a populist, militarist agenda that was at odds with the moderate preferences of President Ouedraogo. The sharp, insurmountable differences between Sankara and Ouedraogo led to the arrest of the former, along with other members of the CSP's leftist faction, on May 17, 1983. Ouedraogo accused Sankara of "following step by step the program of the LIPAD, and that program was to lead to a communist society."[10] Compaore, a key member of the CSP's leftist faction, was able to escape arrest and find his way to Po, from where he mobilized a rebellion against the CSP that resulted in Sankara's release from prison and the overthrow of Ouedraogo's government.

The CNR Coup

Factionalism, ideological cleavages within the army, economic crisis, and widening social disparities, were among the main factors behind the Burkina Faso coup of 1983. This coup represented "the first time in the political history of the country" that "a regime was clearly asserting its intention of transforming society by transferring power from the hands of the bourgeoisie to those of the popular classes."[11] The junior rank, populist ideology and mobilizational thrust of the *Conseil National de la Revolution* (CNR) distinguished it from previous military regimes in the country. Compared to the 1966, 1980 and 1982 takeovers, which were orchestrated by the army's top brass, the CNR coup was spurred by the ranks and led by young junior officers. These officers denounced the CSP for "serving the interests of the enemies of the people, the interests of foreign domination and neocolonialism" and vowed, in the words of Sankara, to "restore independence and liberty to our country and dignity to our people."[12]

In the speech announcing the CSP's dethronement, Sankara called on "the Voltaic people to form Committees for the Defense of the Revolution everywhere in order to fully participate in the CNR's great patriotic struggle and to prevent our enemies here and abroad from harming our people."[13] Involving the people in governance was portrayed as "the best way to avoid the army seizing power for itself."[14] The purpose of the coup/revolution was to "transfer . . . power from the hands of the Voltaic bourgeoisie allied with imperialism into the hands of the alliance of popular classes that make up the people."[15] As envisioned by Sankara, the CNR revolution had a dual character:

> It is a democratic and popular revolution. Its primary tasks are to liquidate imperialist domination and exploitation and cleanse the countryside of all

> social, economic and cultural obstacles that keep it in a backward state. From this flows its democratic character. Its popular character arises from the full participation of the Voltaic masses in the revolution and their consistent mobilization around democratic and revolutionary slogans that express in concrete terms their own interests as opposed to those of the reactionary classes allied with imperialism. The popular character of the August revolution also lies in the fact that, in place of the old state machinery, a new machinery is being constructed that will guaranteee the democratic exercise of power by the people and for the people.[16]

The distinction between "reactionary forces" or "enemies of the people" (state, comprador and middle bourgeoisies, "reactionary feudal forces"), on the one hand, and "the people" or popular sectors (working class, peasantry, lumpens), on the other, was an important ingredient of the CNR's populist ideology.[17] Moreover, whereas "the social base of every regime, one after another, had comprised in the main the public administration, the traditional chiefs and the Catholic and Muslim religious hierarchies," the 1983 coup sought to dismantle this pact and establish a new alliance with the peasantry.[18]

The CNR's populism represented an eccletic blend of nationalism, Marxism-Leninism, Pan-Africanism and anti-imperialism. This ideological orientation was reflected in the original composition and societal base of the Junta. The original CNR junta included Captains Thomas Sankara, Blaise Compaore, Henri Zongo and Jean-Baptiste Lingani, all of whom were identified with the radical wing of the army. Compaore had led the force of 250 paratroopers from Po that freed Sankara and others from house arrest. Two radical civilian organizations, *Union des Luttes Communistes* (ULC) and *Ligue Patriotique pour le developpement* (LIPAD), were also represented on the junta. The ULC was established in 1978 as a breakaway faction of the *Organization Communiste Voltaique* (OCV). Unlike the ULC, the *Parti Communiste Revolutionnaire Voltaique* (PCRV) declined to participate in the CNR because of doubts it had about the latter's revolutionary credentials. Founded in 1973, LIPAD was at the time of the coup one of the most influential leftist organizations in the country. An offshoot of the Marxist *Parti Africain pour l'Independence* (PAI), LIPAD was politically linked to the *Confederation Syndicale Voltaique* (CSV), whose chairman, Soumane Toure, doubled as LIPAD chief in Ouagadougou. This extensive involvement of leftist organizations in the CNR parallels similar alliances in Ghana (1981) and Liberia (1980) but not in Sierra Leone and Gambia.

Sankara and the CNR in Power

Symbolic of the CNR's radical agenda of cultural reaffirmation was its decision to change the country's name from Upper Volta to Burkina Faso. This change was justified on the grounds that it was "in harmony with a rebirth we are currently experiencing." According to this reasoning, Upper Volta had to be put

> to death in order to allow Burkina Faso to be reborn. For us, the name Upper Volta is a symbol of colonization. We feel we have no more interest in an Upper Volta than we would have in a Lower, Western, or eastern Volta.[19]

Burkina stands for "noble, upright" while "Faso" denotes community—"a nation that upholds integrity, nobility and uprightness."[20] Complementing this name change was the policy of promoting literacy by teaching in the local languages (Moore, Fulde, Gurunsi, Jula, Gulimansi) and serving local food at all official banquets.[21] Later, in 1987, all civil servants were required to wear local cotton suits and dresses known locally as *Faso Dan Fani*. Promotion of a sense of pride in Burkina culture was a key component of the CNR's attempt to map a new beginning and direction for Burkinabe society.

Three missions were prescribed for the army by the CNR: to combat internal and external enemies of the revolution and provide military training for the entire population; to become more involved in productive actitivities, and; to develop each soldier into a revolutionary cadre. Such an army was to "have no place for any soldier who despises, looks down on, and brutalizes the people."[22] And, "contrary to the point of view of officers filled with the colonial spirit, the politicization and revolutionization of the army" was not supposed to mean the "end of discipline."[23]

Economically, the goal of the CNR was to create an independent, self-sufficient, and planned national economy at the service of a democratic and popular society. This goal was to be pursued through agrarian, administrative, and educational reforms and reforms of the structures of production and distribution in the modern sector.[24] Women were to be among the beneficiaries of this transformative project because, according to Sankara,

> Our revolution is in the interests of all the oppressed and all those who are exploited in today's society. It is therefore in the interests of women, since the basis of their domination by men lies in the way society's system

> of political and economic life is organized. By changing the social order that oppresses women, the revolution creates the conditions for their genuine emancipation.[25]

Pursuant to the junta's declared revolutionary objective of instilling honesty, integrity and commitment to service among public officials, many public servants were dismissed from their jobs for reasons that ranged from "counter-revolutionary activities" to drunkeness and theft of office supplies. Every Burkina citizen, irrespective of rank or position, was required to provide voluntary service that sometimes bordered on gross misallocation of human resources by the revolution. As one professor complained about the type of voluntary service he was required to perform,

> Quite frankly, I don't think my skills are best used in sweeping the streets in the voluntary work for common interest they ask us to do. I would gladly give my services to literacy classes rather than waste my energy out on the street.[26]

A major instrument in the CNR's attempt to mobilize and transform society was the CDRs, which were inspired by a similar experiment in Ghana. This new organization, according to Sankara, created fear among

> those who do not have a calm conscience since they know that everywhere, at the house and office, there are people who can give proof of their guilt. . . . The revolution doesn't take place with white gloves and protocol. When someone has gone several days without eating, and you ask him to the table, he doesn't follow protocol and worry whether the cutlery is on the left or right, and whether he eats the *hors d'ouevres* first. He eats in disorder and later there is protocol.[27]

Bureaucrats and so-called enemies of the revolution were not the only targets of the CDRs. CDRs in the workplace threatened the power and autonomy of unions, whose members were identified as a privileged minority required by the CNR leadership to be among the first to make sacrifices. When trade unions began to express reservations about some of the sacrifices their members were asked to make, such as losing a month's salary, Sankara's response was to suspend union leaders and dismiss their opposition as "pure demagogy." In justifying the CNR's efforts to squeeze workers, Sankara noted,

> Must we continue to demand that 90 percent of the population, who live in rural areas, pay taxes, so that we can augment the salaries of a

> minority of workers in town or must we courageously decide to diminish the salaries of those in town so that peasants don't have to pay taxes?[28]

Alienation of the unions was to eventually prove costly for Sankara's leadership. But before addressing the factors that helped derail the CNR revolution, it is necessary to profile the junta's tenure in power, especially its performance in the critical areas of corruption, human rights, democratization and economic development.

Corruption

If the CNR was to be taken seriously on the issue of corruption, it was imperative for its leaders to set examples others could follow. In contrast to Liberia where Sergeant Doe and his men refused to declare their assets, all top officials in Burkina Faso, including Sankara, were required to declare their assets and sources of income before an anticorruption commission, otherwise known as *Commission du Peuple pour la Prevention de la Corruption* (CPPC). Sankara's assets included an old Renault car, a refrigerator, a few guitars and bicycles and $560 in the bank. The CNR Chairman was paid the local equivalent of $100 a week and had an outstanding home mortage of $2,200.[29] Sankara drove around town in his Renault and donated all the Mercedes and Chevrolet his government inherited to the national lottery, whose proceeds were earmarked for public spending. According to one account, Sankara was "one of the few leaders in contemporary Africa who could find himself without cash, and to have cheques 'bounced' for lack of funds."[30]

The significance of austerity to the transformative agenda of the CNR cannot be overstated. The two sectors that bore the brunt of the regime's emphasis on personal sacrifice for the collective good and the need for public officials to set an example were civil servants and the urban working class. Civil servants were forced to make huge sacrifices, including a 40 percent reduction in salaries, the tithing of one month's salary to the government and cancellation of official perks. Civil servants were enjoined "to demonstrate their willingness and determination to endure and overcome with the masses all the problems militating against the development of the people."[31] Scores of civil servants, in Maoist fashion, were dispatched to the rural areas and forced to work among peasants so as to prevent the formation of "petty bourgeois tendencies."[32]

The CNR's main instrument in fighting corruption was the *Tribunaux Populaires de la Revolution* (TPR). Established in October 1983, the TPRs handled cases of embezzlement and mismanagement of public funds as well as those involving "crimes against the state." The TPRs were supposed "to apply the will of the people" in their rulings and judgments. According to Sankara,

> The justification for setting up the People's Revolutionary Courts lies in the fact that the Voltaic people intend to replace the traditional courts and put into practice the principle of genuine participation by the toiling and exploited masses in the administration and management of state affairs in all spheres and sectors of society.[33]

Insisting that "we judge one man inorder to establish the rights of millions," Sankara proclaimed that "the judgements of the People's Revolutionary Courts will allow us to lay bare the sores of the neocolonial regime for all the world to see, providing material for criticism and laying out the elements for the construction of a new society."[34]

Given the regime's antipathy toward lawyers, defendants were not allowed any right to counsel and there were no public prosecutors. TPRs were typically composed of five CDR members, one soldier and a presiding magistrate. These tribunals imposed sentences ranging from confiscation of a defendant's property to imprisonment for up to fifteen years. Many former politicians were dragged before these tribunals and although some, like former president Maurice Yameogo, were cleared of wrongdoing, others, like Gerard Ouedraogo, received jail sentences. Saye Zerbo, another former head of state, was also slapped with a fifteen year jail sentence and Joseph Ki-Zerbo was required to pay several million CFA Francs in fines. Perhaps one of the most important contributions of the TPRs was that they demystified the "power which had held Upper Volta's 95 percent illiterate masses in thrall to one of the smallest and most exploitative elite classes in postcolonial Africa."[35]

Some of the cases heard by the TPRs involved foreigners. One such case featured Mohammed Diawarra, a former minister in the Ivorian government, who was jailed in Burkina Faso for defrauding the *Communaute economique de l'Afrique de l'ouest* (CEAO) despite pleas for leniency by Felix Hophuet-Boigny, then president of Ivory Coast. Two other prominent foreign officials given jail sentences for embezzling CEAO funds were Moussa Diakite, the Malian Director of the CEAO's Solidarity Fund, and Moussa N'Gom, the Senegalese former secretary-general of the CEAO. In addition to their jail sentences (fifteen years each for Diawarra and Diakite and ten years for N'Gom), these individuals were ordered to pay back the amount embezzled, which was estimated at $18m or CFA6.5 bn., to the state. While the outcome of these two cases may have sent a clear signal about the regime's sincerity in fighting corruption, it nonetheless created problems for Burkina Faso's relationship with its Ivorian and Malian neighbors.

The CNR could never claim to have eradicated corruption but its emphasis on "moral integrity and the revaluation of the ideal of public service, acted as a brake in this area, permitting at least a partial realization of the modernist-authoritarian project of the August revolution."[36] Sankara's posture of self-abnegation and moral integrity did not, however, survive his assassination in 1987. Where Sankara drove around town in a Renault, his successor, Blaise Compaore, betrays a preference for the sumptuous comfort of Alfa Romeos. Designer French suits have replaced Sankara's camouflage uniforms and civil servants are no longer required to be attired in *Faso Dan Fanis*.

Human Rights

Unabashedly repressive, the CNR nonetheless introduced significant measures to address the basic needs of the Burkinabe population. Social justice took precedence over individual rights as the regime focused almost exclusively on the rights of the marginalized majority, namely peasants and women. Women, according to Sankara, were

> . . . exploited like dairy cows in our country. They are made to bear children, give milk, work themselves to the bone and then provide a source of pleasure for their husbands. When they become old, they are simply replaced by other dairy cows.[37]

The regime sought to mobilize women through the *Union des femmes Burkina* (UFB) and encourage their participation in CDRs and TPRs. To futher the cause of female emancipation, the CNR banned prostitution and polygamy, began a campaign against female circumcision, appointed five women to ministerial positions, improved educational access for girls and even flirted with the idea of paying half a man's salary to his wife.

Addressing the basic needs of the peasantry was an obssession for Sankara. The peasantry was to be the primary beneficiary of state policies not only because it comprised 87 percent of Burkina Faso's population but because "it is the social layer that has had to pay the highest price for imperialist domination and exploitation."[38] Thus, even while acknowledging its "economic and cultural backwardness" the peasantry was projected as "the principal force" and beneficiary of the CNR revolution. The regime's emphasis on rural development led to the abolition of private land ownership, confiscation and redistribution of land, dispossession of landed proprietors, and abolition of rural taxes and compulsory labor by peasants for village chiefs.

The insertion of CDRs into rural communities also formed part of the CNR's anti-feudal project whose main goal was to supplant the authority of traditional chieftains with new revolutionary structures. But traditional authorities did not simply roll over or play dead; many opportunistically reinserted themselves or their allies in the new structures. As in Ghana under the PNDC, traditional hierarchies managed to take control of most rural CDRs and were "in a position to resist the decrees of the central government, and therefore to block the transformation of social relations on which the success of the agrarian and property reform depended."[39] All said, and "despite his high ideals, Sankara appears to have been too progressive for the peasants he stubbornly championed."[40]

Making health care available to all citizens was another important human rights goal of the CNR leadership. The main emphasis in this area was on primary health care (*Soins de sante primaires*). Main hospitals functioned as regional referral centres while local clinics provided primary health care under the supervision of district clinics. The government's plan to have a local health centre in each of Burkina Faso's 7,500 villages, staffed by a community health worker and a midwife, was all but realized by 1987. Providing maternal and infant care and vaccination against communicable diseases were also key elements of the government's health policy. In one immunization campaign, the government in November 1984 vaccinated over three million children against yellow fever, meningitis and measles. The impact of this and other measures were immediately felt, especially in the areas of infant mortality and river blindness.

Education was defined by the CNR regime as a right of all Burkinabe citizens. The problem to be tackled was making access available to all citizens. Hundreds of schools were constructed in the rual areas and literacy campaigns were launched throughout the country. But while primary schooling was made readily available, the paucity of secondary schools was not adequately addressed, a fact that reflected the regime's obssession with primary or basic need satisfaction. Even so, the regime claimed that its campaign to eradicate illiteracy led to an increase in literacy from 5 to 15 percent during the course of the CNR revolution.

Housing, like health and education, was seen as a basic human right of all Burkinabe citizens. The government took steps to provide affordable housing for citizens by regulating rents and constructing modern residential units for urban workers. Many families, however, were forced to evacuate their homes to make room for the new projects. To combat excessive rents, Sankara suspended residential rent payments for a year and began a massive project to build public housing. The regime's housing initiatives did not, however, produce the desired results. In the urban areas, the housing reconstruction program "drove the majority of the *deguerpis* (the urban poor or those "chased off") to the periphery of Ouagadougou where they reconstructed those 'spontaneous neighborhoods' that the reform proposed to suppress."[41]

While the regime was sincerely committed to improving the lot of the average Burkinabe citizen, it also trampled on the rights of those considered "enemies of the revolution." Many civil servants were arbitrarily dismissed from their jobs during the early days of the revolution. Although the CNR did not follow the footsteps of Rawlings and Doe in executing people for corruption, it nonetheless carried out its own fair share of executions, albeit for treasonable offenses that did not include corruption. The most notable of these executions took place in 1985 when seven unionists and army officers were executed for allegedly plotting a coup. Many trade union leaders, once allied to the CNR, found themselves on several occasions in jail for a variety of reasons. In 1985, over 1,000 teachers were imprisoned for daring to go on strike. The *Moro Naba* (Mossi Chief) was denounced as a feudal relic and stripped of most of his powers. Efforts to curb panhandling by clearing the streets of beggars created tensions with the Muslim community for whom random charity constitutes a religious obligation. Maraboutage was also denounced as feudalistic and efforts to undermine the authority of Muslim Marabouts created tensions between the regime and the Muslim community. The recourse to sorcery by those seeking to preserve the privileges of the traditional order prompted the regime to identify fetishism as "one of the principal social hindrances that plunge our countryside into obscurantism . . . thus preventing minds from liberating themselves and opening themselves up to the progress brought by the August revolution."[42]

Compared to Ghana and Liberia, human rights abuses under the CNR were less atrocious and indiscriminate but by no means less arbitrary. Sankara had very little patience with what he described as "bourgeois justice" but his efforts to popularize justice through the TPRs were often subverted by some of the very forces these new institutions were supposed to expose and bring to justice. Unlike Ghana and Liberia, no one was executed for corruption and in contrast to Liberia, there were no mass killings in Burkina Faso under Sankara.

Democratization

The CNR leadership came to power with no immediate plans of returning to the barracks. Sankara rejected the very notion of military disengagement from politics because he saw the army as a "component of the people."[43] As was true of its social conception of human rights, the CNR approach to democracy emphasized social justice and popular participation. Popularizing political power took precedence over the protection of individual rights and liberities. With this as ideological backdrop, one of the first steps taken by the regime to promote popular participation was the establishment of a variety of mass organizations, the most important of which was the *Comites pour la defense de la Revolution* (CDR). Touted as avenues of popular participation and an alternative source of power, CDRs were formed in every urban neighborhood and in each of the thousands of villages that dotted the Burkina rural landscape.

The main purpose of the CDR was to democratize political power. In Sankara's own words, the CDRs were to serve as

> . . . the authentic organization of the people for wielding revolutionary power. . . . The CDRs are the shock troops that will attack all the strongholds of resistance. They are the builders of a revolutionary Upper Volta. . . . Their main task is to organize the Voltaic people as a whole and draw them into the revolutionary struggle.[44]

At the same time that he was calling for the formation of CDRs throughout the country, Sankara also expressed his contempt for political parties. According to him,

> You cannot create a party with the will of leaders alone. This opens the door to all kinds of opportunism. ... We must at all costs avoid the opportunist temptation to create a made-to-measure party. The creation of a party after the seizure of power is a truly tricky undertaking. There's also a disadvantage to parties. They become too restrictive, overly selective in relation to the masses who are mobilized. From the moment you begin to base yourself on a mere minority, the masses become disconnected from the struggle you are waging.[45]

To complement the CDRs, a plethora of mass organizations were formed to help mobilize popular sectors. The more prominent of these organizations were the *Union des Femmes Burkina* (UFB), the *Union Nationale des Anciens du Burkina* (UNAB), the *Mouvement National des Pionniers* (MNP), and the *Union Nationale des Paysans du Burkina* (UNPB). Women were identified as a marginalized group whose emancipation was to be promoted by greater access to educational opportunities and involvement in CDRs and mass organizations like the UFB. The UNAB, whose main objective was to relate the goals of the CNR revolution to the elderly, attracted the participation and membership of two former heads of state—Maurice Yameogo and Sangoule Lamizana. Peasants were likewise encouraged to channel participation through CDRs and later, the UNPB.

The performance of the CDRs, however, failed to approximate the good intentions and lofty expectations of Sankara. CDRs were in many instances used by local officials to extort money and settle personal scores. At a national CDR conference in 1986, Sankara berated CDR officials who acted like "potentates" and abused their position to enrich themselves.[46] Infiltration of CDRs by forces opposed to the revolutionary process led to their subversion as customary chiefs, leftist trade unionists and civil servants fought for control. Like the CDRs of the PNDC period in Ghana, the CDRs established by the CNR evolved into instruments of repression. This repression, wrote Pierre Englebert, had a dual character:

> It was the expression of near totalitarian control by the CNR over every sector of society and it was the fruit of some of its members' excesses. The use of the CDRs as instruments of repression, control, and mobilization made them deeply unpopular.[47]

The struggle for control of the CDRs created a rift between the CNR and leftist trade unions formerly allied with the regime. The most important confrontation was between the regime and LIPAD, whose Secretary-General, Soumane Toure, had lobbied for the position of secretary-general of the CDRs. Having failed in its bid to control the CDRs, LIPAD developed a more critical posture toward these new structures. Growing confrontation between LIPAD and the military leadership of the CNR led to the purging of all but one LIPAD member from the CNR cabinet in 1984. Soumane Toure, LIPAD's leader, was arrested in 1985 for accusing the CNR of corruption. LIPAD's ouster from the regime left the *Union des Luttes Communistes* (ULC) as the only remaining civilian faction of the regime.

The ULC, later renamed ULCR, was closely aligned with Sankara. To counter the growing influence of the ULCR in the CNR, two new organizations were formed: the *Union des Communistes Burkinabe* (UCB) and the *Groupe Communiste Burkinabe* (GCB). Although originally promoted by Sankara as a counterweight to civilian leftist organizations, Blaise Compaore used the UCB "as a stalking horse in his developing conflict with Sankara."[48] Aligned to the UCB within the CNR was the *Organisation Militaire Revolutionaire* (OMR), a group of radical military officers. Both the UCB and OMR were militarist in their approach to policy issues and, with

Compaore serving as their patron, were able to determine policy outcomes in the waning months of the CNR dictatorship. After the 1987 coup in which Sankara was assassinated, the reconstituted junta moved quickly to purge its ranks of all ULCR members, many of who went into hiding after Sankara's elimination.

There are conflicting accounts of the position of CNR members on the issue of forming a political party. One version states that "Compaore and his supporters pressed for the formation of a single, official vanguard party" that would include the four factions of the CNR (ULCR, UCB, OMR, GCB).[49] Another account claims that it was Sankara that "first pushed for the creation of a single party to merge all CNR groupings, a suggestion poorly received by other factions, who feared for their independence, power and careers."[50] As it turned out, the main disagreement between Sankara and other CNR members had less to do with the formation of a political party than with the form this party should take. Sankara favored a more inclusionary, diverse organization that would transcend the tendencies represented by the four factions in the CNR; his opponents, on the other hand, preferred a more exlusionary, tightly controlled, vanguardist party. Whatever the schisms within the CNR, none of its factions or tendencies favored liberal-pluralist democracy.

Like Ghana's PNDC under Rawlings, Burkina Faso's CNR under Sankara was less protective of the rights and freedoms of the individual (see Table 6.1) than it was of social rights. The regime subscribed to an egalitarian rather than a libertarian view of human and political rights, which was at least preferable to what transpired in Liberia, where the inegalitarianism of Doe's dictatorship was surpassed only by the ferocity of its brutality.

Economic Performance

Twenty years of leadership corruption and economic mismanagement contributed to making Burkina faso one of the poorest nations on earth. At the time of the coup in 1983, Burkina Faso had one of the lowest GNP per capita ($180) and average life expectancy (44 years) in the world. To

Table 6.1 Index of civil and political liberty under the CRN

1983/84	*1984/85*	*1985/86*	*1986/87*	*1987/88*
P6/C5	P7/C5	P7/C6	P7/C6	P7/C6

Source: Freedom House Country Ratings at http://www.freedomhouse.org.
P = Political Rights; C = Civil Rights; 1 = Most Free; 7 = Least Free.

overcome the legacy of abject poverty, the economic policy of the CNR emphasized food sufficiency and investment in basic infrastructure. The economic goal of the revolution was to create a self-sufficient and planned national economy that would cater to the most urgent needs of the rural and urban massees. Toward this end, the CNR launched a fifteen-month Popular Development Program (PDP) in 1984 that was later followed by a more comprehensive five-year plan.

The PDP was "clearly the expression of the needs of the rural masses" and a "concrete translation of the principles of self reliance and popular participation which lay at the core of the Burkinabe development strategy" under Sankara.[51] This program provided for 1607 billion CFA francs (CFA471 = $1 US) to be invested between October 1984 and December 1985. Twenty percent of this investment was to be financed by national resources. Formulated after intensive consultations with rural dwellers, the PDP had two components: a base program that emphasized improvement of water and food supplies and a support program that focused on animal husbandry, crop development, education, and health. In addition to the base and support programs, three other projects were given priority in the plan—the Kompienga dam and hydroelectic power scheme, the Bagre irrigation dam and the Ouagadougou-Tambao railway project. The railway project was considered crucial to developing the Manganese deposits at Tambao and promoting agricultural development in the Sahelian north. The areas earmarked for major reforms were agriculture, education, production, distribution, and administration.

The CNR's agrarian reform policy aimed at increasing labor productivity, diversifying the agricultural sector, abolishing cultural obstacles to peasant production and making agriculture the basis of industrial development. Private land ownership and rural taxes (including the poll tax or *impot de capitation*) were abolished and emphasis was placed on self-sufficiency in food and the provision of clean water for the rural population. Women were given the same rights as men to lease land; given the migration of rural men to urban centers and neighboring countries, it was hoped that this reform would give women a greater stake in the land and help increase food production. The commitment to self-sufficiency in food production led the government to embark on the Sourou Valley Project, which covered the provinces of Sourou, Passore and Yatenga. A 714 kilometer canal was to be constructed by local labor during the first phase of the project; the second phase envisaged the establishment of 40,000 hectares of irrigated land, 28,900 hectares of which was to be in the Sourou valley and 10,810 in the upper valley of the Mouhoun. The producer price for food staples was also increased with a view to providing an added incentive for farmers to increase production.

The administrative reforms of the CNR were aimed at purging the bureaucracy of "all the evils that characterize it" and creating "an administration that is inexpensive, more effective, and more flexible."[52] Many of the regime's administrative reforms had the effect of alienating the vast majority of bureaucrats, some of who were summarily dismissed from their jobs. In education, the goal was to transform educational institutions into tools of the revolution and health policy was geared toward making health care available to everyone. Immunization of the population against yellow fever, measles, and meningitis were among the early actions taken by the regime to address the appalling health conditions of the average Burkinabe citizen.

By far the most ambitious economic project launched by the CNR was the Ouagadougou-Tambao railway project. This project was supposed to facilitate the exploitation of the country's manganese reserves (estimated at 17.7 million tons) and establish a rail link to Niger. Considered by many experts to be an unviable project, the decision to proceed with the construction of this railway was illustrative of the CNR's populist approach to development. The government saw the *Bataille du Rail* "as part of the people's struggle" and "a symbol of the country's self-sufficiency and national pride."[53] Sankara laid the first rail and challenged his compatriots to build the rail line through self-help. CDR members, soldiers, civil servants, traders of Quagadougous's *Grande Marche*, and even American Peace Corps volunteers, participated in this project. Throughout, the government maintained that it was the patriotic duty of every citizen to contribute a day's work at the tracks. In addition to providing free labor, voluntary financial contributions were also solicited from citizens by the government. While the project encountered many glitches due to the lack of adequate supervision, the idea of building a railway through voluntary labor was unprecedented in independent Africa.[54]

The steadfast commitment to a developmental approach that emphasized self-reliance also shaped the CNR's policy on foreign aid. As Sankara pointedly observed,

> Few other countries have been inundated with as many types of aid as mine has been. This aid is in principle to favor development. Yet you will look in vain for any signs in what was Upper Volta, of anything connected with development.[55]

Sankara believed aid that could not help Burkina Faso lessen its dependency must be rejected. As he put it,

> Aid to Burkina Faso must serve to strengthen, not undermine, our sovereignty. It should help to destroy the need for further aid. All aid that

> puts further aid to death is welcome in Burkina faso. But all aid that creates a beggar mentality, we will have to do without.[56]

The CNR's populist critique of aid was also extended to the country's foreign debt, which at the time of the CNR coup stood at $461 million. Sankara was defiant, insisting that the country's

> . . . foreign debt should not be repaid. To repay it would be unjust. It would be like paying war reparations two times over. . . . deciding not to pay requires united front action. Either we resist collectively and refuse categorically to repay the debt or, if we are not able to do this, one by one, isolated, we will suffer death.[57]

Diversification of foreign economic relations and reduction of Burkina Faso's dependence on France and neighboring Ivory Coast were key priorities for the government. Economic cooperation with Libya, Ghana and Benin were expanded, as were relations with the European Community, Japan, China, USSR, North Korea, and Cuba. The West German *Kreditanstalt fur Wiederraufbau* agreed in 1985 to contribute $12 million toward the $73 million estimated cost of the PDP. Others contributing to the PDP were the African Development Bank ($23.5 million), the Saudi Fund for Development ($11.1 million), the French *Caisse Centrale de Cooperation* ($9.5 million), the European Development Fund ($6.5 million) and Canada's International Development Agency ($7.1 million).[58]

Although the CNR was able to diversify its external sources of development support, the continued reliance on external development assistance seemed to undermine the government's gospel of self-reliance. Guy Martin, for example, could not help but notice the "obvious contradiction between the proclaimed objective of economic self-reliance and the fact that 80 percent of the development program [was] to be externally financed."[59] Further compounding the problem of self-reliance was the dependency of the Burkinabe economy on receipts from Burkinabe migrant workers in Cote d'Ivoire. Yves Lacoste argued that it was virtually impossible to "initiate a self-reliant development strategy when most of the work force finds more profitable working conditions in a neighboring country."[60]

From a macro-economic perspective, the economy did not perform any better under the CNR than when its predecessors were in charge. One area of dramatic improvement, however, was in the country's international reserves, which climbed from $85 m. in 1983 to $233.5 m. in 1987 (see table 6.02).

Table 6.2 Burkina Faso: Basic economic indicators (1983–1997)

Basic indicators	*1983*	*1984*	*1985*	*1986*	*1987*
Population (m)	7.5	7.7	7.9	8.1	8.3
GDP (CFA-Afr, bn)	381.8	390.6	455.4	455.8	492.3
GDP Growth (%)	−4.8	−2.1	NA	NA	NA
Exports ($m)	57.0	79.8	69.3	82.8	NA
Imports ($m)	287.5	254.6	325.5	403.6	NA
Intl. Resv ($m)	85.0	106.3	139.5	233.5	322.6
External Debt ($m)	394.8	407.0	497.2	615.7	NA
Debt Service Ratio	9.8	9.7	16.9	14.8	16.4
Current Acct. ($m)					

Source: Economist Intelligence Unit, *World Outlook 1989*, p. 137.

On the flip side of the economic ledger, the country experienced a sharp increase in its external indebtedness, a development that somewhat contradicted the regime's self-reliance posture. Both the rising levels of imports, which continued to outstrip exports by a wide margin, and the escalating debt burden, reflected the regime's commitment and impatience to transform Burkina society. This sometimes meant investing in unprofitable ventures that nonetheless created jobs, enhanced communication, and improved the lot of subaltern masses.

Compaore's Front Populaire

On October 15, 1987, soldiers loyal to Blaise Compaore assassinated Sankara. This event marked the end of Burkina Faso's revolutionary experiment. Compaore cited Sankara's growing personalization of political power and his tempestuous relations with the unions as reasons for his elimination. Compaore apparently felt overshadowed by Sankara and had complained that Sankara's "very dominating personality, his charisma, his desire for stardom and his manipulative talents drove him progressively to gain personal power."[61] While Sankara was always the first to admit that mistakes had been made in his zeal to transform Burkinabe society, many felt his shortcomings did not justify his violent end. Even as the revolution faltered, Sankara remained the most popular of CNR members. And it was precisely those who consistently sought to subvert the course of the revolution that "chose to resolve their differences with Sankara through the method they knew best-military force."[62]

To replace the CNR, Compaore announced the formation of a twenty-four member *Front Populaire* (FP). This reconstituted junta included

Compaore as Chairman and two other leaders of the 1983 CNR takeover—Jean-Baptiste Lingani and Henry Zongo. Prominent UCB and GCB leaders were also rewarded with positions in the junta. Two prominent leftwing organizations excluded from the FP were the ULCR, which had supported Sankara to the very end, and LIPAD, with whom Sankara had a falling out. Many ULCR members and "Sankaristas" were targets of FP repression in the aftermath of Sankara's murder. In addition to the twelve or so Sankara aides killed in the volley of bullets that cut down the CNR leader, many others were imprisoned, tortured, and forced into exile. Scores of students were arrested and held *incommunicado* and Guillaume Sessouma, a University lecturer and ULCR member, died in prison under mysterious circumstances.

The hostile domestic reaction to Compaore's power grab was led by students whose protests forced the new junta to close all schools nationwide. The FP sought to demonize Sankara and make life difficult for his widow, Mariam, by denying her employment and preventing her from leaving the country. There was a sharp rise in the number of executions as Compaore went about consolidating his grip on power. He first executed nineteen pro-Sankara soldiers from the Koudougou battalion for resisting the FP takeover. As is usually the case under these circumstances, it did not take long for the FP to turn on itself. Zongo and Ligani, two of the four core leaders of the CNR coup, were executed on September 20, 1989 after they were found guilty by a military tribunal of plotting to overthrow Compaore. Both Lingani and Zongo had complained about the "rightist deviationism" of the FP and may have been eliminated for their growing disagreements with Compaore rather than because they were planning a coup. At any rate, many observers believed that the coup plot was concocted for the sole purpose of getting rid of the last remaining members of the CNR leadership quartet, besides Compaore. In effect, Compaore rose to and consolidated his power by first eliminating the three other individuals with whom he staged the 1983 coup.

Compaore's policy of rectification brought an end to Burkina Faso's revolutionary experiment. Disconnected from the military underclass by virtue of class position and ideological persuasion, the FP was not linked to the CNR era in the same way that the PNDC represented continuity with the AFRC period in Ghana. Despite Compaore's claim that ". . . the Popular Front came to power primarily to enlarge and broaden political freedom by allowing pluralism and multi-partyism,"[63] events in post-Sankara Burkina Faso leave no doubt about the wholsale departure from the populist ideology and direction that shaped CNR policies under Sankara.

Conclusion

Of all the subaltern leaders covered in this study, Sankara was perhaps the most forthright and sincere in his commitment to improve the lot of subordinate classes. Francois Mitterand aptly summed up this endearing aspect of Sankara's personality and leadership:

> President Sankara is a very disconcerting man. He titillates you, asks questions and prevents you from sleeping in peace. But he ought to know that I am like him, with thirty-five years more experience. He has the earnestness of a vibrant youth, and is devoted to his people, but he is too earnest. If he was not like that at thirty-seven years old, how would he be at seventy years old?[64]

That the CNR fell short in its mission to transform Burkina Faso had a lot more to do with the schisms and factionalism that characterized the junta than the sincerity and integrity of Sankara in following through on the revolutionary goals set for society by the regime. Though vanguardist, Sankara was nonetheless more inclusionary in his approach to organizing and exercising power than were his leftist and rightist opponents.

CHAPTER 7

Sierra Leone: "Sobels" and "Foot of State"

This chapter examines the National Provisional Ruling Council (NPRC) and Armed Forces Revolutionary Council (AFRC) coups and dictatorships in Sierra Leone. Both interventions were linked by the social background and false populism of leadership elements and by a shared hostility toward senior officers. The farcical euphoria generated by the 1992 coup dissipated into criminal terror after the 1997 takeover, leaving in its wake a sprawling debris of devastation and human suffering. In many ways similar to the PRC of Liberia, Sierra Leone's AFRC criminalized the state by establishing a direct linkage between subaltern terror and resource extraction. With violence displacing patronage as mode of accumulation, it is little wonder why Sierra Leone and Liberia degenerated into such hellish environments dominated by marauding gangs of brigands. But why did armed subalterns perform so horribly in Sierra Leone and Liberia but not in Ghana and Burkina Faso (under Sankara)? Before taking up some of these issues in the conclusion, it is necessary to first describe what happened under subaltern dictatorships in Sierra Leone and Gambia.

Martial Law, the NRC and ACRM

Sierra Leone has experienced five successful coups since the country gained independence in 1961.[1] Two of these takeovers occurred within forty-eight hours of each other in 1967, followed by yet another coup a year later in 1968. The 1967 interventions took place against a background of growing factionalism within the army. Albert Margai's (prime minister from 1964 to 1967) politicization of the army as an instrument of his rule created dissension and exercerbated tensions among officers and between some officers and the political leadership. The force commander of the army, Brigadier David Lansana, was the prime minister's protégé and ethnic compatriot (both were Mende). Lansana, however, did not command the respect and loyalty of his immediate subordinates, many of who possessed better educational and professional credentials than the brigadier. Differences between Lansana and one of these subordinates, Lt. Col. Ambrose Genda, led to the latter's discharge from the army on the orders of Albert Margai. Genda's dismissal ruffled the feathers of many officers who resented both the prime minister's meddling in military affairs and the force commander's use of his position to promote the fortunes of his political patron.

Relations between Lansana and senior officers continued to deteriorate in the wake of Genda's departure from the army. A group of officers led by Major Andrew Juxon-Smith called for the brigadier's resignation, accusing him of "nepotism, tribalism, immorality, drunkenness and the inability to administer."[2] Northern officers felt particularly alienated by Lansana's ethnic favoritism in promotion and other important decisions affecting the army. Unease among northern officers and ranks at the entrenchment of Mende officers in the army was not helped by the marginalization of Lt. Col. John Bangura, the most senior northern officer in the army at the time. Although Bangura was battalion commander prior to his departure for professional studies in England, he was unable to retain his old job upon his return home. Instead, Bangura was appointed deputy force commander while the post of battalion commander went to Captain Sandi Jumu, a Mende officer.

The rivalry between Lansana and Bangura exposed serious political divisions within the officer corps. Lansana was a tool of Margai's attempt to subjectively control the army while Bangura, on the other hand, was in the opposition APC camp and was believed to enjoy strong support among northern officers. Political lines were further drawn when, in February 1967, Margai implicated the APC and some army officers (mostly northerners) in a coup plot to overthrow his government. Lansana proceeded to arrest Bangura and seven other officers on charges of plotting to overthrow the government.[3] The trials of these officers never got underway as Margai lost the 1967 elections and Lansana was toppled less than forty-eight hours after his brazen imposition of martial law.

Civilian incumbents determined to hold on to power were behind Sierra Leone's first military intervention. After Albert Margai's defeat in the 1967 elections, Lansana must have reckoned that his days as force commander were numbered but this realization alone cannot explain his praetorian intervention. Rather, what happened was that ". . . the Margai group, acting through the force commander staged a coup that was meant to be preemptive" and whose "initial purpose . . . was to use a limited period of martial law to annul the governor general's action and somehow to create a majority in parliament."[4] That the brigadier accused the governor general of acting unconstitutionally in appointing a new prime minister before the final tallies of the 1967 elections were announced did not offset the perception that his actions were politically motivated.

Outflanked by his subordinates, with whom he shared a common ethnic background, Lansana was arrested together with Albert Margai on March 23, 1967 and placed in protective custody. Two of the counter-coup leaders, Majors Sandi Jumu and Bockarie Kaisamba, had benefited from the brigadier's patronage while a third, Major Charles Blake, had seen his career stall under Lansana's leadership. The political loyalties of all three officers lay with the SLPP camp but not with Albert Margai. Kaisamba's brother, Kutubu Kaisamba, was not only a thorn in Albert Margai's political flesh, his defection from the SLPP actually cost Margai the 1967 elections. The two coups of 1967 were, nonetheless, similar in that they represented "the continuation of civilian party politics by other means."[5] The officers who removed Lansana from office were certainly not Margai loyalists but they were even less sympathetic to the prospect of an All Peoples Congress (APC) government, the party that won the 1967 elections. Thus, rather than return the country to constitutional rule, the trio of coup leaders decided to form a junta, the National Reformation Council (NRC), which ruled the country for a year.

Led by Brigadier Andrew Juxon-Smith, the NRC

> Represented the sentiments of a non-Margai faction within the SLPP, which recognized his unpopularity and considered him a political liability. The overwhelming pro-SLPP bias of the new rulers and their commitment to the basic status quo were confirmed by the appointment of P. Tucker, former secretary to the prime minister and one of the chief engineers of the Lansana coup, as secretary-general to the junta.[6]

The NRC was composed of five senior army officers (Juxon-Smith, Blake, Jumu, Kaisamba, and A.R. Turay) and two senior police officers (William Leigh and Alpha Kamara). Tensions later emerged between Juxon-Smith, who had played no role in the NRC coup, and the other members of the Junta. Juxon-Smith was well known for his religious sermonizing and bizarre flights of visionary fancy. His style of leadership, which was highly arbitrary and dictatorial, did not go over well with his colleagues. The sanctimonious chairman clashed repeatedly with Blake, Jumu, and Leigh over a wide variety of issues, from what to do with the northern officers arrested by Lansana on treason charges to Juxon-Smith's "Operation Spring Clean"—anticorruption crusade that targeted members of the previous SLPP government, some of whom were civilian patrons and allies of the officers behind the NRC counter-coup.

After thirteen months in office, the NRC was overthrown in April 1968 by northern ranks of the Sierra Leone army. This mutiny-coup was largely the work of privates in the army who recruited two warrant officers, Patrick Conteh and Emadu Rogers, to lead them. NRC neglect of the other ranks was the primary reason given for the coup. Patrick Conteh's radio broadcast announcing the coup stated: "the rank and file of the army and police have been ignored" by an NRC junta that was "more corrupt and selfish than the ousted civilian regime." The NRC was accused of wanting "to remain in office indefinitely" even though "soldiers and police have no business running this country."[7] While grievances internal to the army prompted Sierra Leone's first subaltern coup, the goal of this intervention, unlike subsequent interventions, was military disengagement and the restoration of constitutional authority. A new junta, the Anti-Corruption Revolutionary Movement (ACRM), briefly took charge of the state. Membership of the ACRM consisted of eleven warrant officers (including Emadu Rogers and Patrick Conteh) and two police sub-inspectors. The first order of business for this group of insurgent subalterns was to arrest and detain all military and police officers. In all, seventy-six army and forty-eight police officers were arrested and detained at Pademba Road prisons. All but one member (Jumu) of the NRC was apprehended.

Although the ACRM coup was carried out by the ranks, the ethnoregional and partisan dimensions of this coup cannot be overlooked. Most of the participants in the coup were from the north and generally sympathetic to the APC cause. The man they chose to lead the National Interim Council (NIC) was as known for his allegiance to the APC as Lansana was for his loyalty to the SLPP. Bangura was reportedly in contact with the coup plotters prior to the coup and elements of the APC were poised to launch an armed insurrection against the NRC at the time of the coup. It is highly unlikely, for example, that the ACRM or NIC would have relinquished power to the SLPP. The APC, on the other hand, "trusted and believed" Bangura's promise to restore constitutional government "because he was reputed . . . to have the . . . interests of the APC at heart."[8]

With the APC finally in power, the most urgent task facing the new government was the restoration of civilian control of the military. Toward this end, Siaka Stevens purged the officer corps after only two months in office. Among those dismissed were Patrick Conteh and Amadu Rogers. Genda, who like Rogers and Conteh were Mende, was also forced into early retirement. As Thomas Cox wrote,

> Throughout 1968 and 1969, the APC eliminated as many Mendes as possible from the officer corps. Apart from those called upon to answer charges of treason, other Mendes were simply pensioned off without explanation. The result was that by the Fall of 1969 there remained a single Mende among the ten most senior army officers.[9]

Retribalization of the officer corps by the APC leadership could not, however, prevent a coup by the very man who, as chairman of the NIC, had earlier handed over power to Siaka Stevens. On March 23 1971, the force commander of the army, Brigadier John Bangura, led an abortive coup against the APC government for which he and three others were executed. The army was disarmed after Bangura's failed coup and Guinean troops were brought in to serve as guarantors of state security.

The restoration of civilian rule in 1968 led to "redictatorialization" rather than the democratic renewal expected by the populace. In a bid to consolidate power, Siaka Stevens declared Sierra Leone a republic in 1971 and a one-party state in 1978. He also established a paramilitary force, the Internal Security Unit (ISU)—later renamed the Special Security Division (SSD)—, which was extensively used to intimidate and brutalize political opponents. The emergency provisions of the constitution were also routinely abused to eliminate political opponents and shrink the political arena.

Stevens retired from the presidency in 1985 but not before handpicking General Joseph Momoh, the army force commander, to replace him as APC leader and president of Sierra Leone. The transition from Stevens to Momoh was highlighted by a coronation presidential election in which Momoh was the only candidate on the ballot. Momoh's presidency, among other things, directly involved the military in politics and blurred civil-military boundaries. Although he inherited a failed political system and an economy in shambles, Momoh's faltering leadership was a resounding disaster. Cronies of the president in the army, APC hierarchy and from his hometown of Binkolo outpaced him in the frenzy to loot public offices and resources. As predatory accumulation by ruling sectors spun out of control, and as the state became less capable of performing its basic functions, a restive civil society took it upon itself to force the issue of democratization onto the political agenda.

NPRC Coup and Dictatorship

As was the case in Ghana (1979) and Liberia (1980), the 1992 coup in Sierra Leone was preceded by years of social unrest and deteriorating socioeconomic conditions. Public protest in the late 1980s and early 1990s focused on problems of declining living standards, leadership corruption, and the need to democratize the political system. Leading the struggle for democracy were university students, teachers, the labor movement, the Sierra Leone Bar Association, independent newspapers, and representatives of the external estate. Faced with growing internal and external pressures to dismantle the one-party system, the incumbent APC government reluctantly agreed to do so in 1991 and promised to hold multi-party elections. Uncertainty over whether these elections would be held, and public fears that the APC would rig them, mirrored doubts about the party's deathbed conversion to multi-party democracy.

While the APC was busy devising a strategy to remain in power, a group calling itself the Revolutionary United Front (RUF) launched an armed insurgency against the government in 1991. This insurgency, according to Major-General M.S. Tarawallie (force commander of the Sierra Leone Army at the time) caught the Momoh government with its "pants down."[10] Ever since the Bangura-led coup against Siaka Stevens in 1971, the army had been poorly equipped and was virtually disarmed by Stevens as a precaution against coups. The RUF rebellion, however, changed all of this by necessitating the enlargement of the Sierra Leone military and providing the rank and file with greater access to the national armory. Moreover, whereas army recruitment in the past had been based on ethnoregional identity and loyalty to the APC, the desperate need for troops created by the RUF insurgency led to a relaxation of these requirements and the extensive recruitment of thugs, social misfits, and hardened criminals into the armed forces. As Momoh observed in exile after the 1992 coup,

> . . . in the quest to increase numbers, training standards dropped and discipline may have subsided also, because not much time was given to screening entrants. The result is that a large number of undesirables, waifs, strays, layabouts and bandits may now be in the nation's military uniform.[11]

Poorly trained but heavily armed, scores of newly recruited soldiers (mainly urban lumpens) were deployed in the countryside where they did more to terrorize innocent civilians than engage rebels. It was "when the civilians figured out that their attackers were not only rebels but also government soldiers gone foul, that they took to calling anyone in uniform a sobel—a soldier who took the guise of rebels to pillage, rape, maim and murder."[12]

Grinding poverty, economic devastation, unbridled corruption among public officials, and the failure of the Momoh government to pay its soldiers were among the reasons cited by the NPRC leadership for the 1992 coup. In his first major broadcast to the nation, Captain Valentine Strasser, who emerged as NPRC chairman and head of state, described the 1992 coup as a "clean-up exercise" designed to eradicate "an oppressive, corrupt, exploitative, tribalistic bunch of crooks and traitors."[13] The twenty-six year old leader identified two main objectives of the coup: to end the rebel war and return the country to "true multi-party democracy."

With the exception of Strasser, the other leaders of the NPRC coup (Solomon Musa, Maada Bio, Charles M'bayo, Komba Kambo, Komba Mondeh, Tom Nyuma) were lieutenants from southern and eastern Sierra Leone—regions generally considered hostile to the APC. All the coup leaders were in their twenties and a good number were high school dropouts. In what Joe Opala termed an "ecstatic revolution," scores of students and youths rallied in support of the new junta.[14] Reporting on the general mood in the country at the time of the coup, Chris Simpson wrote:

> Sierra Leoneans will need no reminding that their country was named last year as the poorest on earth. Rapacious mining interests, a colossal debt burden and a vicious border war have all played their part in the decline, but a consistently losing side is surely entitled to pick a new captain. Momoh is at least alive and well, so from that point of view he can be said to have had a 'good coup'.[15]

The initial popularity of the coup obscured, at least for the first few months, the youth and inexperience of the new leaders. Those who were skeptical chose to suspend their misgivings, especially in light of Strasser's promise that "as soon as we put this rebel incursion behind us, a broad-based committee of dedicated and committed citizens will be set up to ensure the realization of our return to true multi-party system of government."[16]

External reactions to the coup were far less supportive. Chief Emeka Anyaoku, the Commonwealth secretary-general, described the coup "as a set back for democracy" and called on NPRC leaders "to make the realization of multi-party democracy, to which they have committed themselves in their first announcement, among their highest priorities."[17] By far the most negative reaction came from Nigeria whose leader at the time, General Ibrahim Babangida, was a friend of Momoh. Since Sierra Leone was a base for ECOMOG military operations in neighboring Liberia, the implications of the coup for Sierra Leone's continued participation in ECOMOG was of concern to the Nigerians. A press release by the Nigerian Foreign Affairs Ministry stated that "the Federal Government . . . expects that the new rulers of Sierra Leone will take urgent steps to ensure that the democratization process continues" and "that Sierra Leone's role in the peace process in Liberia will continue uninterrupted."[18] Although the donor community took exception to the fact that Momoh was overthrown just as he was making plans to hold multi-party elections, the unpopularity of the ousted government, combined with the euphoria that greeted the NPRC coup, abated such concerns.

The original NPRC junta was established by Decree No. 1 (Appointment of Representatives) of 1992. This decree created a twenty-member ruling council consisting of fourteen soldiers and six civilians. Two of the six civilians (Jim Funna and Ahmed Dumbuya) were holdovers from the Momoh government; their retention was designed to reassure the international community and allay donor fears and anxieties. Three other civilian NPRC members (John Benjamin, John Karimu, Arthur Abraham) belonged to what became known as the *Segbwema Mafia*, a cabal of NPRC military/civilian insiders who hailed from Segbwema in the Kenema district, Eastern province. Arnold Gooding, a lawyer from Freetown, was the sixth civilian named to the junta. Five of the fourteen military officers on the junta were lieutenants (S.A.J. Musa, J.M. Bio, K. Kambo, C. Mbayo, T. Nyuma). The other nine junta members consisted of five majors (A.A. Gibril, A.K. Sesay. J. Gbondo, G.T. Mani, S.F.Y. Koroma), one lieutenant colonel (Daniel Anderson), a retired colonel (A.O. Kamara), and two captains (Strasser and Fallah Sewah). Some of these officers (S.F.Y. Koroma, A.K. Sesay, D. Anderson and G.T. Mani) later resurfaced as key players in the AFRC junta (1997–1998).

The Rebel War

One of the NPRC's primary objectives in seizing power was to end the rebel war. The NPRC initially expected the RUF to lay down its arms because, as Strasser put it,

> Foday Sankoh claimed that he was fighting to overthrow the corrupt and oppressive APC regime. Since we overthrew that regime, one would have hoped that our action was enough to bring the rebels to the negotiating table, but that has not been the case inspite of overtures from us.[19]

Hopes that the forced departure of the APC would bring an end to the war were dashed when the RUF refused to recognize the NPRC government. Foday Sankoh, the RUF leader, dismissed the NPRC as a "rebel government" whose leaders "hijacked the revolution" and were incapable of democratizing the political system "because they are not politically conscious."[20]

In response to rebel intransigence and in an attempt to "conclude the rebel war in the shortest possible time," the NPRC went on the offensive against the RUF. A series of military expeditions were undertaken in the first year of junta rule, leading to the recapture of Pujehun from the rebels in March 1993. By the end of 1993, the RUF had suffered major setbacks at the hands of the SLA and Guinean soldiers. Government troops, with assistance from Guinean and Nigerian soldiers, were able to liberate most of the areas under RUF control. Kono, Kailahun town, Pendembu, and Koindu were retaken, as were most major towns in the Kailahun district. In the Pujehun district, the towns of Faro, Wai, Bo Njeila, Blama Massaquoi, Massam Kpaka, Yoni, Bumpeh, Kporwubu, and Fonikoh were recaptured.[21] Recaptured areas continued to experience sporadic RUF attacks but by the end of 1993, the NPRC was so confident of victory that it declared a unilateral cease-fire.

This unilateral cease-fire played into the hands of a battered RUF, who took full advantage of the lull in fighting to regroup. Arthur Abraham, a former civilian minister in the NPRC government, attributes the NPRC's cease-fire declaration to the determination of its leadership to stay in power. According to Abraham, "once the NPRC . . . set themselves to plundering the resources of the state to enrich themselves, they had to keep the war going in order to stay in power and thus maintain the opportunity to plunder."[22] Echoing this sentiment, Joseph Opala contends that the elimination of the RUF would have stripped "the NPRC of its raison d'etre;" hence "winning the 'rebel war' was the last thing the NPRC wanted."[23]

Julius Maada Bio, who briefly succeeded Strasser as head of state before handing over power to the elected of government of Ahmad Tejan Kabba, vehemently disagrees with Abraham and Opala's characterization of the NPRC's war effort. Bio maintains that he and his colleagues on the junta could not have been more eager to end the war, even resorting to hiring mercenaries, but were sabotaged at every opportunity by APC loyalists and rogue elements in the army.[24] APC loyalists dominated both the officer corps and ranks of the SLA in 1992 and Momoh's front organization, the National Forum for the Restoration of Democracy (NAFORD), was reportedly behind some of the *sobel* activities of SLA personnel. One account, for example, noted the growing "evidence that supporters of Momoh are active in fomenting dissension in the SLA."[25] Amnesty International also blamed some of the armed attacks against innocent civilians on "factions within the army who were supporters of the APC, the former ruling party of the government of President Momoh . . . who were opposed to the NPRC."[26] Scores of APC loyalists defected from the army after the NPRC takeover; some joined the ranks of rebels while others formed their own marauding gangs. Many APC loyalists (from top officers to the lowest rank) who remained in the army under the NPRC doubled as *sobels*. By 1994, as many as three battalions of the army were said to be sympathetic to the rebels. Many of these *sobels* provided intelligence to the RUF, sold them weapons and uniforms and made it virtually impossible for the NPRC to win the war.

In addition to this core of APC loyalists were two other identifiable groups of soldiers, namely supporters of the NPRC and those with ambivalent or uncertain loyalties. For the most part, the allegiance of soldiers recruited into the SLA after the 1991 invasion tended to be more ambivalent than those whose enlistment predated the war. Soldiers with questionable loyalties as well as NPRC loyalists may have had less of a political motivation to engage in *sobel* activities but many nonetheless did so for personal gain. In effect, all three groups of soldiers and their officers were not immune from *sobelization*, a process that was set in motion not only by subversive and predatory calculations but also by the sudden transformation of formerly destitute NPRC leaders into profligate tycoons. As Joseph Opala recounts,

> The NPRC reached a tacit understanding with its troops upcountry. If the soldiers refrained from making trouble in Freetown, NPRC leaders would deny every report of government forces terrorizing civilians and attribute every outrage to the RUF. That deal worked well until soldiers seized control of key diamond mining areas in Kono district, depriving NPRC leaders of its greatest source of wealth.[27]

The threat posed by sobels to the NPRC leadership called into question the state's ability to protect its citizens from rebel and sobel atrocities. Unable to protect its citizens against mass atrocities, the NPRC subcontracted some of its security functions to foreign mercenary firms.

The first group of mercenaries, the Gurkhas, proved to be ineffective against the rebels and was replaced by Executive Outcomes, a South African security agency with interests in the diamond industry. Executive Outcomes fought alongside the regular army and local militias and within a short period was able to flush the rebels from most of their camps in the hinterland. A rebel attempt to invade Freetown in early 1995 was repelled by the combined forces of Executive Outcomes, loyalist soldiers, and local militias. The mercenaries, however, distrusted SLA soldiers and preferred to work with members of the *Kamajor* militia, some of whom received basic military training from their mercenary allies. Much of the NPRC's successes against the rebels in 1995 were due to the mercenaries and the *Kamajor* militia.

The RUF was, for all intents and purposes, a far more formidable military adversary at the end than at the beginning of NPRC rule. By contrast, the SLA was weaker and more discordant in 1996 than in 1992. The state, as a result, was less secure under the NPRC than the APC against whom the war was first launched. The NPRC could not win the war because it lost the confidence and support of the population. Leadership corruption and the compradorization of NPRC leaders, together with the sobelization of the SLA, destroyed confidence in the NPRC's ability to end the war. Rather than end the war, it was under NPRC leadership that the war migrated from the Liberian border to the interior of the country and the outskirts of its capital.

Corruption

Next to ending the war, eradicating official corruption ranked highest on the NPRC's inaugural agenda. One of the first steps taken in its short-lived campaign against corruption was to freeze the assets of top APC politicians and bureaucrats. NPRC Decree No. 2 (The Freezing of Assets Decree, May 1992) impounded the assets of key members of Momoh's government, including the former president, vice presidents, ministers, parliamentary special assistants, public officers and board members of state corporations who served between June 1, 1986 and September 22, 1991. Not only were the assets of individuals covered by this decree confiscated, all but a few were detained without charges at the Pademba Road prisons where they languished for long periods of time.

Reminiscent of Doe's PRC in Liberia, NPRC leaders rejected calls to declare their assets but wasted no time confiscating the possessions of some of their predecessors. The Sierra Leone Bar Association (SLBA) had recommened that the "failure to make such statutory declaration on the part of any government official or senior public official should result in loss of office of the said government official or senior public officer in addition to any lawful action which government may feel disposed to take."[28] The failure of NPRC leaders to declare their assets could not be reconciled with the zeal with which they went about seizing the ill-gotten wealth of their predecessors.

The NPRC also established commissions of inquiry to investigate charges of "corruption, mismanagement, and indiscipline in the public service" and to recover "all state assets and other properties improperly obtained . . ." during the period June 1986 to September 1991.[29] The reports of these commissions (three in all) were never published and by the time the whole exercise was concluded, public opinion had turned against the NPRC. Although the commissions uncovered cases of gross misuse and embezzlement of public funds, the *White Papers* issued by the NPRC were in many areas inconsistent with the findings and recommendations of the commissions. A Reconciliation Commission set up by the SLPP government in 1996 to review the petitions of parties aggrieved by NPRC decisions concluded that NPRC penalties were "in most cases . . . arbitrary, draconian and independent of any rationale."[30] The Reconciliation Commission overturned some of these penalties but accepted the original findings of the Beccles Davies Commission, noting that there was a preponderance of evidence regarding ". . . the subterfuges adopted by Dr. Momoh to convert government property to his own benefit and to attempt to conceal that he had done so." In a particularly scathing indictment, the commission surmised that "Momoh appeared to treat Sierra Leone as his personal fiefdom and felt that he was at liberty to act as if its finances were at his disposal no matter what contrary advise was tendered."[31]

The 1986–1991 period covered by the commissions of inquiry left untouched some of the most corrupt officials who served under Siaka Stevens. Investigating Stevens while exempting his ministers surprised a baffled public that was already becoming increasingly suspicious of junta motives and activities. The NPRC apparently decided not to investigate ministers who served under Stevens because of "known relationships between junta members and former APC ministers, as well as the deep involvement of some civilian members of the NPRC in criminal acts with the past APC regime."[32] A well-known APC patron of the NPRC was Edward Kargbo (former minister under Stevens) whose younger brother, Franklin Kargbo, served briefly as the NPRC's Attorney General. Although Edward Kargbo, like Momoh, is Limba, the two men had fallen out during the 1985 transition from Stevens to Momoh. Kargbo, unlike Momoh and Stevens, was never investigated.

Commissions of Inquiry and asset seizures became meaningless gestures as NPRC leaders fell prey to the temptations of office. After a brief period of modest restraint, NPRC leaders began lining their pockets with public funds and living visibly opulent lifestyles that were incommensurate with their social background, official salaries, and positions of responsibility. Junta leaders transformed *Kabasa* lodge mansion into "a private disco where they danced, smoked pot and snorted cocaine through the night."[33] They openly sold the country's passport to foreign nationals, especially Hong Kong

Chinese, for personal gain. Dispatched on an overseas mission to buy arms, Lt. Komba Kambo absconded with the money and settled in Texas, USA. A report that first appeared in a Swedish newspaper, *Sunday Express*, with the headline "Sierra Leone's 'Great Redeemer' Becomes a Millionaire Whilst the People Continue to Starve" was reprinted in Sierra Leone by a local newspaper, the *New Breed*. The *New Breed* editorial accompanying the *Sunday Express* report lamented the fact that

> Eighteen months after the so-called revolution, the promise land is still not in sight. If anything, the status of the common man has worsened due to the NPRC's slavish adherence to IMF and World Bank conceived programs. If this were all, we would not be unduly upset. However, recent events reported by the international press have caused us to despair.[34]

NPRC junta operatives promptly arrested the entire editorial staff of the newspaper, confiscated copies of the paper, and harassed vendors selling this particular edition. In the words of Karefa Kargbo, the NPRC spokesperson,

> The arrest and detention of the *New Breed* journalists is as a result of legal action taken against them. I tell you, that article not only spoilt our characters but did a great deal of damage to the integrity of the NPRC and the country as a whole.[35]

The *Mountain Fat-Foot* anti-smuggling campaign is another illustrative example of how the NPRC went about expropriating the state. The *Mountain Fat-Foot* scheme was designed to curb diamond smuggling by creating an incentive for citizens to provide information leading to the arrest of diamond smugglers. Those providing such information were entitled to 40 percent of the value of the seized diamond. In most instances where the 40 percent commission was collected, the identities of the informants were never disclosed and the sums in question were routinely paid into the accounts of key junta members, including Reginald Glover, the NPRC secretary of state for Mineral Resources. Even gemstones that were not recovered through the *Mountain Fat-Foot* campaign became subject to the 40 percent commission, thus transforming the campaign into a diamond laundry scheme for NPRC leaders.[36]

NPRC corruption unleashed hordes of armed subaltern predators on the countryside. As Strasser and his cohorts

> . . . took up a life of partying, womanizing, and diamond dealing in the capital city, their soldiers cut loose, taking to banditry and terror up

> country. Unable to justify itself as a military government if it could not control the military, NPRC leaders covered for their soldiers, insisting that the mayhem was entirely the work of the RUF."[37]

In no time, "SLA soldiers, backed by powerful patrons, replaced the rebels and also dug for alluvial gold and diamonds which were illicitly exported through Liberian territory."[38] A new mining policy that banned military personnel from "directly or indirectly" acquiring "any right or interest in any mineral" was rendered ineffective by the wholesale involvement of the top echelon of the NPRC leadership in diamond mining and smuggling.[39] By the time the NPRC left office, its leaders had "looted everything they could lay hands on-not a cent was left in the treasury; they stole everything."[40]

The corruption and compradorization of NPRC officials were directly related to the junta's failure to end the war. As Solomon Musa, one of the architects of the NPRC coup, self-servingly observed,

> Selfishness, greed, the desire to acquire wealth at the expense of the people by the Mondeh's and others turned a popular revolution into an unpopular one to the extent that the NPRC lost respect and credibility and was virtually chased out of office.[41]

Without the support of the populace, not to mention its own army, the NPRC could not defeat the rebels because the enemy was within the regular military establishment. Corruption, more than any other single factor, was the major reason the NPRC lost public support and was unable to end the RUF's criminal insurgency.

Human Rights

As was the case in Ghana, Liberia, and Burkina Faso, there was a sharp increase in human rights abuses after subaltern upstarts seized control of the state apparatus in Sierra Leone. Summary executions, harassment, molestation of civilians, detentions without trial, and the maiming and displacement of villagers were commonplace under the NPRC. A major turning point in the escalation of human rights abuses was the December 1992 summary execution of twenty-nine prisoners, many of whom were in detention on charges of plotting to overthrow the junta. Among those executed were Bambay Kamara (Momoh's Police Chief), Lt. Cols. Yaya Kanu and Kawuta Dumbuya, Salami Coker (a playwright), and Coker's pregnant girlfriend. This was the largest group of people executed in Sierra Leone since independence, not to mention the first woman put to death by the state. Although local groups and the international community condemned the NPRC, more executions for alleged treason and collusion with rebels were to follow. The arbitrary manner in which these executions were carried out distinguished the NPRC from the APC, under whose rule executions, though not rare, were only carried out after court proceedings that at least had the appearance of due process.

Soldiers under NPRC rule routinely committed atrocities against innocent civilians and blamed them on rebels. In one such incident, renegade soldiers in Panguma murdered an Irish priest (Felim McAllister) and a Dutch family of three (Elco, Karen, and Zita Krijn) in March 1994.[42] Reacting to these murders, the religious leaders of Kenema, whose diocese includes the St. Kizito parish of Panguma, called on the NPRC government to stop "all looting by armed men in military uniform" and deplored the "continued presence of the army in the mining areas."[43] Two soldiers, Lieutenant James Forbie and Sergeant Mohamed Jawara, were arrested in connection with these murders but were later released for lack of sufficient evidence.[44] This episode, like many others involving disloyal soldiers or *sobels*, blurred the distinction between soldier and rebel and solidified the hostility of local communities toward the NPRC and the army.

The mysterious circumstances surrounding the 1993 death of Dr. Alpha Lavalie, one of the early organizers of the *Kamajor* civil defense militia in Kenema district, and the lingering suspicion that he was ambushed by rogue soldiers who saw him as a threat, further widened the chasm between the national army and civil society. By 1994, the people of Bo (headquarter of the southern province) and Kenema (headquarter of the eastern province) had started calling on the NPRC government to withdraw its soldiers from their towns. In a related development, tanker drivers went on strike in 1995 and refused to haul fuel to the provinces unless the government provided Nigerian and Guinean troops to escort their convoys. The drivers specifically rejected protection by national army regulars because the latter were known to moonlight as *sobels*.

The assault on civilians by *sobels* and rebels created a humanitarian disaster. Over a third of the country's five million inhabitants were displaced. Uprooted from their homes, Sierra Leoneans overcrowded urban centers and sought refuge in neighboring countries. Over 250,000 Sierra Leoneans became refugees in Guinea while another 600,000 were internally displaced.[45] Displacement worsened an already lawless environment as those fleeing rebel/sobel banditry either became brigands themselves or joined the teeming ranks of the destitute, starving, and dying.

In the area of freedom of expression, the proliferation of newspapers that began under the Momoh government continued during the NPRC period.

NPRC press guidelines, however, threatened to destroy the independent press. The NPRC, for example, decreed that "any person who publishes any report or statement which is likely to cause harm or despondency or be prejudicial to the public safety, public tranquility or the maintenance of public order, shall be guilty of an offense and liable on summary conviction to a fine not exceeding Le5000,000 . . . or to imprisonment for a term not exceeding five years or to both a fine and imprisonment."[46] Stiff academic, professional, and financial requirements for the registration of newspapers were also introduced, resulting in the closure of almost half of the thirty newspapers in circulation at the time of the NPRC coup.

Democratization

The NPRC coup forced the democratic transition that began in 1991 into a holding pattern. At the time of the coup, Captain Valentine Strasser committed "the NPRC government . . . to returning the country to multi-party democracy in the shortest possible time."[47] During its second year in office, a National Advisory Commission (NAC) was appointed to review the 1991 constitution and advise the government on the transition to constitutional democratic rule. The junta also established an Interim National Electoral Council (INEC) under whose supervision the 1996 elections were held. James Jonah, the man chosen to head the INEC, was a retired United Nations under-secretary for political affairs and candidate for secretary-general of the world body in 1992. Jonah accepted the challenge of piloting the democratic transition because he wanted to, in his words, "give some service to my country" after "having worked for thirty years in the UN."[48] Before taking the job, Jonah received assurances from the NPRC that the INEC would be allowed to operate autonomously of the government.[49]

Prior to lifting the ban on political parties in preparation for multi-party elections, the NPRC banned fifty-seven politicians from holding public office and participating in the political process. The list of outlawed politicians included former president Momoh, Abdulai Conteh, Salia Jusu-Sheriff, Wiltshire Johnson, Alhaji Musa Kabia, Joe Amara Bangali, Moses Dumbuya, Abdul Karim Koroma, A.K. Turay, and all politicians investigated by the NPRC's commissions of inquiry.[50] Some of these banned politicians (Momoh, Bangali, Johnson, Kabia) later closed ranks with the AFRC after the 1997 coup.

Among the political parties to make their debut on the national political scene in 1995 was the National Unity Party (NUP). The NUP was widely identified as the NPRC party since it was founded and supported by the NPRC junta and its civilian supplicants, notably the *Segbwema Mafia*. John

Karimu, the party's presidential candidate in the 1996 elections, acknowledged that "the NUP was initiated by some people who have served in the NPRC."[51] The other contenders (Valentine Strasser, Hindolo Trye, Steven Bio) for the party's presidential nomination were all from the NPRC. Strasser's desire to contest the 1996 presidential election was made known when some of his supporters stormed an NUP convention with placards that read: "Strasser For President Or No NUP;" "For Me Strasser Ah Go Die;" "Only Strasser Can Lead Us Through;" "No Strasser, No Sierra Leone;" "Who Are Saying Our Leader Is A Child."[52] In the end, it was the balance of power within the NPRC junta that ultimately determined what transpired in the NUP. Led by John Benjamin, the *Segbwema Mafia* orchestrated both the ouster of Strasser as head of state in January 1996 and the choice of John Karimu (NPRC finance minister) as the NUP presidential candidate. Assuming his colleagues are to be believed, Strasser's unceremonious removal from power—he was actually beaten up and sent packing to neighboring Guinea in a helicopter—was prompted by his "blatant attempt to make some major legislative changes in the electoral laws . . . and start machinations to ensure that he is installed as the next president come February 26."[53]

Upon replacing Strasser as head of state in January 1996, Julius Maada Bio first announced that elections would be held on schedule. He later tried to postpone the elections by initiating dialogue with Foday Sankoh, the RUF leader. While dismissing Bio's belated *entente* with Sankoh as a ploy designed to derail the elections, Jonah nonetheless went along with the NPRC's request to convene a consultative conference to revisit the issue of whether to postpone or proceed with the elections.

The prevalent view among the delegates at the Bintumani II consultative conference was that the NPRC was desperately seeking to prolong its incumbency. Bio actively campaigned and reportedly bribed traditional rulers to support postponement of the elections.[54] On the day of the conference, soldiers tore down banners proclaiming "Elections Now" while those calling for "Peace Before Elections" festooned the entrance to the conference hall. Politicians on their way to the conference were manhandled and beaten by soldiers but this did not deter many delegates and their supporters from making the trek to the conference site at Aberdeen. Of the seventy delegates who attended the February 12, 1996 consultative conference, fifty-six voted for elections to be held as scheduled. Fourteen delegates, mainly representatives of the NPRC and the RUF (the RUF sent a letter that was read at the conference), voted to postpone the elections until the attainment of peace. Those favoring elections included representatives of the Bar Association, Petty Traders Association, the Sierra Leone Labor Congress (SLLC), the

Sierra Leone Teachers Union (SLTU), National Union of Sierra Leone Students (NUSS), political parties, and women's organizations.

Consultative conferences (Bintumani I and II) provided an effective forum for public consultation on crucial issues affecting the timing and conduct of the 1996 elections. By opting for consultative conferences, the composition of which it had no control over, the NPRC unwittingly ceded control of the transition process to the INEC. The INEC's position and autonomy were in turn bolstered by these conferences whose deliberations and outcome the NPRC could not skew to its liking. As Jonah insisted during the second consultative conference,

> A small band of people are playing with the lives of the majority of the people of this country. People of goodwill should not allow this to happen. The People's wish must be obeyed.[55]

A few intimidating incidents prior to Election Day renewed doubts as to whether the election would in fact be held. On February 10, 1996, there were three grenade attacks in which the offices and residence of the INEC Chairman were targeted as well as the residence of Ahmad Tejan Kabba, the SLPP presidential candidate. Although there were no casualties and physical damage was slight, these attacks were clearly aimed at derailing the elections by intimidating some of the key players in the process. But if the intention of the NPRC and the SLA was to intimidate and scare voters away from polling stations, the shootings and other acts of intimidation and violence backfired. Demonstrations by women's organizations, students, petty traders, and unemployed youth became the order of the day. Unflattering songs depicting NPRC leaders as rebels and crooks enlivened most of these demonstrations. In the end, people came out in droves not so much to elect a new government as to retire a loathed military dictatorship.

The international community played a very important role in insisting that the elections be held on schedule. A European Union official warned the NPRC government that "if the elections are not conducted, and civilian rule is not put in place by the first week in March, we will use all the instruments available to the European Union to isolate Sierra Leone."[56] Such threats were, however, accompanied by the announcement of packages designed to induce NPRC chieftains to relinquish power. One such controversial package, put together by the African-American Institute (AAI), provided scholarships for NPRC junta members to study abroad.

Thirteen political parties participated in Sierra Leone's transfer elections of 1966.[57] Only five of these parties—Sierra Leone People's Party (SLPP),

United National People's Party (UNPP), People's Democratic Party (PDP), National Unity Party (NUP), All People's Congress (APC)—were serious contenders. Both the presidential and parliamentary elections came down to a contest between the SLPP and its leader, Ahmad Tejan Kabba, and the UNPP and its leader, John Karefa-Smart. In the presidential run-off, Kabba bested Smart with almost 60 percent of the popular vote and was duly elected president of Sierra Leone. The SLPP also won twenty-nine parliamentary seats, followed by the UNPP with eighteen and the PDP with twelve. An electoral alliance between the SLPP and PDP carried over into parliament, giving the SLPP-led coalition government a formidable majority in the legislature.

Economic Performance

Sierra Leone was the poorest country in the world at the time of the NPRC coup in 1992. This ranking was largely due not to the effects of war, which only started in 1991, but to decades of unmitigated malfeasance on the part of public officials. All vital economic indicators were negative in 1992. GDP had fallen from $1.3 billion in 1985 to $857 million in 1990. Government revenue and expenditure as percentages of a declining GDP were down in the same period from 5.3 to 3.9 percent and 11.5 to 5.5 percent respectively. The country's international reserves stood at a paltry $11 million in 1985, bottoming out at $5 million in 1990. The external debt grew from $723 million in 1985 to $1.2 billion in 1990.[58] Dismantling the public sector created financial windfalls for political cronies but the informalization of the economy, particularly the diamond sector, wiped out the revenue base of the state. Chronic delays in the payment of public officials became the order of the day, with salary arrears owed by the government sometimes running into months if not years.

In his first full address to the nation, Valentine Strasser bemoaned the "collapse of our economic, education, health, transport and communications system" under the APC. In the fatuous words of the NPRC chairman, the NPRC coup was supposed to signal "the final death of nepotism, gross mismanagement, corruption, injustice, tribalism and economic decay."[59] The stated objectives of NPRC economic policy were to improve economic performance, control government spending, revive the agricultural sector by emphasizing self-sufficiency in food production, negotiate external debt relief, increase state income from mining by regaining control over mining areas, and rehabilitate the country's infrastructure. These policy goals were in broad conformity with the Rights Accumulation Program (RAP) designed by the IMF and to which the NPRC was committed.

The NPRC was initially successful in controlling expenditures and lowering inflation. Inflation averaged 72.3 percent during the period 1985 to 1993, but was 35 percent in early 1993 and 24 percent at the start of 1994.[60] The Paris Club in 1992 wrote off half of Sierra Leone's debt service obligations on non-concessionary loans. Debt arrears dropped from $279 million at the beginning of 1992 to $162 million by the end of the year. Part of this improvement was due to debt rescheduling and debt cancellations by France, Germany, United States, China and Belgium. There was a 61.2 percent increase in the country's international reserve, from $5 million in 1990 to $52 million in 1995. Government revenue as a percentage of a declining GDP nearly quadrupled from 3.9 percent in 1990 to 14.5 in 1995.[61] Price and trade restrictions were lifted and liberalized, although this resulted in sharp increases in the prices of basic commodities. For their part, western donors and investors poured roughly $324 million into NPRC coffers between 1992 and 1995.[62]

Notwithstanding few areas of nominal improvement, the overall economic outlook of the country under the NPRC remained bleak (see Table 7.1). Real GDP grew from −9.6 percent in 1992 to 1 percent in 1993 but per capita income continued its downward slide from $220 in 1991 to $160 in 1992 and $140 in 1993.[63] The value of exports plummeted from $139 million in 1990 to $24 million in 1995. A major cause of the depressed economy under the NPRC was the rebel insurrection. The rebel war devastated the country's agricultural breadbasket and terminated official mining activities. Many villagers had their limbs severed by rebels and renegade soldiers, thus rendering them (if they survived) useless as farmers. In many areas, farmers were unable to plant crops because of pervasive insecurity and this disrupted both food

Table 7.1 Sierra Leone: Basic economic indicators (1992–1996)

Basic indicators	*1992*	*1993*	*1994*	*1995*	*1996*
Population (m)	4.2	4.3	4.4	4.4	4.4
GDP (Le, m)	327,259	467,188	543,711	710,389	Na
GDP growth(%)	−14.6	−6.9	0.1	−3.6	−3.6
Exports ($m)	150.4	118.3	115.8	39.3	43.06
Diamond Ex(Cts)	329,000	201,000	174,000	266,000	327,000
Imports ($m)	139.0	187.1	149.9	140.0	193,936
Intl. resv. ($m)	20.6	32.8	49.7	51.7	32.9
Ext. Debt ($m)	1,313	1,452	1,532	1,226	1,079
Debt serv. ratio	20.3	16.3	100.0	Na	Na
Current($m) act	−5.5	−58.3	−89.1	−160.5	Na

Source: Economist Intelligence Unit, *World Outlook, 1998.*

and cash crop production. The output of coffee, for example, dropped by over 50 percent in 1996.[64]

Official production of diamond, which once contributed 70 percent of export earnings, all but ceased even before the NPRC came to power. Illegal mining and smuggling, the depletion of alluvial mining fields and the breakdown of security in mining areas were all contributory factors. As the war progressed, illegal mining spun out of control as diamonds distracted soldiers of all ranks. William Reno observed how "some strongmen, including army commanders, refashioned themselves as 'warlords', leading youthful miners, rebel and soldiers . . . in independent mining operations."[65] Not to be left out of the diamond bonanza, Strasser's father resigned his position as headmaster of a school in Waterloo to devote himself to full-time mining.

Sobelization of the Sierra Leone army undermined the regulative capacity of the state and fostered its extractive and allocative contraction. The Sierra Rutile Company and the Sierra Leone Ore and Metal Company (SIEROMCO), which together accounted for 60 percent of the country's export earnings in the early 1990s, were forced to close down their operations following attacks by rebels and renegade soldiers in early 1995. Sierra Rutile, the world's largest producer of high-grade titanium ore, was the country's largest private sector company. That both the rutile and bauxite operations were forced to close down destroyed any hope of economic recovery under the NPRC.

The AFRC and the Felonization of the State

Compared to the NPRC coup, which ousted an unpopular one-party dictatorship, or the 1968 ACRM coup that overthrew a military dictatorship, the May 1997 intervention toppled a democratically elected government. Before this coup, there were at least three attempts made by soldiers to wrest power from the democratically elected government. Common to all of these attempts was the army's refusal to accept its relegation to the barracks in the second republic. As Olu Awoonor-Gordon argued at the time,

> The origins of the May 25 coup lay in the reluctance of a section of the army to give up power in the first place. Although the AFRC Chairman denies that his regime is a re-run of the NPRC, there is no doubt that since the SLPP took power in March 1996, sections of the military have been unrelenting in their attempts to reverse the verdict of democracy.[66]

Awoonor-Gordon's assessment is consistent with the army's image of itself as the most powerful trade union in the country. In an ominously revealing letter sent to President Kabba by a disgruntled soldier, the former was warned that ". . . after God in this country is the army; If you don't believe try to disturb us."[67]

Some of the former bodyguards and errand boys of NPRC leaders initiated the AFRC coup. Tamba Gborie, a semi-illiterate army corporal, freed Major Johnny Paul Koroma from prison before announcing that the ranks of the Sierra Leone army had ousted the fourteen-month-old government of President Kabba. Gborie was a high school dropout who had served in ECOMOG in Liberia and was a personal bodyguard to Colonel Fallah Sewah, a former NPRC Secretary of State.[68] The other principal architects of the 1997 coup were Sergeant Abu "Zagalo" Sankoh, Staff Sergeant Alex Brima, twelve other soldiers and two civilians.[69] The two civilians, Abdul Sesay and Bios Sesay, were laborers (grass-cutters) attached to the Wilberforce barracks of the First battalion.[70] The only senior officer to join the coup right from the beginning was Victor King, the squadron leader of the Air wing of the military. With the exception of King and a few others, the AFRC leadership was "drawn from a group of young, poorly educated and poorly trained junior officers and other ranks."[71]

According to the leaders of the AFRC coup, it was the deplorable conditions of the rank and file and the indifference of senior officers to their plight that prompted their seizure of power. The government's decision to reduce rice subsidies for the army and rumors that the president was planning to downsize the army incensed an already disaffected rank and file.[72] The Government's decision to retire 26 officers and 155 NCOs after an attempted coup in September 1996 angered supporters of the dismissed officers.[73] Gborie revealed that Brigadier Hassan Conteh (the army chief of staff) had advised soldiers that the SLPP government was not in a position to meet their demands because it had to also provide for the *Kamajor* militia.[74] Given the animosity between the SLA and *Kamajors*, Conteh's spin was clearly designed to incite the ranks into taking action. Conteh later joined the AFRC after reassuring the president that the coup would be foiled.

Although "the soldiers who struck claimed to be acting in the interests of the 'nation' as a whole and gave populist reasons for intervention . . . their motives and actions were almost wholly self-serving . . ."[75] Major Johnny Paul Koroma, who was freed from prison to head the junta, stated in his first address to the nation that the army had acted "as committed custodians of state security and defenders of the constitution." He went on to identify three main reasons for the coup: "the fear of having Sierra Leone disintegrate into factional conflicts; the inability of the executive to bring sanity to the situation . . ." and; "the inability of our commanders to convey to the head of state the welfare problems and other administrative constraints within the armed forces."[76] The first point was a clear reference to the escalating feud between the SLA and the *Kamajors*; the second reflected perceptions that the government was using the *Kamajors* as a counterweight to the army and, as such, was incapable of resolving the rift between the two armed factions, and; the third point expressed deep-seated corporate grievances within the army. In short, Johnny Paul Koroma claimed he and his men "took over power . . . to bring peace to our war-torn country and arrest the ugly situation."[77]

But the AFRC coup was at bottom a *sobel* coup that brought together rogue soldiers, discredited APC politicians, remnants of the NPRC and the leadership of the RUF. Johnny Paul Koroma had been suspected of *sobel* activities under the NPRC and prior to his arrest on coup charges in September 1996. Koroma was in charge of securing and protecting the rutile mines when it was overran by rebel forces in January 1995. Reports that most of the attackers at the mines were government troops posing as rebels seem to validate Koroma's *sobel* credentials. Gborie, the man who announced the coup, was a member of Koroma's unit at the time and based on his brazen looting activities after the coup, it is not unreasonable to surmise that he was among those who ransacked the rutile mines.[78]

Related to the *sobel* character of the 1997 coup was the involvement of the RUF in the execution of the coup and the maintenance of the AFRC in power. According to *The Democrat* newspaper, RUF commandos participated in the storming of the state house during the early hours of the AFRC coup. Charles Taylor, the RUF's principal backer and warlord-turn-president of Liberia, also backed the coup by dispatching some of his fighters to Sierra Leone to help keep the AFRC in power.[79] In addition to Taylor, Stephen Bio (NPRC patron/beneficiary) and Omrie Golley (RUF spokesman and legal representative) played key roles in facilitating the marriage of convenience between soldiers and RUF irregulars. During his court martial on treason charges, Gborie revealed that Omrie Golley was among the first people he contacted after the coup. Golley applauded the coup and was instrumental in connecting Gborie and Koroma to Foday Sankoh, the RUF leader.[80]

The AFRC coup of 1997 in many ways represented an undisguised attempt to sequelize the NPRC regime. It was no secret that relations between the Kabba government and former NPRC chieftains had become strained after the forced retirement of NPRC junta members from the army in September 1996. Tom Nyuma, one of the retired NPRC chieftains, and Stephen Bio, the NPRC power broker, were implicated in the first coup attempt against Kabba. Although Nyuma escaped prosecution and was allowed to leave the country, one of his close associates, Paul Thomas, emerged as an important player in the AFRC. Solomon Musa, one of the original architects of the NPRC coup, was appointed the AFRC's *de facto* prime minister. Among other prominent NPRC operatives who resurfaced as members of the AFRC were Colonels. S.F.Y. Koroma, A.K. Sesay, G.T. Mani, S.O. Williams, Captains Paul Thomas and John Milton, Victor Brandon, and Stephen Bio.

In an interview with Johnny Paul Koroma, the former AFRC chairman claimed that the real mastermind of the 1997 coup was Solomon Musa, former vice chairman of the NPRC.[81] Eyewitness accounts of the early hours of the 1997 coup describe soldiers dancing in the streets with pictures of Solomon Musa.[82] Musa, according to Koroma, was the preference of the coup leaders as head of state but Musa was out of the country at the time of the coup and could not easily return, at least not in a timely manner, given the blockade of Sierra Leone by the Nigerian navy and the occupation of its airport by Nigerian-led Ecomog forces. To circumvent this hurdle, Musa duped Kabba and other SLPP leaders in Guinea into facilitating his return to Sierra Leone under the pretext that he would convince AFRC leaders to reinstate Kabba. Johnny Paul Koroma, on the other hand, was in Freetown, albeit in jail, and it was logistically easier to release him from prison than return Musa from London to Freetown. By the time Musa arrived in Sierra Leone, Johnny Paul Koroma was already chairman of the AFRC and Musa had to settle for the position of chief secretary and secretary of mineral resources.[83]

The AFRC also attracted hordes of discredited APC politicians who stood no chance of gaining political power through the ballot box. One such politician was Abass Bundu, an old APC and NPRC hand who could only muster 3 percent of the popular vote in the 1996 presidential election. In addition to Abass Bundu, the list of prominent APC politicians who collaborated with the AFRC junta included former president Momoh, Alhaji Musa Kabia, I.B. Kargbo, Wiltshire Johnson, Nancy Steele, Victor Foh, Alikali Bangura, Dauda Kamara, Joe Amara Bangali, Sani Sesay, and Hassan Barrie. Like the APC, the AFRC was opposed to the democratic wishes of the populace and was prepared to vandalize the state if its leaders could not control or access its offices and resources.

Given the amalgam of unpatriotic elements (APC, NPRC, RUF) supporting the 1997 coup, it is not surprising why this coup was so unpopular. External reactions to the coup were predictably negative. The OAU secretary-general, Salim Ahmed Salim, described the coup as a setback for Africa. Chief Emeka Anyaoku, the Commonwealth secretary-general, denounced the AFRC usurpation as "totally unacceptable to the

Commonwealth" and "a particularly retrograde step for Sierra Leone after the advances made . . . in the last year in building democracy, peace and reconciliation."[84] The coup was also condemned by Kofi Annan, the UN secretary-general, as well as by the donor community upon whom Sierra Leone had become increasingly dependent since the onset of the rebel war in 1991. Not a single country officially recognized the junta, although it was no secret that Liberia's Charles Taylor and Blaise Compaore of Burkina faso supported the AFRC. Sanctions imposed by ECOWAS and the international community on the AFRC were often busted with the help of Taylor and Compaore; this support, more than anything else, helped stiffen the resolve of the AFRC leaders to hang on to power.

Local reactions to the coup were intensely hostile. Although Kabba had squandered his popularity in the months leading to the coup, Sierra Leoneans remained implacably opposed to military rule. Apparently, the coup leaders miscalculated in their expectation that the erosion of public support for the Kabba government would translate into public approval of the AFRC coup. Not only were the political contexts of the AFRC and NPRC coups different, the reasons given for the AFRC coup failed to resonate with the public. Workers refused to return to work even in the face of threats by the junta to sack all employees who failed to do so. For the first time in the country's history, civil society was prepared to resist an unpopular coup not simply through civil disobedience and flight but also through the force of arms. Rejected by civil society and the international community, the AFRC embarked upon the systematic vandalization of the state under the slogan "If you don't want us, you'll die."

Dialogue and Armed Resistance

Efforts to broker a deal between the AFRC and ECOWAS, which would have allowed the ousted government of president Kabba to be reinstated, fell through after the RUF refused to go along with the agreement. Although rumors that the AFRC junta was demanding $45 million as payment for reinstating the ousted government were denied, monetary considerations and a desire to duplicate the predations of the NPRC were uppermost in the minds of the coup plotters. According to Desmond Luke, one of the participants at the talks held to convince the AFRC to relinquish power, "the last thing Johnny Paul Koroma said to me before he left the room after the agreement had been reached, when we were drafting the announcement, was that the amount for himself was too small." The accord, according to Luke, unraveled because the AFRC "could not get the agreement of the RUF who had already come to town at their invitation."[85]

Differences between the SLA and RUF factions of the AFRC over the issue of handing over power to the elected government resurfaced again after the signing of the Conakry Accord between the AFRC and ECOWAS. The RUF opposed this agreement, which called for the immediate cessation of hostilities, the disarmament, demobilization, and reintegration of combatants, the return of refugees and displaced peoples to their homes and the restoration of the elected government of Ahmad Tejan Kabba by April 22, 1998. Signed on October 23, 1997, the Conakry agreement also indemnified members of the junta but the immunities were predicated on the reinstatement of Kabba by April 22, 1998. Its Secretary-General, Colonel A.K. Sesay, and Secretary of State for Foreign Affairs, Paolo Bangura, signed the agreement on behalf of the AFRC.

As it turned out, the junta had no intention of adhering to the terms of the Conakry agreement. Less than thirty-six hours after the agreement was signed, Johnny Paul Koroma was waxing belligerent, demanding that ECOMOG, which was supposed to enforce the agreement, should leave the country. A few days later, the AFRC Secretary of State for Information, Allieu Kamara, advised Kabba to seek asylum in a country of his choice and give up on the idea of returning to power.[86] Later, the SLA element of the junta insisted that it was not required to disarm under the terms of the Conakry agreement while the RUF vowed not to disarm unless its leader, Foday Sankoh, was released from detention in Nigeria. In the end, only a few child soldiers were temporarily disarmed.

One of the most outrageous claims made by the AFRC was that the SLA-RUF merger had finally brought peace to the country. According to Colonel A.K. Sesay,

> There are many good things about the AFRC that are hardly positively mentioned . . . These include: the removal of the RUF from the bush which brought us relief at least on the highways . . . ; the continuous provision of basic necessities like fuel, rice, electricity, until recently, when the sanctions have bitten harder; reopening schools even in Freetown except for the orchestrated threats from ECOMOG which have hampered schooling further.[87]

The notion that the war was over simply because the army and rebels had closed ranks against the civilian population was instantly dispelled by the refusal of the *Kamajors* to lay down their arms or accept the AFRC's invitation to become part of the junta. Counterinsurgents under the NPRC and SLPP governments, the *Kamajors* found themselves recasted as insurgents under the AFRC. *Kamajor* armed resistance to the junta was backed by ECOMOG and the ousted civilian government.

Armed resistance by the civilian population had its limitations. For one thing, the ousted president was reluctant to fully arm and support the *Kamajors* out of fear they could become too powerful and pose a threat to what remained of his authority. Unlike many SLPP barons who clearly sought to strengthen and utilize the *Kamajors* as an adjunct of their party, Kabba was uncomfortable with the *Kamajors* for two main reasons. He saw them not only as a potential threat to his authority but as a force that, if not handled properly, could divide and possibly plunge the country into an ethnic war. Kabba was more accommodating of the *Kamajors* when he was out of power than when in power. Without adequate support from the government on whose behalf it was fighting, and given the lack of proper training, it was highly unlikely that *Kamajor* resistance alone could have dislodged the AFRC from power.

In the final analysis, the AFRC outed the SLA as the military wing of the APC in much the same way that the *Kamajor* militia became identified as a paramilitary wing of the SLPP. The SLA was a key pillar of the house that the APC built and the fact that the sentries of this political edifice became uncontrollable after the overthrow of the APC in 1992 and the election of the SLPP in 1996, only confirm the extent to which APC rule sowed the seeds of lawlessness and destruction in Sierra Leone.

Corruption and Looting

The AFRC coup launched the SLA and its RUF allies on an indiscriminate looting spree that lasted the entire duration of the junta's ten-month stay in power. With the RUF in town, hardly anyone was spared the effects of the looting rampage that gripped the capital and other parts of the country. Soldiers and rebels systematically looted government offices, hotels, banks, restaurants, and shops. The public treasury was razed to the ground and parts of the central bank were also gutted by fire. In contrast to the looting that followed the NPRC coup, whose main targets were APC leaders, AFRC looting was indiscriminate and accompanied by very high levels of violence directed at innocent civilians. In the "gospel" according to Johnny Paul Koroma, looting by AFRC operatives was justified because "that's what happens in revolutions-*looting*."[88]

AFRC subalterns and their leaders expropriated whatever state and society held up as valuable. Major public buildings were ransacked and set on fire. Sierra Leone's prestigious Bintumani and Mammy Yoko hotels were asset stripped, as were many other public and private businesses and institutions.

Peter Penfold, the British High Commissioner in Sierra Leone, reported during the first few days of the coup on the

> . . . need for a degree of control over military elements here. I saw with my own eyes a lot of the looting, especially at the Mammy Yoko hotel, an international hotel which has been stripped bare.[89]

The looting, however, and the atrocities that accompanied it, never abated. In one particular incident, Johnny Paul Koroma felt compelled to compensate his Spur Loop neighbors (the Austrian Consul and the Director of Living World Ministries) after soldiers looted their premises in September 1997.[90]

So pervasive was looting under the AFRC that the junta, in a public relations stunt, issued an anti-looting decree to curb the problem. AFRC Decree No. 6 (Anti-Looting Decree) came into effect on November 20, 1997. The decree established an anti-looting squad with specific functions, powers and duties."[91] It further stated that "any person who is found guilty of an offense under subsections (1), (2) and (5) of Section 15 shall be sentenced to death by firing squad."[92] Section 15 lists five categories of offenses, three of which are punishable by death. The three death categories were: looting and commandeering any vehicle or property without authority; knowingly receiving looted and commandeered property; and occupying, "with or without force and without lawful authority, . . . the premises of another person."[93]

This decree, however, was unenforceable because AFRC leaders were among the chief looters. It seemed hypocritical for Johnny Paul Koroma to take issue with the commandeering of vehicles when he was himself cavorting around town in a stolen jeep. But even Johnny Paul Koroma's thievery paled in comparison to the exploits of Tamba Gborie, the junta's "looter-in-chief" who first announced the AFRC coup on a local radio station and was involved in emptying Pademba Road prisons of its inmates and burning down the treasury building.[94] In one of his most brazen acts of plunder, Gborie led a group of uniformed men to the Iranian embassy where they ransacked the premises and took away every valuable item they could lay hands on.[95] Gborie was subsequently dismissed from the junta's ruling council and demoted to the rank of corporal (he had been promoted sergeant after the coup) after this incident. He was an inmate at Pademba Road prison, where he was being held on treason charges, at the time the AFRC was dislodged from power by ECOMOG forces in 1998.

Soldiers on the rampage repeatedly targeted the premises of foreign NGOs and aid agencies. Together with their rebel allies, they reportedly commandeered over 490 United Nations and NGO vehicles. The offices of

Medecin Sans Frontiers at 18 Lab Lane (off Wilkinson Road) was broken into by armed gunmen who took away drugs, furniture, communication equipment, and cash.[96] One of the favorite targets of the looters was property, especially vehicles, belonging to the European Union.[97] World Food Program warehouses and the offices of the International Committee of the Red Cross and other relief agencies were thoroughly looted in the first week following the coup. Although a few soldiers were summarily executed for looting, execution was less a deterrent than an attempt to find scapegoats for a problem that was endemic to the junta.

Junta members and their operatives went about expropriating the state and private individuals with as much menacing bluster as they did foreign NGOs. Government offices and supplies were among the juicy targets—office equipment and materials, generators, computers, and office furniture were routinely carted away from state offices and sold by soldiers.[98] Private residences were not spared either. Lt. Marouf Sesay, a junta member, led the group of soldiers who looted the residence of President Kabba on June 3, 1997, taking away a variety of items, including TV sets, suitcases, office and household items.[99] The home of the Bishop of the United Methodist Church at Kissy was also repeatedly burglarized by gunmen who took away many of the Bishop's personal possessions at gunpoint.[100] Even the indigent and displaced were targets in what amounted to an endless orgy of instant deprivation at gunpoint. In one incident, the displaced, after abandoning the old Fourah Bay College building at Cline Town during a bombing raid by ECOMOG jets, returned to their temporary shelter only to find out that their belongings had been stolen by soldiers who now occupied what had been their makeshift abode.[101]

Since the undeclared motive of the 1997 coup was the criminal expropriation of public and private property, no attempt was made by the AFRC to address the problem of bureaucratic corruption. In the first week after the coup, junta leaders demanded cash payments, in addition to houses and cars, in exchange for Kabba's reinstatement as President. In the end, the junta gambled that it could ride out domestic and international opposition and gain more by hanging on to power than by stepping aside. Diamond mining, which became every soldier and rebel's obsession, was to provide the resources that would make possible the transformation of previously destitute armed subaltern leaders into freshly minted tycoons.

Human Rights

The AFRC's human rights record was the most appalling of the regimes examined in this study. Crimes against humanity committed by junta operatives included summary executions, mutilation and torture, arbitrary arrests, *incommunicado* detentions, sexual abuse and enslavement, abductions, forced labor, forced recruitment, and the extensive use of child soldiers. All of these violations occurred on a massive scale and were in many instances videotaped by the perpetrators themselves.

The main targets of AFRC terror were supporters and associates of President Kabba, members of the SLPP, suspected *Kamajor* sympathizers, students, teachers, journalists, Nigerian nationals, and even listeners of FM 98.1 (Radio Democracy). Fifteen individuals (eight retired senior military officers and seven civilians) with close ties to the SLPP were arrested, severely beaten, and accused of conspiring to overthrow the AFRC dictatorship in 1997. Soldiers on the hunt for *Kamajors* and their supporters murdered Albert Demby, the ninety-year-old blind father of Vice President Joe Demby, in Gerihun on June 26, 1997. Junta operatives who accused him of supporting the *Kamajors* also dismembered B.S. Massaquoi, a prominent SLPP stalwart and community leader in Kenema. Many other prominent and less known citizens were eliminated by the AFRC for their known or assumed ties to the SLPP and *Kamajors*. Individuals with no SLPP or Kamajor connections, but who favored reinstatement of the ousted elected government, were also targeted for mutilation, dispossession, displacement and other sundry abuses.

An eighty-six year old widow's account of her fateful encounter with junta forces in Bonthe (Sherbro Island) captures the mindless brutality of AFRC rule. In her testimony at the court martial of Tamba Gborie and thirty-seven others, Mrs. Cecilia Caulker informed the court that she and her son, Victor Caulker, were arrested on October 14, 1997. She was later taken to a soccer field to witness the gruesome mutilation of her son who happened to be the regional secretary-general of the SLPP. She was forced to watch as soldiers sliced off the ears and other extremities of her son. Then, her son's bleeding heart was shoved into her mouth. After soldiers decapitated the dead man, Mrs Caulker was ordered at gunpoint to take her dead son's head to the charred remains of her house, which had been ransacked and torched by soldiers. There she was instructed to breast-feed the decapitated head.[102] That this old woman survived this ghastly ordeal to tell her story was in itself quite remarkable, demonstrating, as it does, the resilience of the human spirit in the face of dehumanizing terror.

Many other families, individuals and communities were at the receiving end of AFRC atrocities. The entire village of Telu Bongor, hometown of Hinga Norman (the Kamajor leader), was razed to the ground and many of its inhabitants killed by soldiers and their rebel accomplices. Students and teachers were particularly endangered since the organizations representing them (NUSS, SLTU) had come out very strongly in opposition to junta rule. The AFRC threatened to mutilate students if the latter held protest demonstrations, a threat that was carried out when machete-wielding AFRC operatives broke up a student demonstration on August 18, 1997. Six students were reportedly killed in this confrontation and over one hundred of them were arrested and detained. Many female students were taken to the residences of AFRC members where they were sexually assaulted and raped.[103]

The AFRC did not spare journalists or lip-serve the ideals of press freedom. The few independent newspapers that dared to publish during this period risked the lives of their workers. Umaru Fofanah, a BBC stringer, was stripped naked after being shot by soldiers.[104] J.Z. Foray of the *New Storm*, Prince Akpu of the *Financial Times* and Jonathan Leigh of the *Independent Observer* were detained at Cockerill military headquarters in a freight container riddled with bullet holes to provide ventilation. Leigh was arrested for publishing a report implicating a senior AFRC official in the sale of bulgur wheat, a donated relief food item. Foray was docked on suspicion of filing reports to the CNN while Akpu was arrested because he is Nigerian.[105] Abdul Kposowa, a reporter for *Liberty Voice*, was likewise detained for allegedly providing information to FM 98.1 (Radio democracy). BBC correspondent Prince Brima was arrested for reporting that the junta was taking a beating from ECOMOG in their frequent skirmishes.[106] On July 8, 1997, Jeff Bowlay-Williams (a civil engineer and populist activist) and six others were arrested at the premises of the *Democrat* newspaper and detained for what the junta suspected was their involvement with Radio Democracy. Many journalists went into hiding after the AFRC seized power but a few, most notably Ibrahim Shaw and Chernor Sesay, served as fifth columnists for the AFRC.

Newspaper headlines—"Sojas Dance with Kamajoh Penises,"[107] "Military Displays Human Heads in Bo,"[108] "Sojas Beat Imam into Coma,"[109] "Exodus from Bonthe Island"[110]—do not even begin to highlight the severity of human rights violations by the AFRC. Making matters worse was the fact that the judicial system practically ceased to function during this period, as many judges were forced to flee the country out of fear for their lives. Any attempt to reinstitute a semblance of normal judicial proceedings had to come to terms with the massive jailbreak that accompanied the AFRC coup. Hardened criminals comprised the bulk of those who stormed out of prison with Johnny Paul Koroma. Some of these prison escapees went after the judges and prosecutors who sent them to jail, killing and raping the few they could track down. Johnny Paul Koroma's subsequent announcement that former inmates of Pademba Road prison should report to the authorities so that they can be reincarcerated provoked disbelief and derision among former prisoners who were quick to point out that Koroma should be the first to heed his own advice by relocating from state house to the prison cell he occupied before becoming "foot of state."[111]

Thousands of child soldiers were pressed into military service by *sobels* and rebels before and after the AFRC coup. Children were targeted for the simple reason that they are easier to manipulate and more likely to follow orders. Many of these children were drugged and sent on suicide missions to retake Lungi international airport and other positions occupied by Nigerian-led ECOMOG forces. One report described how a boy soldier was ordered by his prison commander to cut off the hands of a handcuffed victim because he could not find the key for the handcuff.[112] As the junta beat a hasty retreat into the jungles of the countryside, children as young as five years old had their hands chopped off and told to take their severed limbs to Kabba so he could replace them.[113] The psychological damage done to some of these desocialized children may be difficult if not impossible to repair.

Democratization

The AFRC came to power with no intention of voluntarily stepping down. The leaders of the coup, and their civilian patrons/supplicants, were antidemocratic to the core. After their failed attempt to scuttle the 1996 elections, the SLA and RUF joined forces in 1997 to reverse the outcome of a process they had opposed. This authoritarian reversal represented more than just another change in government. Compared to previous coups, the AFRC usurpation sowed more discord, wrecked more lives, brutalized more civilians, and transformed the state into an agent of mass terror and plunder.

Unsure of itself, the AFRC gave contradictory signals on the issue of restoring constitutional authority. Initially, Johnny Paul Koroma stated that he expected the international community to finance new elections within a year or so. He later changed his mind and announced that the AFRC planned to stay in power until 2001. In one of his many tirades, Koroma likened President Kabba to a "demon" and vowed never to hand over power to him.[114] The *sobels* and rebels of the AFRC were as opposed to the restoration of an elected government as they were to the electoral process that established this government. In a very real sense, the interests of *sobels* and rebels were incompatible with democratization, respect for basic human rights and social progress.

The main impetus behind democratic restoration during the AFRC interregnum came from civil society, whose campaign of disobedience paralyzed the country for the entire duration of the AFRC dictatorship. Almost the entire professional class fled the country in protest and out of fear. Threats by the junta to dismiss workers who failed to report for work did not elicit the expected response. With the entire country grounded to a complete halt, there was neither work to be done nor was the junta capable of paying salaries. The National Union of Sierra Leone Students (NUSS) maintained a firm position of not returning to the classroom until Kabba's restoration. A communique released by the Sierra Leone Teachers Union (SLTU) instructed teachers not to return to the classroom until "permanent peace is achieved, school premises vacated by armed combatants and all other demands forwarded in our last communique are met."[115] As one clergyman put it, "how do they in fact expect people to go to work when they have taken away our vehicles and emptied filling stations."[116]

Acutely allergic to democracy and isolated from civil society and the international community, the AFRC was opposed to Kabba's restoration and had no plans for new elections. Any talk by the junta of negotiations to end the crisis was merely intended to buy time, which many in the AFRC believed was on their side. This reasoning was based on the assumption that the longer the AFRC stayed in power, the greater the probability that domestic and international opposition will subside. Thus, even as it engaged in negotiations, the AFRC was at the same time constructing a makeshift airport at Magburaka to ferry weapons into the country in violation of a United Nations arms embargo.

The forceful reinstatement of the Kabba government in 1998 was the second time in the country's history that such an event has taken place. The first time was in 1968 when force was used to reinstate the democratically elected government of Siaka Stevens. The difference between the democratic restoration of 1968 and 1998 is two-fold: in contrast to its antidemocratic posture in 1998, the SLA was an agent of democratic restoration in 1968; also, the force used to restore the democratically elected government was internal in 1968 but predominantly external in 1998.

Sierra Leone's formal rating on political and civil rights (see Table 7.2) under the AFRC (1997/98) presents a somewhat mixed and to some extent inaccurate picture of trends in the country in the post NPRC period. The year 1997, which began with a democratically elected government at the helm of state affairs, ended under the most tyrannical dictatorship to emerge in Sierra Leone since independence. Political and civil rights could not have been any worse under the NPRC than the AFRC, yet this is what the Random House ratings seem to suggest. A careful reading of this data, however, would factor in the pendulum swings of both 1997 and 1998, especially

Table 7.2 Index of civil and political liberty: NPRC and AFRC

Regime	*1992/93*	*1993/94*	*1994/95*	*1995/96*	*1997/98*
NPRC	P7/C6	P7/C6	P7/C6	P7/C6	
AFRC					P5/C5

Source: Random House Country Ratings at http://www.freedomhouse.org. P = Political Rights; C = Civil Rights; 1 = Most Free; 7 = Least Free.

how the democratic periods of 1997 and 1998 may have to some degree statistically offset the tyrannical interlude of 1997/98. By no stretch of the imagination, however, were the basic rights of the individual in any better shape under the AFRC than the NPRC.

Economic Performance

Despite the rampant corruption in Kabba's government, signs of a modest economic turnaround were evident in the last quarter of 1996 and first quarter of 1997. Inflation was down from 40 percent in March 1996 to around 6 percent by the end of the year; GDP grew from –10 percent at the start of 1996 to 5.6 percent by the end of the year and the country's external reserves rose from $31 million in 1995 to $55 million in 1996. As of September 1996, the country's external debt stood at $1 billion or 108 percent of GDP, with debt service as a percentage of merchandise exports at a hefty 83.4 percent.[117]

Several projects funded by external agencies were suspended after the coup. These included the European Union's Highway project, the Artisanal Fisheries Program, the Rehabilitation and Resettlement Program and the National Power Authority (NPA) Network Rehabilitation Program. The Freetown Rehabilitation Project, which involved resurfacing the streets of the Freetown business district and its environs, was in full swing at the time of the AFRC coup. A new Peninsular road was also under construction and there was even talk of bringing back the railways (phased out by Siaka Stevens), with India offering to help. Kuwait expressed interest in funding the construction of a $100 million bridge linking Freetown and Lungi, site of the country's international airport. The Guma Valley Water Improvement project, designed to improve the distribution network of the water authority, was also ongoing as were a myriad other projects geared toward infrastructural rehabilitation. All of these projects were suspended after the AFRC coup.

The AFRC coup displaced over 1.5 million people. The country's basic infrastructure, factories, business houses, schools, hospitals, and bridges were destroyed. The closure of factories and businesses caused massive layoffs of workers as the economy went into a tailspin. GDP plummeted by over 22 percent in the first few months of AFRC rule and only Le 8 billion of the government's 1997 revenue total of Le 45 was collected during the seven months of 1997 that the AFRC was in power. The government's budget deficit climbed to 7.2 percent of GDP in 1997, the official exchange rate depreciated by almost 55 percent and inflation skyrocketed from under 1 percent at the end of March 1997 to 67 percent in December 1997.[118] Most significant was the sharp decline in revenue collection-customs and excise duties, for example, had been projected to contribute Le 6.5 billion monthly for 1997 but was down to less than Le1 billion a month under the AFRC.[119]

All commercial banks, with the exception of the Sierra Leone commercial bank, remained closed for the duration of the AFRC dictatorship. As part of an international effort to isolate the junta, the United Kingdom and United States froze accounts held by the Sierra Leone government in their respective countries. Kaifen Kallay, a senior manager at the Bank of Sierra, made several trips to London in an unsuccessful bid to gain access to the country's account.[120] The inability of the AFRC to access the country's foreign accounts was in sharp contrast to Kabba's unimpeded access to these accounts. This differential accesss led the AFRC secretary-general to complain that the decision by the United States to freeze the government's account did not prevent Kabba from withdrawing $8 million of the $12 million that was in the account.[121]

The economic sanctions imposed on the AFRC and enforced by ECOMOG deepened processes of economic contraction and informalization that started under Siaka Stevens. Sam Bockarie, alias "Maskita," spent much of the junta interregnum mining diamonds for his patron, the Liberian warlord Charles Taylor. Under the AFRC, Lebanese diamond dealers became government diamond valuators. The Lebanese tended to undervalue the country's diamonds because of the risks involved doing business with the junta. Reminiscent of the NPRC years, 50 percent of the value of diamonds traded on the black market went to the miners who found the diamond and 50 percent to the state.[122]

Conclusion

In comparing the NPRC and AFRC coups/dictatorships in Sierra Leone, certain facts stand out, especially the parallels in social background of coup leaders, their predatory motivations, anti-democratic stance and personnel continuities. These similarities gave credence to perceptions of the AFRC as a more brutal and anomic version of the NPRC. Some contrasts are also worth mentioning. The AFRC coup overthrew a democratically elected government whereas the NPRC coup replaced a discredited, one-party government; this largely accounts for the popularity of the NPRC coup and the unpopularity of the AFRC coup. Led by southerners, the NPRC coup was anti-APC while the northern-led AFRC coup was anti-SLPP. In terms of casualties, the NPRC coup was less violent and destructive than the AFRC coup. The degree of rebel involvement also separates the two takeovers—the RUF was a key participant in the AFRC but not the NPRC coup. Looting and violence in the immediate aftermath of the AFRC coup was more generalized, diffuse, and indiscriminate than was the case during and after the NPRC seizure of power. The AFRC, unlike the NPRC, coup, occurred in a context in which subalterns had already tasted power. Lastly, external reactions to the AFRC coup were far more hostile in comparison to the NPRC coup.

From the standpoint of the performance of these two dictatorships, a few similarities are noteworthy. Both dictatorships spectacularized corruption but where the NPRC initially pretended to have some interest in fighting corruption, the AFRC betrayed no such pretense. Both leaderships were deeply involved in diamond mining and smuggling and were equally reluctant to hand over power to elected civilians. Although human rights abuses were more systemic under the AFRC than the NPRC, both regimes were extremely arbitrary and prone to summarily execute their real and imagined opponents.

The differences between the NPRC and AFRC dictatorships can be summed up as follows: the NPRC coup was initially populist in pretension while the AFRC coup was from the very beginning anti-populist; the AFRC brought into government two factions (APC and RUF) that were relatively absent or dormant in the NPRC. In contrast to the NPRC, which received generous donor support, the AFRC had to deal with a global oil and arms embargo, as well as a travel ban imposed on its members. The AFRC sought to manipulate ethnic divisions and was more openly "tribalistic" than the NPRC. Where the NPRC's economic performance showed slight improvement over the previous regime, the AFRC reversed the economic turnaround that had begun under the Kabba government. Law and order were more conspicuous for their absence under the AFRC than when the NPRC was in power. Finally, Charles Taylor, the Liberian warlord-turned-president, provided active support and exercised greater influence over the AFRC than the NPRC.

CHAPTER 8

The Gambia: Despot from Kannillai

Gambia is one of three West African states where a coup by armed subalterns toppled a democratically elected government. The country maintained a quasi-democratic political system for almost thirty years and was one of the more stable and least repressive states in Africa. Not only was Gambia Africa's longest surviving constitutional democracy in 1994, only Felix Houphuet-Boigny of Ivory Coast and Hastings Kamuzu Banda of Malawi had been in office longer than Dauda Jawara, Gambia's first postindependence leader. Gambia's positive image as an oasis of stability in a continent riven by internecine strife, military coups, and instability was abruptly shattered by the July 1994 coup.

The July 23, 1994 coup in the Gambia is the country's only successful coup to date. Not unlike Doe in Liberia and Rawlings in Ghana, Gambia's Yayah Jammeh ran for office instead of handing over power to elected civilians. In contrast to post-PNDC Ghana under Rawlings, which was quite liberal and open, Gambia remains a personalist dictatorship masquerading as parliamentary democracy. How long this façade can be maintained remains to be seen but if the examples of Liberia and Sierra Leone are anything to go by, Gambia may not be able to rid itself of subaltern coups and/or dictatorships any time soon. The despot from Kannillai, who is in the habit of threatening to send his opponents "six feet deep," may well be following the career path of Gnassingbe Eyadema, Africa's longest serving head of state, who rose from the ranks of the military to dominate his country's politics for almost forty years. Jammeh's Gambia, like Eyadema's Togo, may be farther away from democracy today than when both lumpen upstarts seized power in their respective states.

Background to the AFPRC Coup

For three decades, the same party, the People's Progressive Party (PPP), and leader, Dauda Kairaba Jawara, ruled Gambia. Although the political system during this period was less exclusionary and repressive than Liberia under the TWP or Sierra Leone under the APC, it was nonetheless neo-patrimonial and corrupt. Regime access depended on the informal clientelistic networks that formed around national, sectoral, and local elites. Like the TWP of Liberia and the APC of Sierra Leone, Jawara's PPP eventually faced a "crisis of clientelism" which "led to, but was not resolved by, military intervention."[1]

The first serious challenge to Jawara's PPP came in July 1981 when a group of civilian radicals, disgruntled field force personnel, and taxi drivers attempted to overthrow the government. This civilian or "taxi drivers" coup was, with the exception of Sudan, unprecedented in the annals of coup making in subsaharan Africa.[2] The main group behind the coup was the Gambia Revolutionary Socialist Party (GRSP) whose founding leader, Gibril "Pengu" George, was an unsuccessful businessman with an axe to grind with the police inspector. Kukoi Samba Sanyang, the leader of the coup, became a member of the GRSP after failing to win a parliamentary seat (Foni East Constiutency) in the 1977 elections as a member of Sheriff Dibba's National Convention Party (NCP). Another group that was active in fomenting rebellion against the Gambian government was the Movement for Justice in Africa (MOJA). Like its counterpart in Liberia, MOJA-Gambia brought together self-proclaimed Marxists and pan-Africanists in a campaign to promote egalitarian causes. The leadership of the movement included Koro Sallah, a school teacher, and Ousman Manjang, a part-time journalist. Both the GRSP and MOJA-Gambia were banned as subversive organizations in October 1980 after the murder of the Field Force commander, Eku Mahoney, by a private with ties to MOJA. It was also around this time that the Libyan embassy was shut down in Banjul for allegedly sponsoring subversive activities.

The core of the group that initiated the 1981 coup consisted mainly of Jolas, an ethnic group that was perhaps the most disadvantaged in Gambian society. With the exception of Sanyang, most of the coup plotters were illiterate taxi drivers from Talinding-Kunjang, the Jola tenement in Serrekunda. With support from members of the field force, the coup plotters (about twelve in all) easily took over the Field Force depot in Bakau and helped themselves to the armory. Although several attempts to take over the central police headquarters in Banjul failed, the Assistant Commissioner of Police, Kikala Baldeh, was shot dead at his house in cold blood.

As the coup began to unravel, Sanyang and his fellow insurgents distributed "self-loading rifles to their supporters and more generally to anyone producing a voter's card."[3] Internal dissension, however, threatened the insurgency, and the first to go was Gibril "Pengu" George, who was shot at the Field Force depot on July 31, 1981. Although Sanyang and his men had detained the wife and children of President Jawara at the depot, nothing was apparently done to harm them. Jawara, who was at the time in London attending the royal wedding of Prince Charles and Princess Diana, was able to crush the coup and reestablish his authority with the help of Senegal and Britain. This restoration was followed by the establishment in 1982 of the Senegambia Confederation, an arrangement that practically ceded responsibility for Gambian security to the Senegalese. Relations between the partners of the confederation deteriorated toward the end of the 1980s, leading to the dissolution of the experiment in 1989.[4]

A key development following the failed coup of 1981 was the establishment of the Gambia National Army (GNA). This new security outfit, which was 800 strong at the time of the 1994 coup, comprised of loyalist elements of the disbanded paramilitary field force and gendarmes trained in Senegal. With the breakup of the Senegambia Confederation, Nigerian commanding officers were brought in to replace Senegalese officers. The denationalization of the commanding ranks of the GNA was, however, counterproductive as it generated discontent among young Gambian officers who came to view their foreign commanding officers as career impediments.

Growing leadership corruption, endemic poverty and public discontent marked the period between the failed coup of 1981 and the successful coup of 1994. Jawara was perceived in the West as a champion of democracy and human rights and under his leadership Gambia seemed the quintessence of social tranquility and political stability in Africa. This stability, however, masked a corrupt political system mired in patronage, nepotism, and cronyism. The "persistence of corruption and mismanagement in government, advanced as reasons for the 1981 coup attempt", were "not . . . resolved by Jawara, despite periodic dismissals of the worst offenders."[5] Rather than view the failed coup of 1981 as a wake-up call to reform the political system and combat corruption, Jawara continued to surround himself with sycophants and opportunists whose abuses damaged the credibility of his government. It was against this background of a complacent and discredited leadership that the AFPRC coup took place.

Prior to the 1994 coup, Jawara, in a trial ballon, had expressed his desire to retire from the presidency but was "persuaded" to contest the 1992 elections by the numerous beneficiaries of his vast patronage network. Jawara's

PPP won 59 percent of the popular vote, as against 22 percent for Sheriff Dibba's National Convention Party (NCP), in what was billed as the president's final electoral contest for political office. With all the patronage resources of the state at its disposal, PPP dominance appeared impregnable. But as Alhaji Joof points out, the fact that there was no resistance to the AFPRC coup demonstrates that "patronage political systems such as those practiced by the PPP can generate nothing but sycophancy, political opportunism and at best, conditional loyalty."[6] In the assessment of Zaya Yeebo, the "biggest failure" of the PPP government "was its inability to control petty theft, corruption and all manner of crimes against ordinary people." Thus,

> . . . its merits notwithstanding, the democracy Sir Dawda championed could easily be described as . . . a neocolonial "casino" capitalist democracy in which the majority of Gambians were bystanders, although not by choice. That would explain why it was so easy for a group of poorly trained, ill-equipped lieutenants, without popular support outside the barracks, to overthrow a thirty year-old government.[7]

The AFPRC Coup

On July 22, 1994, a small group of soldiers led by four lieutenants (Yayah Jammeh, Sana Sabally, Sadibou Hydara, Edward Singhatey) succeeded in overthrowing the only government and leader Gambia had known since independence. The constitution was immediately suspended, political parties were banned, and all ministers were ordered to report to the nearest police station "for their own protection." Airports, seaports and land borders were temporarily closed and a radio broadcast by Lt. Yayah Abdul Aziz Jamus Junkung Jammeh, the new head of state, promised "a new era of freedom, progress, democracy and accountability."[8]

Compared to the 1981 coup, which was carried out by radical civilians and elements of the Gambia Field Force, the 1994 AFPRC coup was planned and executed by four lieutenants of the Gambia National Army (GNA). An important factor in the 1994 coup that was absent in the failed coup of 1981 was resentment felt by junior Gambian officers toward their Nigerian commanding officers. Furthermore, the post-cold war context of the 1994 usurpation distinguished it from the amateurish 1981 civilian coup. Where an estimated 500 lives were lost in the 1981 coup, the 1994 coup was reportedly bloodless. There was no armed resistance to the AFPRC coup, in contrast to the coup of 1981 which was reversed by Senegalese troops working in collaboration with the British. In London at the time of the 1981 coup,

Jawara was in The Gambia in 1994 when Jammeh and his men decided to seize power.

If Lt. Jammeh is to be believed, the leaders of the AFPRC were prompted to seize power because of "the firm belief that there was need to put a halt to the plundering and pillage of this country's resources by a privileged few to the detriment of the downtrodden majority . . . ."[9] As Jammeh would have it, the AFPRC coup "marked the end of an era in which a parasitic minority thrived on the labor and sweat of the toiling majority."[10] Beyond these self-serving pronouncements regarding motives and objectives of the coup, several factors, both internal and external to the GNA, are critical to understanding the underlying and proximate causes of the 1994 coup.

Abdoulaye Saine has identified at least four primary causes of the Gambian coup: the corruption and nepotism of the Jawara government, the personal ambition of coup plotters, discontent within the army over low salaries and deplorable living conditions, and disparities between Gambian (junior) and Nigerian (senior) officers.[11] The *Banjul Mafia* (prominent PPP politicians, ministers, civil servants, and local businessmen) presided over the bureaucratic expropriation of the state by refusing to pay taxes and duties, defaulting on government loans, using government workers for personal projects, paying salaries to ghost workers and collecting per-diem overpayments for foreign trips.[12]

Saihou Sabally, vice president from 1992 to 1994, symbolized the corruption of the Jawara government. Sabally's appointment to the vice presidency, and by implication as heir apparent to Jawara, ignored the fact that he had been implicated in a major corruption scandal at the Gambia Cooperative Union (GCU) and was widely regarded as corrupt by the public. The Gambia Commercial and Development Bank (GCDB) was forced to close down after prominent individuals, including Abu Denton (former accountant-general), defaulted on their loans. The Assets Recovery and Management Company (ARMC), which was established to recover the bank's bad debts, turned out to be a charade under Jawara. It was not until after the AFPRC seized power that efforts to recover some of these debts by confiscating the properties of many of the debtors began to bear fruit.

Conditions within the GNA are also relevant to understanding the 1994 coup. Junior officers were resentful over their subordination to Nigerian commanding officers. This "Nigerian presence," to borrow the words of John Wiseman, "combined maximum irritation with minimum deterrence" and did more to alienate Gambian officers than protect the Jawara regime.[13] Other signs of growing problems within the GNA emerged in 1991 and 1992 when elements of the GNA staged demonstrations over the late payment of salaries to soldiers returning from service in Liberia as part of the ECOMOG contingent. Notwithstanding Jammeh's claim to the contrary, the issue of unpaid allowances was an important precipitating factor in the 1994 coup.

In addition to the corruption of the political class and the corporate grievances of the Gambian soldiery, personal ambitions also motivated the coup leaders. According to one account, ". . . the most obvious possible motivation for the coup was the simple desire on the part of the plotters to seize power in order to gain access to the considerable gains which accrue from controlling the state, and the "rent-seeking" opportunities that such control includes."[14] From this perspective, it comes as no surprise that ". . . Jammeh now lives in the State House and clearly enjoys the privileges of power-the fancy cars, foreign travel allowances, and traffic stops designed to ease the movements of his growing convoy."[15]

An episode that may have influenced the timing of the coup was the "humiliation" felt by Jammeh and his co-conspirators at Yundum airport where they had been deployed to welcome Jawara back home from what turned out to be his last trip abroad as President of Gambia. According to Jammeh's version of events at the airport,

> When we came from the airport where we went to welcome the president from his annual leave, we were humiliated publicly because the politicians accused us of plotting to overthrow the government, and we were searched in public. All soldiers were searched, weapons seized. And that was the last straw.[16]

Although Jammeh claims that the coup was planned in the hours following this incident, the "humiliation" suffered by him and his co-conspirators seem to have merely provided another pretext to seize power.

An important parallel between the failed coup of 1981 and the successful coup of 1994 coup was the leadership role of Jolas. Jammeh, who like Sanyang is a Jola, was born into a cattle-herding family in Kannillai in 1965. The Jolas, as Wassa Fatty explains, "are the most deprived, and most discriminated ethnic group in the Gambia; in fact, the word Jola has become synonymous with domestic servant in the Gambia."[17] Given this social stigma, internal support for the AFPRC coup came mainly from subaltern sectors, irrespective of ethnicity. The social background of Jammeh and the other coup leaders may also explain the initial anti-bureaucratism and anti-elitism of the AFPRC coup.

Internally, the AFPRC coup was not as popular as the "first coming" of Rawlings in Ghana or the PRC and NPRC takeovers in Liberia and Sierra

Leone respectively. Gambian civil society feared a repetition of the violence and destruction that marked the failed 1981 coup. Public response to the coup was, therefore, generally subdued and apprehensive. Unlike Ghana (1979), Liberia (1980) and Sierra Leone (1994), where students took the lead in expressing support for subaltern coups, workers were the first to declare support for the AFPRC coup. The Gambian Workers Confederation (GWC) called on its members to support the AFPRC "as long as the AFPRC maintains the rule of law and, above all, comes up with a timetable for handing over power to a democratically elected government."[18]

Some opposition politicians, notably Sheriff Dibba of the National Convention Party (NCP), applauded the coup. Dibba had opposed Jawara's choice of Saihou Sabally as vice president in 1992 "because it was not in the public interest" to have a "certified thief" (Sabally) serving in such a position.[19] While some politicians saw the AFPRC coup as an opportunity to resurrect their floundering careers, a few notable professional organizations came out in opposition to the coup. The Gambia Medical and Dental Association (GMDA) expressed "alarm . . . at the military takeover of the constitutionally-elected government" and "at the abuse of power which followed." The organization denounced the AFPRC coup as an "unconstitutional act" and called on the junta to "step down immediately."[20] Joining the GMDA was the Gambia Bar Association (GBA), which released a statement condemning both the AFPRC's "usurpation of power by unconstitutional means" and the "spate of unlawful arrests, detentions and unwarranted interference with the freedom of expression."[21] Local opposition to the AFPRC coup was, however, largely confined to elite sectors and urban areas.

Compared to the relatively quiescent internal response to the AFPRC coup, external reactions were uniformly hostile. Britain declined to initiate or join any military effort to reinstate Jawara, as it had done in 1981, but led other Western countries in condemning the coup and pressuring the junta to return the country to constitutional democratic rule. Britain evacuated its nationals from Gambia and warned tourists to avoid travel to Gambia. Special flights were arranged to evacuate over 2,500 British citizens living in or visiting the Gambia at the time of the coup.[22] Tony Baldry of the Foreign and Commonwealth Office justified British reaction to the Gambian coup on the grounds that "it is our judgement that the safety of British tourists in The Gambia is at risk from the unstable internal political situation."[23] The British action, however, seemed to have been taken more in protest than in response to a deteriorating security situation.

Following the British lead, Sweden and Denmark issued travel advisories warning their citizens to stay out of the Gambia.[24] The United States terminated its technical assistance program and aid operations by invoking a U.S. post-cold war policy that prohibits assistance to countries under military dictatorships.[25] The European Union also issued a press release, titled "Declaration on the Gambia", in which it announced the suspension "of all military cooperation and balance of payments support to the Gambia." The Union pledged to "review new aid projects on a case-by-case basis" and predicated the resumption of normal relations upon the restoration of democracy in the Gambia.[26]

The AFPRC's initial response to the refusal by western countries to have normal relations with Gambia was one of anger and defiance. Declaring "we are not in the thirteenth century," Jammeh vowed that the AFPRC "will not tolerate being dictated to (restore Sir Dauda to Power)."[27] The AFPRC chairman insisted "Jawara will never be reinstated unless and until we are all dead."[28] He even went so far as to threaten harm to the citizens of any country whose government sanctions military action to reinstate the ousted president, warning the international community that "the only . . . superpower we are afraid of is Allah."[29] In the words of Yayah Abdul-Aziz Jamus Junkung Jammeh,

> We prefer to suffer in dignity than be seen as pets who are hand-fed by the Europeans who in turn would dictate to us as to how to run our country. Nobody will give us aid and then dictate to us how we run our country. We, Gambians, are not beggars.[30]

The AFPRC in Power

The first cabinet appointed by the AFPRC leadership consisted of seven soldiers and eight civilians. Three of the civilians were women—Santang Jow in Education, Amie Bensouda as acting Minister of Justice, and Amina Faal-Sonko in Youth, Sports, and Culture. Bakary Dabo was briefly retained as Finance minister but was sacked or resigned (depending on whose version of events is believed) from his post in October 1994. Fafa M'bai, one time attorney-general in the Jawara government, was also appointed to the AFPRC cabinet only to be relieved of this position a few months later. Four of the seven soldiers in the fifteen-member cabinet were the original coup plotters; the other three—Lt. Yankuba Touray (Local Government and Lands) and Captains Sheriff Sarr (Trade, Industry, and Employment) and Mamat Cham (Information and Tourism) came on board after the coup. Sarr and Cham were later dismissed from the cabinet and imprisoned on suspicion of being Jawara loyalists.

The attrition rate among ministers in the AFPRC cabinet exceeded that of any other regime examined in this study, with the possible exception of Doe's PRC. Rapid turnover in cabinet reflected dissension and conflicts within the AFPRC and GNA. After the arrest of Hydara and Sabally, the latter's cousin, Fatoumata Tambajang, was fired from her position as Minister of Trade. The justice ministry alone was led by four different ministers (Bensouda, M'bai, Battiye, Ceesay) during the junta's first year in office.

Cracks within the junta and dissension in the GNA provided openings for Jammeh to consolidate his power. After getting rid of Sabally and Hydara for allegedly trying to kill him in order to take over the government, Jammeh moved swiftly to personalize power by constantly changing and shifting around his ministers and by silencing real and potential opponents of his dictatorship. As the AFPRC dictatorship stiffened, top officials in the junta and GNA began to vote with their feet. First to flee the country was Ebou Jallow, the AFPRC spokesperson, who claimed to have defected from the regime in protest over Jammeh's growing corruption and tyranny. Captain Pa Sanneh and Major David Coker, both of the GNA, also fled the country in 1995. Many other officers were detained on suspicion of being loyal to the ousted government; those charged were often court martialed in cases where the "defense attorneys" were serving GNA officers without legal training.

The performance of the AFPRC in office was not markedly different from the other regimes examined in this study. This is particularly true of the regime's record on corruption, human rights, democratization, and the economy. Although Jammeh and his cohorts claimed to be "soldiers with a difference," their "lack of political acumen, crude rhetoric and their distinct inability to inspire confidence and mobilize the people for socioeconomic development—all show that they are not soldiers with a difference'."[31]

Corruption

In his first interview with a local newspaper following the July 22 coup, Jammeh warned the Gambian public that the AFPRC government "will not tolerate any sort of corruption" as it attempts "to set up a just system that is not corruptible."[32] Sounding very much like Liberia's Doe, the AFPRC leader threatened that "anyone convicted of corruption will regret why he was born in the first place."[33] Corrupt officials were classified as "unpatriotic Gambians" who deserve to "be dealt with mercilessly because when they were in power, they had . . . no mercy for the poor."[34] AFPRC members tried to pass themselves off as revolutionaries or, in their own words, "soldiers with a difference" who seized power not to enrich themselves but to improve the lot of the average Gambian. It did not take very long, however, for the AFPRC's populist rhetoric to be contradicted by the growing corruption within its leadership ranks.

In its first few months in office, the AFPRC set about fighting corruption by first discrediting and dispossessing its predecessors. Decree 17 (Freezing of Assets and other Properties Decree) froze the assets of former ministers, managing directors, civil servants, and associates of ex-president Jawara. Among those who had their assets frozen were president Jawara, former vice president Saihou Sabally, former secretary to the president Abdou Janha, former accountant general Abu Denton, former comptroller of customs Mambanyik Jobe, former managing director of Civil Aviation Authority Malick Cham, former managing director of Gambia Produce Marketing Board Kaba Jallow, and former managing director of Gambia Ports Authority Momodou Gaye.[35] In addition to freezing the assets of these and other former government officials, the AFPRC also periodically detained, without charges, officials of the deposed Jawara government.

The AFPRC established Commissions of inquiry to probe the assets and activities of former government officials. Five commissions in all were established. The Public Assets Commission was chaired by Justice Vida Akoto-Bamfo, a Ghanaian judge, who was assigned the task of investigating "the assets, properties, activities and other related matters of public officers." Another commission under the chairmanship of Omar Alghali, a Sierra Leonean judge, was tasked with probing the activities of government departments and their line ministries. Another Sierra Leonean judge, Dunstan Williams, was appointed chairman of the commission in charge of investigating "the financial activities of all public corporations, including Gamtel and the former NIB." A fourth commission chaired by a Gambian judge, Solomon N'jie, investigated issues of land administration.[36]

Revelations at commission hearings discredited the Jawara regime and helped the AFPRC consolidate its hold on power. As John Wiseman wrote, "one of the main ways in which the new regime attempted to legitimize itself was to delegitimize the previous regime, retrospectively by establishing a series of commissions of inquiry to investigate government malpractice and corruption in the Jawara era."[37] Commissions were only empowered to examine past cases of malpractice and corruption, not allegations of AFPRC corruption. Many of the individuals investigated by the commission had already fled the country and were living in exile. Despite many shortcomings, the commissions were able to uncover significant evidence of malfesance among public officials in the Jawara government. But " . . . the failure to date of the AFPRC to bring charges of corruption against many ex-ministers and dismissed top civil servants suggests that the perception of corruption by the military leaders was not commensurate with the practice."[38]

Undercutting the work of the commissions was the growing evidence of corruption within the AFPRC leadership. Ebou Jallow, at one time AFPRC spokesman, fled the country in October 1995 amid allegations that he stole $3 million from state coffers. Jallow flatly denied this allegation and instead pointed a finger at Jammeh, whom he alleged maintained a personal multimillion dollar Swiss bank account. AFPRC leaders also diverted loans from Taiwan ($35 million in 1995) and Libya for personal use. Generally, whereas "mechanisms of government accountability were deficient in the pre-coup period, . . . under military rule mechanisms of accountability . . . all but vanished."[39]

Human Rights

Jawara had deftly managed to promote an image of Gambia as a peaceful and stable country that protected the basic rights and freedoms of the individual. The AFPRC coup and dictatorship shattered this image. The upsurge in cases of civilians beaten by soldiers after the coup prompted a local newspaper to comment on how "hardly any cases of such military brutality had been reported during the days of the deposed Jawara regime."[40] Indeed, Gambian society under the AFPRC was by all accounts less free and less open than when Jawara was in power.

The most intrusive arm of the AFPRC's repressive apparatus was the National Intelligence Agency (NIA), which was established by AFPRC Decree No. 45. This decree, otherwise referred to as the National Intelligence Agency Decree 1995, empowered the NIA to "obtain and provide government with information relating to actions or intentions of persons which may be a threat to state security; to protect the security of the state generally and, in particular, protect the state against threats from espionage, terrorism and activities relating to sabotage undertaken by Gambians or foreigners, agents of foreign powers, organizations or institutions." Decree 45 also authorized the NIA to "take adequate precautions to protect the state against actions which may undermine the government or lead to the overthrow of the government through industrial, violent or other means."[41] Both the establishment of the NIA and the power wielded by this agency were in sharp contrast to the AFPRC's initial pledge to run a transparent government.

Another weapon in the AFPRC's repressive arsenal was Decree 57. Issued on 25 October 1995, this decree was retroactively "deemed to have come into effect on the 22nd day of July, 1995." Decree 57 allowed individuals to be detained without charge for up to ninety days and empowered "the Minister of Interior to arrest and detain any person "in the interest of the security, peace, and stability of the Gambia."[42] Under the provisions of this decree, thirty-five alleged PPP loyalists were arrested and detained in October 1995 for planning a pro-Jawara demonstration. Twenty-five of these individuals were later charged with sedition and released on bail (after ninety days in detention) only to be rearrested on the same day they were granted bail.

The most prominent human rights abuses of the AFPRC involved the harassment and detention of ex-ministers, the mysterious deaths of Sadibou Hydara and Koro Ceesay, molestation and beating of civilians by unruly soldiers and attacks on journalists and the independent press. The circumstances surrounding the June 1995 death of Hydara, one of the original leaders of the July 22 coup, raised concerns that were not resolved by the official explanation of his death. The government's account that Hydara died from acute pulmonary oedema, a condition induced by high blood pressure, was disputed by his widow, who claimed that her husband had never suffered from high blood pressure.[43]

The death of Ousman Koro Ceesay also cast a dark shadow over the AFPRC. Ceesay was an energetic and charismatic young Gambian who was appointed finance minister a few months before his charred remains were found in his car. A post-mortem examination of his skeletal remains revealed fractures in the upper abdomen, suggesting that he was beaten or struck prior to his death.[44] Suspicion of AFPRC involvement in his death was never substantiated but rumors persist that his murder was linked to his knowledge of corrupt financial deals involving the AFPRC leadership. Whatever the motives behind Ceesay's murder, this was the first murder of its kind involving a cabinet minister in postindependence Gambia.

The AFPRC also reintroduced the death penalty after initially voicing opposition to it. Jammeh had earlier stated

> We abhor the death penalty as much as any other Gambian. And let nobody fear, we are not going to set up any military tribunal. We have only suspended the constitution but the judiciary will not be suspended. And all due process will take place without interference.[45]

A "phenomenal rise in . . . treasonable offenses" was the reason given for restoring capital punishment.[46] This made it very obvious that the death penalty was reintroduced for the sole purpose of intimidating, silencing, and eliminating the political opposition.

Summary executions of suspected and alleged coup plotters also became standard fare under the AFPRC. Most of these executions, which involved

GNA personnel, were denied by the government. In November 1994, twenty-three soldiers were executed for allegedly attempting to overthrow the AFPRC government. The coup in question was purportedly led by Lieutenants Bashiru Barrow (at the time commander of the First Infantry Battalion), Gibril Saye, and Abdoulaye Faal. All three men, along with twenty other soldiers, were believed to have been executed, contrary to the government's claim that they died during the coup attempt. Strangely, his family saw Gibril Saye after the shooting incident in which he is supposed to have died.[47] Other summary executions of alleged coup plotters were to follow but these, as in the elimination of Bashiru Barrow and others, were always blamed on gunfire exchanges during coups that seldom involved fatalities on the government side.

An important barometer of the AFPRC's human rights record was its relationship with the independent press. Foreign journalists, particularly Liberians and Sierra Leoneans, were either deported or forced underground. Kenneth Best, the Liberian publisher and editor of the *Daily Observer*, was reclassified as an "undesirable alien" and deported to Monrovia in October 1994. Attempts by Lenrie Peters, the highly respected Gambian surgeon and author, and Robert Collingwood, the E.U. representative in the Gambia, to intercede on behalf of the beleaguered editor were rebuffed by the AFPRC leadership.[48] Best, according to the official line, was deported for violating unspecified immigration laws. Chernor Sesay, another journalist working with the *Daily Observer*, was deported to his native Sierra Leone in 1995 where he was promptly arrested. Other *Daily Observer* journalists who ran foul of the AFPRC included: Alieu N'jie (verbally abused and detained by soldiers); Abdullah Savage (beaten up by soldiers during the arrest of ex-ministers at the Bakau military barracks); Ebrima Ceesay (threatened by Hydara for criticizing AFPRC self-promotions); Justice Fofanah (picked up while covering a conference at the Kairaba Beach Hotel); and Lorraine Forster (detained on charges of distributing Ebou Jallow's post-defection allegations).[49]

Individuals working for or affiliated with the *Daily Observer* were not the only journalists targeted by the AFPRC leadership. The editors of *Foroyaa*, Sidia Jatta and Halifa Sallah, were arrested in August 1994 for "illegally" publishing a newspaper affiliated with a political party. Jatta and Sallah were subsequently arraigned before a Magistrate who turned out to be sympathetic to the defendants, requiring them to pay only 1,000 dalasi to cover court costs. Several other journalists, most notably from *The Point* (Ebrima Sankareh, Ernest Brima, Pap Saine and Alieu Badara) were at various times arrested and held in detention for long periods without charges. The Voice of America (VOA) correspondent in Banjul, Chikeluba Kenechuku, was declared an "undesirable alien" and ordered deported in April 1996 by Captain Lamin Bajo (minister of interior at the time).[50] So widespread and pervasive were the harassment, beating and detention of journalists that *Reporters Sans Frontiers* issued a strongly worded statement denouncing such actions and calling on the government to prosecute soldiers involved in these abuses.[51]

There was no letting up on human rights violations during the 1996 election period. A call by Gabriel Roberts, the provisional interim electoral commissioner, on the government to release all political prisoners so that they could participate in the electoral process was ignored. Some of these politicians had been in detention since the July 22 coup while others were incarcerated in October 1995 for planning a pro-Jawara demonstration. Of the political parties taking part in the elections, the United Democratic Party (UDP) of Ousainou Darboe received the most attention from Jammeh and his supporters. UDP members were harassed, beaten, detained, and tortured by agents of the state. Kemeseng Jammeh (UDP candidate for Jarra West) Wassa Janneh, Dembo Bojang, Ansumana Bojang, Buba Sanneh, and Fabakary Taal, were among a long list of UDP supporters beaten and/or detained by the AFPRC leadership in the months leading to the 1996 elections. Soldiers who broke up a UDP rally at Lamin on September 22, 1996, inflicted severe injuries on UDP supporters. Perhaps by far the most threatening incident before the elections was the confrontation between UDP supporters (estimated at close to 200) and armed soldiers on Denton bridge during the evening hours of September 22, 1996. The soldiers ordered the UDP partisans to lie face down on the ground as they proceeded to manhandle and beat them; at least three deaths resulted from this incident.[52]

Although the human rights abuses of the AFPRC pale in comparison to those committed in Liberia, Sierra Leone and Ghana, they nonetheless represented a radical departure from past practices in the Gambia. To protect its members against prosecution, the AFPRC junta inserted an indemnity clause into the 1996 constitution which states that "No member of the Armed Forces Provisional Ruling Council, any person appointed Minister by the AFPRC or other appointees of the AFPRC, shall be held liable whether jointly or severally for any act or omission in the performance of their official duties."[53] A common practice in Latin America and Africa, the immunization of AFPRC leaders was consistent with similar provisions in Ghana, Liberia, Sierra Leone, and a host of other African countries that have been ruled by the military. Such indemnity clauses, however, make it very difficult for governments to prevent future human rights abuses.

Democratization

The AFPRC stormed into office with a rather dismissive attitude toward democratic governance. Jammeh viewed democracy as a western invention and was clearly ambivalent on the issue of returning Gambia to constitutional rule.[54] He strenuously argued that although the AFPRC dictatorship was transitional, it would "have to make sure that Gambians are aware of what their rights are, what kind of leaders they want and what kind of system they want to put into effect in this country" before returning to the barracks.[55] The AFPRC sought to make a distinction between what it termed "real democracy" and "apparent democracy." In the words of Lt. Edward Singhatey, who later emerged as Jammeh's deputy, "all we wanted to do was come to state house, take over and put in place a new government that would rule with real democracy and not apparent democracy."[56]

The AFPRC's lack of commitment to democratization was underscored by Jammeh's equivocal assertion that although "we are not giving any timetable for free and fair elections, that does not mean that we are here to stay too long."[57] A few months later, after pressure from the international community forced the junta to rethink its position, Jammeh claimed that he was misquoted as saying the AFPRC would be in power for "four years" when he in fact meant "for years." Four years, as it turned out, was the transition period called for in the junta's Program of Rectification and Transition to Democratic Constitutional Rule.

The international community and influential local organizations rejected the four-year transition plan proposed by the AFPRC. The European Union issued a statement calling the plan "unsatisfactory and counter-productive" while the United States demanded a one-year transition period.[58] Joining these external voices in demanding a speedy return to civilan rule were the Gambia Bar Association (GBA), the Gambia Teachers Union (GTU), and the Gambia Workers Confederation (GWC).[59] It was in response to these demands, especially those emanating from the international community, that the AFPRC announced the establishment of a National Consultative Committee (NCC) to examine the issue of a transition timetable.

Chaired by Lenrie Peters, a prominent Gambian physician and writer, the twenty-three member NCC included representatives of religious groups, trade unions, womens organizations, professional associations, and traditional authorities (local chiefs). The Committee began its work in December 1994 by holding meetings throughout the country to gauge the mood of the public regarding the AFPRC's four-year transition plan. In its report to the AFPRC, the NCC recommended a two year transition period and the establishment of an interim civilian government. Jammeh had no interest in the interim government proposal, which he outrightly rejected; he nonetheless chose to shorten the transition period from four to two years. This transition, however, turned out to be fraudulent as Jammeh was able to civilianize his authority by contesting and allegedly winning the 1996 presidential election.

The next step in the AFPRC's transition plan was the establishment of a Constitutional Review Commission (CRC) in April 1995 under the chairmanship of Justice Gilbert Mensah Quaye. The commission submitted its recommendations to the AFPRC in December 1995 but the public remained unaware of its details until March 1996. The document that emerged was tailored to the AFPRC's liking, with some of its provisions clearly intended to make it difficult for opponents to participate freely in the political process. There was a 1,500 percent increase in the deposit required from candidates in parliamentary elections and a 200 percent hike in the fee for presidential candidates. Even more outrageous than the new electoral fees, which were written into the new constitution by the AFPRC without consultation, was the risk candidates faced of losing their deposits if they failed to capture at least 40 percent of the vote in their contests. As a keen observer of the Gambian political scene remarked, the requirement that candidates gain at least 40 percent of the vote in order to "save" their deposits "raised the bizarre prospect of even some winning candidates losing their deposits in tightly contested constituencies with more than two candidates."[60]

As if the above measures were not enough to limit genuine participation, the AFPRC also decided to disenfranchise the political class. Decree No. 89 banned all persons who held the offices of president, vice president and minister in the Gambian government during the thirty years preceding the 1994 coup from participating in any form or manner of political activity. The ousted PPP, Sheriff Dibba's NCP and Musa Camara's Gambia People's Party (GPP) were outlawed and prevented from participating in the electoral process.[61] Reflecting the position of banned parties and individuals, Musa Camara, the GPP leader, denounced Decree 89 as "very unfair and without justification."[62] Chief Emeka Anyaoku, the Commonwealth secretary-general, decried the banning of "a whole generation of public servants, politicians and political parties," calling it "a very retrogressive stand."[63] In protest over this and other moves to limit participation, the Commonwealth Ministers Action Group (CMAG) declined to endorse what it described as a "flawed" transition process in the Gambia.

A key player in the AFPRC's transition program was the Provisional Independent Electoral Commission (PIEC), which organized both the referendum on the draft constitution and the presidential and parliamentary elections of 1996. Turnout for the August 8, 1996 referendum on the new constitution was 87 percent, with 70.3 percent voting to adopt the new constitution and 29.6 percent rejecting it. Thirty-six of a total forty-one constituencies voted to adopt the constitution. The five constituencies rejecting the new constitution were Central Badibu, Lower Badibu, Jarra West, Kiang East and Kiang West.[64]

After significantly contracting the political space by banning potential opponents from participating in the electoral process, the AFPRC reconstituted itself into a political party to contest the presidential election of September 1996 and the parliamentary elections of January 1997. Jammeh officially retired from the GNA (after promoting himself to the rank of Colonel) to contest the presidential election as flag-bearer of the Alliance for Patriotic Re-orientation and Construction (APRC). In his campaign for the presidency, Jammeh touted his "achievements" in office such as the building of schools, hospitals, and skills training centers, fisheries projects, decentralization of essential services, roads network, national Youth Service Scheme, National television, attitudinal orientation, international airport terminal and Arch 22-a colossal monument erected to commemorate the July 22 1994 coup.[65]

Three other political parties were allowed to participate in the elections. These were: the United Democratic Party (UDP) of Ousainou Darboe; the National Reconciliation Party (NRP) of Hamat Bah; and the People's Democratic Organization for Independence and Socialism (PDOIS) led by Halifa Sallah, Sidia Jatta, Sam Sarr, Amie Sillah, and Adama Bah. Like Jammeh's APRC, the UDP and NRP were personalist vehicles established for the sole purpose of furthering the ambition of their leaders. The UDP leader accused the junta of corruption and blamed it for the death of Koro Seesay, the AFPRC's one-time finance minister.[66] Hamat Bah, who admitted that he was chiefly attracted to the pomp and pageantry of the presidential office, wanted all foreign judges sacked even though there was a dearth of qualified Gambians to fill such positions.[67] The NRP leader accused the AFPRC of corruption and misallocation of resources in the construction of the $10 million Arch 22 and the $10 million new airport terminal. Bah also called on the AFPRC leadership to reinstate dismissed civil servants.[68]

The PDOIS was the only pre-coup political party allowed to participate in the elections. Founded in 1987, the party was fiercly critical of the Jawara government but declined an offer from the AFPRC to work with the latter. The party emphasized national independence, sovereignty, and the creation of a productive economic base in its electoral campaign. According to Sidia Jatta, the PDOIS presidential candidate in the 1996 elections,

> It is important to know PDOIS is fundamentally different from other political parties. Our approach to politics is equally different. The differences lie

> in the fact that the PDOIS sees it as a necessity first to enlighten the people. Then put our programs to them. We do not induce anyone to vote for us or buy votes or do anything that will undermine the integrity of the voter. . . . Those who beat drums have nothing to tell the people. . . . There is no euphoria about our meetings, no clapping because people want to hear. Our drums are excellent ideas on how to solve our problems. These are the drums we beat.[69]

In the end, Jammeh was declared the winner of the 1996 presidential election with 56 percent of the popular vote; Darboe came in second with 35 percent. In the parliamentary elections, Jammeh's APRC was also the winner with 33 seats (including five unopposed); the UDP and NRP each won seven seats, independents won two seats and the PDOIS won one seat.

The marked deterioration in political and civil rights under the AFPRC was captured by the Freedom House ranking of Gambia as one of the least free and open societies from 1994 to 1998 (see Table 8.1). Compared to Jawara's tenure, which was corrupt but protective of basic political and civil rights, Jammeh's dictatorship turned out to be no less corrupt but far more repressive than his predecessor. As was true of the other subaltern dictatorships examined in this study, AFPRC rule in the Gambia resulted in contraction of the political space and the extensive abuse of individual rights and freedoms. Compared to Ghana, Liberia, Burkina Faso, and Sierra Leone, however, AFPRC repression in the Gambia was more discontinuous with the country's past and at odds with preexisting political practices.

Economic Performance

At the time of the AFPRC coup, Gambia's economy was in far better shape than any of the other countries examined in this study. Official development assistance as a percentage of the country's GDP was only 25.5 percent in 1993, compared to 164.4 percent in Sierra Leone for the same year. Gambia's external debt grew modestly from $137 million in 1980 to $386 million in 1993; this compared favorably to Sierra Leone's external debt, which

Table 8.1 Index of civil and political liberty under the AFPRC

1994/95	*1995/96*	*1996/97*	*1997/98*
P7/C6	P7/C6	P7/C6	P7/C6

Source: Freedom House Country Ratings at http://www.freedomhouse.org.
P = Political Rights; C = Civil Rights; 1 = Most Free; 7 = Least Free.

skyrocketed from $435 million in 1980 to $1.6 billion in 1993. Gambia's international reserve was also respectable for a country its size—at $94 million, it was almost three times the combined reserves of Liberia and Sierra Leone.[70]

The AFPRC coup led many observers to predict dire economic consequences for the Gambia. Especially worrisome was the Western campaign to pressure the new junta to either reinstate the ousted president or hold democratic elections in the shortest possible time. Tourism, in particular, was adversely affected by the change in government. Many European governments and tour operators declared Gambia unsafe after the coup and sought to dissuade their nationals from vacationing there. This campaign resulted in massive lay-offs in the hotel industry and the loss of a critical source of revenue for the government. Job loss in tourism, where an estimated 10,000 workers were laid-off, also affected taxi drivers, handicraft traders, horticulturists, and the extended Gambian family. Compounding the loss of jobs and revenue from the tourist sector was the suspension of economic aid by the European Union, the United States and the World Bank. The AFPRC reaction to the strong-arm tactics of the donor community was to question the very nature and character of Gambia's dependence on the international community. As Jammeh phrased the issue, "if a government relies solely and wholly on international assistance to pay its workers, then what happens to the money generated by the local economy?"[71]

The AFPRC decision to shorten its transition timetable from four to two years allowed its leadership to negotiate a relaxation of the suspension on bilateral and multilateral aid from the West. Taiwan and Libya also stepped in and helped the junta ride the storm of its revenue shortfall. The regime then proceeded to embark on several projects, including the building of a new hospital in Farafeni, the construction of a new airport terminal, as well as several schools and recreational facilities throughout the country. At an estimated cost of $10 million, the Arch 22 project was the most ostentatious misallocation of Gambian resources by the state in recent memory. Expressive of the AFPRC leader's delusions of grandeur, Arch 22 also suggested a leadership that was growing out of touch with the masses.

In terms of macro-economic performance, the AFPRC dictatorship was able to reverse the sharp fall in GDP growth and the number of charter tourists visiting the country during the first year of its rule (see Table 8.2). As external resistance to the regime receded, the AFPRC began putting its economic house in order through policies of monetary stability and fiscal discipline.

Whereas GDP growth was −6.5 percent in 1995, there was a remarkable turnaround the following year with a 3.2 percent growth rate. This reversal

Table 8.2 Gambia: Basic economic indicators (1994–96)

Economic indicators	*1994*	*1995*	*1996*
Population	1080	1120	1211
GDP (Dalisi, million)	2886	3400	3700
Real GDP Growth rate	1.5	−6.5	3.2
Exports ($M)	125.0	123.0	130.0
Imports ($M)	181.6	162.5	168.0
International Reserves ($M)	98.0	106.2	101.8
Total External Debt ($M)	421.3	425.6	451.9
External Debt Service Ratio	14.4	14.0	12.7
Current Account ($M)	8.2	−8.2	−47.7
Groundnut Production ('000 tons)	76.7	80.8	32.0
Charter Tourists ('000)	90.00	43.3	70.00

Source: Economist Intelligence Unit, *World Outlook* 1998, p. 154; ibid., 1999, p. 156.

of fortune was largely due to sharp increases in the number of tourists visiting the country, which dropped from 90,000 in 1994 to 43,000 in 1995 before rising to 70,000 in 1996. The value of exports held steady during the first two years of AFPRC rule while the value of imports showed a modest decline. The country's international reserves, total external debt and debt service ratio also remained essentially the same. The value of the dalasi, the country's currency, was also stable, making it one of West Africa's strongest currencies. Groundnut production, however, showed a marked decline from 76,700 tons in 1994 to 32,000 tons in 1996, as did the country's current account, which dipped from $8.2 m. to −$8.2m within a year of the AFPRC's coming to power.

Taken together, the AFPRC did a better job of not ruining the economy of Gambia than the PRC of Liberia or the NPRC and AFRC of Sierra Leone. Like the PNDC of Ghana, the economic performance of the AFPRC surpassed that of its predecessors, especially in the area of welfare provisioning. After negotiating an end to the suspension of multilateral and bilateral aid, the AFPRC went ahead with several projects that were beneficial to the average Gambian.

Conclusion

Gambia under the AFPRC resembled the NPRC of Sierra Leone more than any of the other juntas covered in this study. In contrast to the NPRC, however, the AFPRC became a personalist dictatorship that did not completely abandon its populist fancy even as its leaders became compradorized. Gambia also became more repressive the longer Jammeh stayed in power. If Rawlings and Sankara represented the best in armed subaltern leadership and Doe and Johnny Paul Koroma the worst, then Jammeh can be slotted somewhere in the middle, as he was neither the finest nor the most retrograde of lumpen leaders to emerge in West Africa.

Conclusion

Five of the preceding chapters examine the causes (both underlying and proximate) of subaltern coups and the performance of dictatorships of the militariat in five West African states. While there were significant variations in both the circumstances that led to these interventions and the overall conduct of the regimes they gave rise to, the parallels are compelling enough to warrant a few preliminary generalizations regarding the role of armed regulars in contemporary West African politics.

One of the distinctive features of subaltern coups is the relative youth and lumpen social background of many of the leaders who are, without exception, relative youngsters. Rawlings was thirty-two, Doe twenty-eight, Sankara thirty-four, Strasser twenty-six and Jammeh thirty, at the time they catapulted themselves to power. Reinforcing this chronological deficit are the rank, lumpen cultural outlook, and low educational levels of armed subaltern leaders. With the exception of Rawlings and Sankara, the leaders of dictatorships of the militariat in the cases examined were poorly educated and trained. Most were elementary and high school dropouts and many could barely read or write. Doe was functionally illiterate when he became head of state and the corporal who announced the AFRC coup in Sierra Leone could not utter a coherent sentence in English. Even in cases like Ghana and Burkina Faso, where radical junior officers provided leadership and direction, what brought some of these officers into the militariat's fold was their identification with the plight of the ordinary soldier and their willingness to embrace violence as political tool.

Another commonality of subaltern coups is the character of the regimes they depose. All the ousted regimes, without exception, were patronage or spoils-based oligarchies. These regimes were uniformly elitist, exclusionary, corrupt, and unresponsive to popular demands and aspirations. Although three (PNDC of Ghana, AFPRC of Gambia, and AFRC of Sierra Leone) of the seven coups examined replaced democratically elected governments, the ousted governments were no less corrupt and disconnected from popular currents than their authoritarian counterparts. Replacing unpopular governments, on the other hand, did not herald a new dawn in the politics of the countries affected.

Subaltern coups are, without exception, extremely violent affairs. The least violent of the cases examined was the Gambian coup but even Gambia experienced a dramatic upsurge in the level of violence after the AFPRC seized power. The AFRC coup in Sierra Leone was the bloodiest and most destructive; it indiscriminately targeted civilians and summarily dispossessed, mutilated, and dismembered thousands of them. The AFRC coup in Ghana and the PRC coup in Liberia were also extremely violent, albeit less indiscriminate in the selection of victims. Thus, whereas most of the victims of AFRC atrocities in Ghana were senior military officers, smugglers, and market women, the victims of AFRC atrocities in Sierra Leone were an undifferentiated assortment of politicians, local notables, teachers, students, workers, peasants, and even the homeless. From the outset, the violence of Sierra Leone's AFRC coup was driven by the logic of plunder rather than by the need to right the wrongs of society or consolidate political power.

The main targets of subaltern coups are, to varying degrees, the political class and, more generally, the privileged of society. In the cases examined, civilian politicians and senior military officers were molested, ridiculed, severely beaten, tortured, and, in some instances, executed. Class envy, rather than revulsion at the corruption of senior military officers and civilian politicians, partly explains the militariat's animus toward senior officers. This was evidenced by the sudden enrichment of previously destitute subalterns like Doe, Jammeh, and their vast coterie of lumpen supplicants and beneficiaries. Subaltern mimicry of predatory modes of elite accumulation negated the transformative potential of subaltern coups and refocused the relevance of class factors in explaining the conduct of coup leaders. Stated differently, the class factors that are relevant to understanding the politics of subordinate class resistance are less germane to comprehending the performance of subaltern dictatorships.

Related to the above is the populist rhetoric of these usurpations. Populist sloganeering and the myriad publicity stunts of these regimes are for the most part deceptive. The false populism of the juntas in Liberia, Sierra Leone, and Gambia squandered any chance these regimes may have had to break decisively with the past. The PRC of Liberia was the most deviationist while the AFRC of Sierra Leone was the most anti-populist. The Rawlings and Sankara coups were broadly populist, nothwitstanding the subsequent adoption of neoliberal economic policies by the Rawlings regime. In three of the five countries examined, populist pretensions were belied by the plundering exactions of subaltern leaders and their armed supporters.

Many factors, including timing, separated the coups in this study. The Ghana, Liberia, and Burkina Faso interventions were carried out during the cold war, making their reversal more difficult than the coups of the post–cold war era. Doe, in particular, was able to exploit the rivalry between the United States and the Soviet Union to his advantage. The role of the Libyan strongman, Muamar Gaddafi, whose cultivation of close ties with Rawlings and Sankara did not sit well with the West, was a major factor in U.S. decision to support rather than ostracize Doe. The coups in Sierra Leone and Gambia were post–cold war events that were more amenable to reversal than their cold war precedents. Sanctions imposed on subaltern dictatorships that usurped power during the cold war were generally not as tough as those imposed in the post–cold war period.

Internal and external reactions to these coups also varied considerably. Because of the unpopularity of the ousted governments, and given the populist rhetoric of coup leaders, all but one of these interventions were greeted with some degree of public approval. Internally, the most popular coups were in Ghana (1979), Liberia (1980), and Sierra Leone (1992). The CNR coup was also warmly received by popular sectors but the same could not be said for the PNDC and AFPRC coups. Public reactions to the PNDC coup in Ghana and the AFPRC coup in Gambia were muted, reflecting in part the legacy of previous interventions. The 1997 coup in Sierra Leone was by far the most unpopular and degenerate. External reactions to this coup and the AFPRC coup in the Gambia were far more hostile than external responses to the coups in Ghana, Liberia, and Burkina Faso. While differential external reactions may have something to do with the end of the cold war, the extreme brutality of the Sierra Leone coup compelled the international community to isolate the AFRC and support its forcible removal from power.

Differences in the level of training of officers and in the degree of professionalism separate two coups from the rest. The coup leaders in Ghana and Burkina Faso had better education and professional training than their counterparts in Liberia, Sierra Leone, and Gambia. Both Sankara and Rawlings embraced a "subjective" view of military professionalism, according to which a soldier must serve as agent of revolutionary transformation. Sankara expressed this position as follows:

> Contrary to the point of view of officers filled with the colonial spirit, the politicization and revolutionization of the army does not mean the end of discipline. Discipline within a politicized army will have a new content. It will be a revolutionary discipline, that is, a discipline that derives its strength from the fact that the officer and soldier, commissioned and

> non-commissioned personnel, are valued on the basis of human dignity and are distinguished from one another only by their concrete tasks and by their respective responsibilities.[1]

This approach to military discipline and professionalism, although not objective, was conspicuously absent in the cases of Liberia, Sierra Leone, and Gambia.

Somewhat related to the above was the role of ideology in shaping the direction of these coups and regimes. Ghana and Burkina Faso had a more recognizable leftist tradition than the other countries. Sankara was the most ideological and least pragmatic of subaltern leaders to emerge in West Africa. He, and to a lesser extent Rawlings, had been exposed to the writings of Karl Marx and was committed to transforming Burkinabe society along some of the lines envisaged by Marx. As events would later prove, Rawlings was no ideologue and his reading of Marx was essentially humanist rather than determinist. But even as he embraced liberal economic policies, Rawlings did not completely abandon his populist orientation or lose rapport with the masses. By contrast, ideology was irrelevant to understanding the coups in Liberia, Sierra Leone, and Gambia.

The role of civilian groups in either fomenting or orchestrating subaltern coups represents another significant variable. While there is no evidence of any direct civilian role in the AFRC (Ghana) and NPRC (Sierra Leone) coups, civilian radicals and politicians played prominent roles in the PNDC (Ghana), CNR (Burkina Faso), PRC (Liberia), and AFRC (Sierra Leone) coups. Civilian radicals and leftist intellectuals masterminded the PNDC coup and leftist intellectuals played a critical role in undermining the Tolbert presidency and hastening its demise. The close ties between junior officers and leftist trade unions and organizations in Burkina Faso paved the way for the 1983 CNR takeover and in Sierra Leone the AFRC coup attracted quite an array of discredited politicians from previous governments. In general, the ideological orientation of the civilians who participated in the PNDC, PRC, and CNR coups was radically different from those involved or identified with the AFRC coup in Sierra Leone. While the civilians implicated in the PNDC, PRC, and CNR coups were mostly leftist radicals, reformists, and trade unionists, the AFRC coup in Sierra Leone was mainly supported by disgruntled and opportunistic elements of the political class.

The dictatorships installed by these subaltern takeovers were, with the exception of Ghana and Burkina Faso, unmitigated disasters. Doe's abuses and excesses destroyed the Liberian State, which had been on life support from the United States during much of the 1980s. Although it inherited a state on the verge of collapse, it was the NPRC's inability to distinguish itself from the dictatorship it dethroned that ultimately accelerated its demise. Jammeh's Gambia turned out to be no less corrupt than Jawara's but it was certainly more repressive. Rawlings and Sankara were, to varying degrees, exceptions to this pattern of degeneracy that often afflicts countries ruled by the militariat. Processes of state decomposition were reversed in Ghana and Sankara launched an authentic revolutionary project in Burkina Faso that had its shortcomings but whose aim was to uplift the peasantry and transform society in the process.

On the issue of combating corruption, which all but the AFRC of Sierra Leone claimed as priority, only the AFRC/PNDC of Ghana and the CNR of Burkina Faso had a decent record to show for their effort. Much of the success in the anti-corruption crusade of the two juntas stemmed from the personal integrity and examples set by Rawlings and Sankara. Although these campaigns sometimes involved gross human rights abuses, such as the executions in Ghana, the AFRC/PNDC and CNR were less corrupt than their predecessors and in comparison to the other regimes examined in this study. Liberia and Sierra Leone, and to a lesser degree Gambia, are perfect examples of how armed subaltern rule often results in the compradorization of leadership elements. In all three countries, subaltern juntas turned out to be more rapacious than the governments they replaced. Thus, while subaltern rule can be uniformly repressive, they can sometimes differ in the sincerity with which the problem of corruption is tackled.

The human rights record of these dictatorships does not show much variation, as these regimes were extremely despotic and, in at least two cases, downright brutal. The worst abuses were in Liberia and Sierra Leone, where civil wars formed the backdrop of subaltern atrocities. The conjuncture of accumulation and violence, however, separated the human rights abuses in Sierra Leone and Liberia from those in Ghana and Burkina Faso. Repression in pursuit of a populist agenda, however misguided, is not the same as violence in furtherance of predatory objectives. The former tends to target so-called enemies of the people while the latter often degenerates into looting expeditions that make no distinction between public and private property. Executing corrupt officials, as in Ghana, does not alienate popular sectors provided the executioners do not turn out to be corrupt themselves, as in Liberia. Random maiming and dismemberment of civilians, on the other hand, is bound to trigger the ire and vengeance of mass publics. In short, while subaltern juntas are notorious for committing gross human rights abuses, the impact of these atrocities on public support varies depending on the motivation and target of the abuses.

The victims of subaltern terror in Liberia and Sierra Leone were often mutilated, amputated, decapitated, disembowled, and sometimes consumed. Child soldiers were heavily recruited in both countries by all armed factions, resulting in the social death of a whole generation of Liberian and Sierra Leonean youth. With the transformation of the wars in both countries into profitable enterprises by key players, it became almost impossible to separate the dynamics of violence from those of accumulation. Civil wars provided a cover for pillage and atrocities that were frequently blamed on the opposition. The criminal terror that convulsed these two countries serve as telling reminders of what the militariat does when it rules.

Armed subalterns have shown no greater inclination than senior officers to hand over power to democratically elected civilian governments. Doe, Rawlings, and Jammeh succeeded themselves after contesting multi-party elections. The elections in Liberia and the Gambia, however, were fraudulent affairs whose outcomes were never in doubt. Doe's refusal to relinquish power and the brazen manner in which he stole the 1985 elections led some elements of Liberian society to take up arms against his government. In the Gambia, where Jammeh stacked the polls in his favor by preventing First Republic politicians from participating, the outcome of the 1996 election was no less contrived. With Rawlings, it was the performance of the PNDC, rather than any attempt to rig the elections, that ensured victory for the PNDC Chairman in the 1992 elections. Sierra Leone's Valentine Strasser flirted with the idea of contesting presidential elections in 1996 but his ouster in a palace coup thwarted his plans. Sankara also showed some interest in prolonging his incumbency but his tenure at the helm was abruptly cut short by assassins acting on the orders of Blaise Compaore.

On the related issues of military disengagement and democratization, these case studies underscore the relative weight of internal and external factors in processes of democratization. The differential outcome of efforts to demilitarize politics can be analyzed from the standpoint of the contrasting interplay of local and external forces and pressures. Internal pressures for democratization were much stronger in Sierra Leone than in Ghana and Gambia where the main sources of democratic pressure were external. Popular sectors in Sierra Leone were galvanized by the prospect of removing the military from power through the ballot box. In Ghana, and to a lesser extent Gambia, the main source of internal opposition came from elites, many of whom were out of touch with the masses. Donor pressures, as in the case of Ghana and Gambia, may force subaltern juntas to hold multi-party elections but they cannot prevent their leaders from reinventing themselves as popularly elected presidents. The metamorphization of military dictators into elected presidents is more likely to occur where internal demands for military disengagement lag behind external pressures.

After corruption, it is in the area of economic performance that subaltern dictatorships show the most variation. Liberia and Sierra Leone were economically worse off at the end than at the beginning of rule by the militariat. The untrammeled rapacity of subaltern rule in these countries devoured the state and deprived it of its capacity to carry out basic functions. In Ghana, on the other hand, processes of economic decline were reversed, albeit along lines dictated by the World Bank and IMF. Sankara's efforts to uplift Burkina Faso's peasantry, and his pursuit of economic development through self-reliance, led to modest improvements in the welfare and lives of ordinary citizens. The corruption and repression of Jammeh's dictatorship seems to have turned the clock back on Gambia, where the economy was in relatively better shape in 1994 than it is today.

Three broad conclusions can be drawn from this study of armed subaltern interventions and leadership in West Africa. First, subaltern coups are by their very nature more violent and destabilizing than coups led by senior army officers. *Coups from below* invariably decapitate rank hierarchy, the repercussions of which are often felt far beyond the confines of the military. With multitudes of armed marginals fancying themselves to be presidential material, it is little wonder why subaltern coups have attracted so many copycats. The dual inversion of leadership roles in both the military and political establishment brings into office hordes of culturally *declasse* elements who tend to glamorize violence, disorder, and gangsterism.

Second, the militariat's rise to power has resulted in greater convergence between violence and accumulation. This intersection is key to understanding the "criminalization of the state" and society's "refeudalization." With collapse of the boundaries separating political from criminal violence, civilians are now victimized by a form of praetorian violence that has less to do with political domination than criminal expropriation of private and public property. As Chabal and Daloz point out:

> . . . the notion of criminal civil conflict does not imply that some sections of the population, chiefly the disaffected youth who benefit, do not find instrumental use (rather than legitimacy) in the violence in which they are involved. Force here becomes most narrowly instrumental and is used, as required, to ensure immediate compliance regardless of the social and political consequences. At its most extreme, as in Sierra Leone, such violence violates most of the commonly held social, communal or religious boundaries.[2]

Third, the underlying cause of the militariat's seizure of political power has been the failure of non-hegemonic political elites to legitimize political power, curb corruption, and promote socioeconomic development. The repressive and corrupt manner in which political classes have governed paved the way for the political ascendancy of armed subalterns. Without exception, the five states covered in this study were all governed by patronage oligarchies that were unresponsive to popular demands and currents. Past strategies of containment—informer networks, material rewards, the establishment of paramilitary units as a counter-force, ethnicization of recruitment and promotions, to name just a few—have simply not worked. Spoils enticements, such as providing access to rent-seeking opportunities and coopting military personnel into the government, have mostly benefited senior officers and sharpened class differences within armies. Access to state offices and resources identifies senior officers with ruling classes but it also makes them prime targets of armed subaltern insurgencies.

The objective of deterring coups of any kind can only be achieved through a radical transformation in the organization and exercise of political power. West African states have been unstable and prone to subaltern coups partly "because the principles of governmental legitimacy have yet to be fully espoused or understood."[3] Consequently, these states have failed to "establish institutions that are capable of constraining and outlasting the individuals who occupy their offices."[4] What is needed, therefore, is not so much changes of government as a change of regime.

To the degree that regime determines how state power is organized and exercised, there can be no respite from subaltern coups in West Africa until concrete and meaningful steps are taken to disavow the spoils logic or predatory imperatives of governance. *Coups from below* can be prevented, or at the very least their incidence can be considerably lessened, if government is subordinated to the state, processes of accumulation are decoupled from the exercise of state power, and the relationship between state and society is radically transformed. Regime transformation in West Africa, however, is unlikely in the absence of hegemonic ruling classes whose interests are compatible with popular sectors.

Notes

Introduction

1. Kenneth Grundy, *Conflicting Images of the Military in Africa* (Nairobi: East African Publishing House, 1968), pp. 5, 8.
2. Lucien Pye, "Armies in the Process of Political Modernization," in John J. Johnson (ed.) *The Role of the Military in Underdeveloped Countries* (Princeton: Princeton University Press, 1962), p. 80.
3. Marion Levy, *Modernization and the Structure of Society* (Princeton: Princeton University Press, 1966), p. 603.
4. Sierra Leoneans referred to Johnny Paul Koroma, chairman of the AFRC as a "foot of state" to underscore his unsuitability for office and the inversion of authority patterns occasioned by subaltern coups.
5. Eric Nordlinger, "Soldiers in Mufti: The Impact of Military Rule Upon Economic and Social Change in the Non-Western States," *American Political Science Review*, vol. 64 (1970), p. 1,134.
6. See Achille Mbembe, *On The Postcolony* (Berkeley: University of California Press, 2001), pp. 83–85, for a discussion of "tonton-macoutism" in the African context.
7. Samuel Huntington, *The Soldier and the State* (New York: Vintage Books, 1964), pp. 17–18.
8. See Amos Perlmutter, *The Military and Politics in Modern Times* (New Haven: Yale University Press, 1977), p. 26.
9. Samuel Huntington, op. cit., p. 14.
10. Amos Perlmutter, op. cit.
11. Hannah Arendt, *On Violence* (New York: Harcourt Brace Jovanovich, 1970), p. 55.
12. Robert Fatton, *Predatory Rule in Africa* (Boulder: Lynne Rienner, 1992), p. 20.
13. Basil Davidson, *The Black Man's Burden* (New York: Times Books, 1992), p. 86.
14. See Patrick Chabal and Jean-Francois Daloz, *Africa Works: Disorder as Political Instrument* (London: James Currey, 1999), p. 79.
15. David Keen, "Incentives and Disincentives for Violence," in Mats Berdal and David Malone (eds.), *Greed and Grievance: Economic Agendas in Civil Wars* (Boulder: Lynne Rienner, 2000), p. 25.
16. See "Trial Starts," *Daily Graphic* (Accra) July 13, 1979, p. 1.

17. Christopher Clapham, "Analysing African Insurgencies," in Christopher Clapham (ed.), *African Guerrillas* (Oxford: James Currey, 1998), p. 3.
18. Thandika Mkandawire, "The Terrible Toll of Post-Colonial 'Rebel Movements' in Africa: Towards an Explanation of the Violence Against the Peasantry," *Journal of Modern African Studies*, 40/2 (2002), pp. 207–208.
19. Charles Tilly, "War Making and State Making as Organized Crime," in Peter Evans et. al (eds.), *Bringing the State Back In* (Cambridge: Cambridge University Press, 1985), p. 171.
20. As Nii K. Bentsi-Enchil observed in the case of the 1979 coup in Ghana, "the ranks organized themselves and allowed certain officers to participate and lead. Yet they watched those officers carefully, and still do." See "Notes of the Latest Revolution," *West Africa*, July 23 (1979), p. 1,300.
21. See Pat MCGowan and Thomas Johnson, "Sixty Coups in Thirty Years-Further Evidence Regarding African Military Coups d'Etat," *Journal of Modern African Studies*, 24/3 (1986), p. 542.

Chapter 1

1. See, for example, Samuel Huntington, *The Soldier and the State: The Theory and Politics of Civi-Military Relations* (New York: Vintage Books, 1957); Amos Perlmutter, *The Military and Politics in Modern Times* (New Haven: Yale University Press, 1977) and; Samuel Finer, *The Man on Horseback: The Role of the Military in Politics* (London: Pinter, 1988).
2. See Morris Janowitz, *Military Institutions and Coercion in the Developing Nations* (Chicago: University of Chicago Press, 1977), and Samuel Decalo, *Coups and Army Rule in Africa: Studies in Military Style* (New Haven: Yale University Press, 1976).
3. See Pat MCGowan and Thomas Johnson, "African Military Coups d'Etat and Underdevelopment: a Quantitative Historical Analysis," *Journal of Modern African Studies*, 22/4 (1984), pp. 633–666, and Julius Ihonvbere, "A Critical Evaluation of the Failed 1990 Coup in Nigeria," *Journal of Modern African Studies*, 29/4 (1991), pp. 601–626.
4. Ruth First, *Power in Africa* (New York: Penguin, 1971), p. 430.
5. See Robin Luckham, "The Military, Militarization and Democratization in Africa: A Survey of Literature and Issues," *African Studies Review*, 37/2 (1994), pp. 13–75.
6. See Eboe Hutchful, "A Tale of Two Regimes: Imperialism, the Military and Class in Ghana," *Review of African Political Economy*, vol. 11 (1979), pp. 36–55, and "Instituional Decomposition and Junior Ranks' Political Action in Ghana," in Eboe Hutchul and Abdoulaye Bathily (eds.), *The Military and Militarism in Africa* (Dakar: Codesria, 1998), pp. 211–256.
7. See Emmanuel Hansen, "The Military and Revolution in Ghana," *Journal of African Marxists*, vol. 2 (August 1982), p. 8.

8. One of the best examples of this is Sierra Leone, where military coups in the 1960s showcased extensive collaboration between civilian politicians and senior military officers. For a detailed account of the coups, see Thomas Cox, *Civil–Military Relations in Sierra Leone* (Cambridge: Harvard University Press, 1976).
9. For a discussion of how African states are formatively functional but reproductively dysfunctional from the standpoint of ruling class interests, see Jimmy D. Kandeh, "Sierra Leone: Contradictory Class Functionality of the 'Soft' State," *Review of African Political Economy*, no. 55 (November 1992), pp. 30–43.
10. See Adam Przeworski, "Proletariat into a Class: The Process of Class Formation from Karl Kautsky's The Class Struggle to Recent Controversies," *Politics and Society*, 7/4 (1977), p. 367.
11. Richard Sklar, "The Nature of Class Domination in Africa," *Journal of Modern African Studies*, 17/4 (1979), p. 537.
12. Jean-Francois Bayart, *The State in Africa: The Politics of the Belly* (London: Longman, 1993), p. 87.
13. Excerpt from Claude Ake's address to the annual meeting of the Nigerian Political Science Association, reproduced in *West Africa*, 25 May 1981, pp. 1162–1163.
14. Goran Hyden, *No Shortcuts to Progress* (Berkeley: University of California Press, 1983), pp. 36–45.
15. Robert Fatton, "Bringing the Ruling Class Back In: Class, State and Hegemony in Africa," *Comparative Politics*, 20/3 (1988), p. 257.
16. Thomas Callaghy, *The State-Society Struggle: Zaire in Comparative Perspective* (New York: Columbia University Press, 1984), p. 191.
17. Sara Berry, *Fatther's Work for their Sons: Accumulation, Mobility and Class Formation in an Extended Yoruba Community* (Berkeley: University of California Press, 1985), p. 13.
18. John Lonsdale, "Political Accountability in African History," in Patrick Chabal (ed.), *Political Domination in Africa* (Cambridge: Cambridge University Press, 1986), p. 155.
19. Roger Murray, "Militarism in Africa," *New Left Review*, 38, (July/August 1966), p. 54.
20. Ibid.
21. Shehu Othman, "Classes, Crises and Coup: The Demise of Shagari's Regime," *African Affairs*, 83/333 (1984), p. 441.
22. Bjorn Beckman, "The Military as Revolutionary Vanguard: a Critique," *Review of African Political Economy*, 37 (1986), p. 55.
23. John Mbaku, "Military Coups as Rent-Seeking Behavior," *Journal of Political and Military Sociology*, 22 (Winter, 1994), p. 241.
24. Ibid., p. 243.
25. Richard Jeffries, "Rawlings and the Political Economy of Underdevelopment in Ghana," *African Affairs* 81/324 (1982), p. 315.
26. Michael Lofchie, "The Uganda Coup-Class Action By The Military," *Journal of Modern African Studies*, 10/1 (1972), p. 23.

27. William Gutteridge, *Military Regimes in Africa* (London: Methuen, 1975), p. 8.
28. Rebecca Schiff, "Civil–Military Relations Reconsidered: A Theory of Concordance," *Armed Forces and Society*, 22/1 (1995), p. 21.
29. Robin Luckham, "The Military, Militarization and Democratization in Africa: A Survey of Literature and Issues," *African Studies Review*, 37/2 (September 1994), p. 39.
30. Ibid., p. 38.
31. Emmanuel Hansen, "The Military and Revolution in Ghana," *Journal of African Marxists*, vol. 2, (August 1982), p. 22.
32. Robin Luckham, op. cit., p. 22.
33. William Graf, *The Nigerian State* (Portsmouth: Heinemann, 1988), p. 156. Although Nigeria has never experienced a successful coup by subaltern ranks, the social polarization within the army described by Graf is consistent with patterns in other African states.
34. Eric Nordlinger, op. cit., p.1,142.
35. On the issue of state felonization, see Jean-Francois Bayart et al., *The Criminalization of the State in Africa* (London: James Currey, 1999).
36. See Adam Przeworski, "Proletariat into Class: The Process of Class Formation from Karl Kautsky's The Class Struggle to Recent Controversies," op. cit, p. 371.
37. See Nii K. Bentsi-Enchil, "Losing Illusions at Makola Market," *West Africa*, September 3 (1979), p. 1,592.
38. See "Warning to Politicians," *West Africa*, July 16 (1979), p. 1,287.
39. See Eboe Hutchful's Introduction to John Hansen's *Ghana Under Rawlings* (Lagos: Malthouse, 1991), p. xii.
40. See "Ghana's New Strong Man Gains Support," *West Africa*, June 18 (1979), p. 1,061.
41. Quoted in *Daily Mail*, April 19, 1968 (Freetown), p. 1. See also "The Sergeant's Coup," *West Africa*, April 27 (1968), pp. 498–499 for a detailed report on the 1968 coup.

Chapter 2

1. Ali Mazrui, "The Lumpen Proletariat and the Lumpen Militariat: African Soldiers as a New Political Class," *Political Studies*, 21/1 (1973), p. 1.
2. Antonio Gramsci, *Selections From the Prison Notebooks* (New York: International Publishers, 1971), p. 198.
3. Ibid., p. 199.
4. See David Arnold, "Gramsci and Peasant Subalternity in India," *The Journal of Peasant Studies*, 11/4, 1984, pp. 155–177, for a superb analysis of subaltern attributes and traits.
5. Alberto Maria Cirese, "Gramsci's Observations on Folklore," in A.S. Sasson (ed.), *Approaches to Gramsci* (London: Writers and Readers, 1982).
6. Antonio Gramsci, *Selections From the Prison Notebooks*, op. cit., p. 327.

7. See D.N. Dhanagare, "Subaltern Consciousness and Populism: Two Approaches in the Study of Social Movements in India," *Social Scientist*, 16/11 (Nov. 1988), pp. 18–35.
8. See James Scott, *The Moral Economy of the Peasant: Rebellion and Subsistence in Southeast Asia* (New Haven: Yale University Press, 1976), *Domination and the Arts of Resistance: Hidden Transcripts* (New Haven: Yale University Press, 1990), and Goran Hyden, *Beyond Ujamma in Tanzania* (Berkeley: University of California press, 1980).
9. Claus Offe and Helmut Wiesenthal, "Two Logics of Collective Action: Theoretical Notes on Social Class and Organizational Form," in M. Zeitlin (ed.), *Political Power and Social Theory: A Research Annual*, vol. 1 (Greenwich, Conn: JAI Press, 1980).
10. Karl Marx and Friederick Engels, *Collected Works*, vol. 10 (New York: International Publishers, 1978), p. 62.
11. Ibid.
12. Frederick Engels, *The Peasant War in Germany* (New York: International Publishers, 1976), pp. 18, 45.
13. Sam Dolgoff (ed.), *Bakunin on Anarchy: Selected Works* (New York: Alfred A. Knopf, 1972), p. 334.
14. For a comprehensive overview of the historical and conceptual uses of the term lumpen, see Peter Stallybrass, "Marx and Heterogeneity: Thinking the Lumpenproletariat," *Representations*, vol. 31, 1990.
15. See Vivek Dhareshwar and R. Srivatsan, "Rowdy-Sheeters: An Essay on Subalternity and Politics," *Subaltern Studies*, vol. 9 (1996), p. 202.
16. Frantz Fanon, *The Wretched of the Earth* (New York: Grove Weidenfeld, 1963), p. 129.
17. Ibid., pp. 129–130.
18. Amilcar Cabral, *Revolution in Guinea* (New York: Monthly Review Press, 1969), p. 62.
19. Ibid., p. 59.
20. Ibid. For a comparative discussion of Cabral and Fanon, see Robert Blackey, "Fanon and Cabral: A Contrast in Theories of Revolution for Africa," *Journal of Modern African Studies* 12/2 (1974), pp. 191–209.
21. James Scott, *Weapons of the Weak: Everyday Forms of Peasant Resistance* (New Haven: Yale University Press, 1985), p. 335.
22. Robert Fatton, *Predatory Rule in Africa* (Boulder: Lynne Rienner, 1992), p. 9.
23. Ibid.
24. Ibid.
25. Ibid., p. 10.
26. Nelson Kasfir (ed.), *State and Class in Africa* (London: Frank Cass, 1984), p. 17.
27. Robert Fatton, op. cit., p. 54.
28. Eric Nordlinger, "Soldiers in Mufti," *American Polical Science Review*, vol. 64 (1970), p. 1134.

29. The Burkina Faso incident referred to here was the general strike of December 1965, during which the police and army deliberately refused to suppress strikers, thus paving the way for the overthrow of Maurice Yameogo's government by General Sangoule Lamizana. In Liberia, local troops refused to open fire on demonstrators protesting a rice price hike in 1980. This led the government of William Tolbert to bring in Guinean troops to quell the mounting social unrest. A year later, the government was overthrown by subaltern elements of the very army that refused to carry out its orders.
30. Kenneth Noble, "Liberia's Government Plans to Hold Peace Talks," *New York Times International*, 10 June 1990, p. 16.
31. See Ali Mazrui, "The Lumpen Proletariat and the Lumpen Militariat: African Soldiers as a New Political Class," op. cit., p. 2.
32. Eboe Hutchful and Abdoulaye Bathily (eds.), *The Military and Militarism in Africa* (Dakar: Codesria, 1998), pp. VI–VII.
33. Henry Bienen, "Populist Military Regimes in West Africa," *Armed Forces and Society*, 11/3 (1985), p. 357.
34. Nii K. Bentsi-Enchil, "Notes on the Latest Revolution," *West Africa*, July 23 1979, p. 1300.
35. Basil Davidson, *The Black Man's Burden* (New York: Times Books, 1992), pp. 246–247.

Chapter 3

1. Ruth First, *Power in Africa* (New York: Penguin, 1971), p. 27.
2. Crawford Young, *The African Colonial State in Comparative Perspective* (New Haven: Yale University Press, 1994), pp. 73–74.
3. See Garnet Wolseley, "The Negro as Soldier," *Forthnightly Review* (December 1888), p. 87. Garnet Wolseley led British forces in the second Ashanti-British war (1869–1874).
4. Crawford Young, op. cit., p. 93.
5. Garnet Wolseley, op. cit., p. 86.
6. War Office 32/5356, Churchill to CIGS, January 11, 1920.
7. See Josiah Wedgwood, *Memoirs of a Fighting Life* (London, 1941), pp. 134–135.
8. Abioseh Nicol, "West Indians in West Africa," *Sierra Leone Studies*, June 13, 1960, p. 15.
9. Ibid.
10. Garnet Wolseley, op. cit, pp. 86–87.
11. Colonial Office 879, African Conference Print no. 565/24, Lugard Memorandum, October 9, 1898.
12. A. Haywood and F.A.S. Clarke, *The History of the Royal West African Frontier Force* (Aldershot: Gale and Polden, 1964), p. 5.
13. Garnet Wolseley, op. cit., p. 86.
14. Ibid.

15. Anthony Clayton and David Killingray, *Khaki and Blue: Military and Police in British Colonial Africa* (Athens: Ohio University Press, 1989), p. 145.
16. Garnet Wolseley, op. cit., p. 92.
17. Haywood and Clarke, op. cit., p. 37.
18. Ibid.
19. Ibid.
20. See *Sierra Leone Weekly News*, February 19, 1898, p. 2.
21. Clayton and Killingray, op. cit., p. 146.
22. Ibid.
23. Ibid., p. 178.
24. Ibid., p. 160.
25. Thomas Cox, *Civil–Military Relations in Sierra Leone* (Cambridge: Harvard University Press, 1976), p. 30.
26. James Coleman and Belmont Brice, "The Role of the Military in Sub-Saharan Africa," in John Johnson (ed.), *The Role of the Military in Underdeveloped Countries* (Princeton: Princeton University Press, 1962), p. 371.
27. Ibid., p. 372.
28. Ruth First, op. cit., p. 74.
29. Patrick Manning, *Francophone Subsaharan Africa 1880–1985* (London: Cambridge University Press, 1988), p. 67.
30. See Myron Echenberg, *Colonial Conscripts: The Tirailleurs Senegalais in French West Africa, 1857–1960* (London: Heinemann, 1991) for a detailed history of the *Tirailleurs Senegalais.*
31. Shelby Davis, *Reservoirs of Men: A History of the Black Troops of French West Africa* (Geneva: Librairie Kundig, 1934), p. 54.
32. Ibid., p. 71.
33. Ibid., p. 145.
34. Ibid., p. 149.
35. Ruth First, op. cit., p. 76.
36. Frantz Fanon, cited in Ruth First, Ibid., p. 49.
37. Ruth First, Ibid., p. 88.
38. Ibid, p. 89.
39. See John Chipman, *French Power in Africa* (London: Basil Blackwell, 1989), p. 117.
40. Ruth First, op. cit., pp. 86–7.
41. Carlos Wiese, quoted in Malyn Newitt, *Portugal in Africa* (London: C. Hurst & Co., 1981), p. 52.
42. See Anne Pitcher, *Politics in the Portuguese Empire* (London: Oxford University Press, 1993), p. 258.
43. See Malyn Newitt, op. cit., p. 230.
44. Crawford Young, op. cit., p. 93.
45. Patrick Manning, op. cit., p. 65.
46. Christopher Fyfe, *A History of Sierra Leone* (London: Cambridge University Press, 1962), pp. 582–3.

47. A. A. Afrifa, *The Ghana Coup: 24th February 1966* (London: Frank Cass, 1966), pp. 93–105.
48. Ruth First, op. cit., p. 84.
49. Simon Baynham, "The Subordination of African Armies to Civilian Control: Theory and Praxis," *Africa Insight*, 22/4 (1992), p. 260.
50. See David Rapoport, "The Praetorian Army: Insecurity, Venality and Impotence," in Roman Kolkowicz and Andrzej Korbonski (eds.), *Soldiers, Peasants and Bureaucrats: Civil Military Relations in Communist and Modernizing Societies* (London: Allen and Unwin, 1982), p. 264.
51. These figures cover the period 1956–2001. For details, see Patrick McGowan, "African Military Coups d'etat, 1956–2001: Frequency, Trends and Distribution," *Journal of Modern African Studies*, 41/3 (2003), pp. 339–370.
52. See Guy Martin, "Francophone Africa in the Context of Franco-American Relations," in John Harbeson and Donald Rothchild (eds.), *Africa in World Politics: Post–Cold War Challenges* (Boulder: Westview Press, 1995, p. 176.
53. For an excellent discussion of Nigeria's role in the maintenance of peace and security in West Africa, see Adekeye Adebajo, *Building Peace in West Africa: Liberia, Sierra Leone and Guinea-Bissau* (Boulder: Lynne Rienner, 2002).
54. See Samuel Decalo, *Coups and Army Rule in Africa: Studies in Military Style* (New Haven: Yale University Press, 1976), p. 70 for details.
55. Anton Bebler, *Military Rule in Africa: Dahomey, Ghana, Sierra Leone and Mali* (New York: Praeger, 1973), p. 79.
56. Jerry Rawlings, quoted in "Not a Coup . . . a Revolution," *West Africa*, January 11, 1982, p. 70.

Chapter 4

1. See Robert Dowse, "Military and Police Rule," in Dennis Austin and Robin Luckham (eds.) *Politicians and Soldiers in Ghana* (London: Frank Cass, 1975), p. 16.
2. See A.K. Ocran, *A Myth is Broken* (London: Longmans, 1968), p. 37.
3. Robert Dowse, op. cit., p. 16.
4. For a discussion of the role of corporate grievances in both the 1966 and 1972 coups, see Valery Bennet's "Epilogue: Malcontents in Uniform," in Dennis Austin and Robin Luckham (eds.), op. cit., pp. 300–314.
5. See John Esseks's chapter on "Economic Policies" in Dennis Austin and Robin Luckham (eds.), op. cit., pp. 37–61, for a discussion of economic conditions leading to the 1966 coup.
6. A.A. Afrifa, *The Ghana Coup* (London: Frank Cass, 1967), p. 37.
7. Simon Baynham, "Divide et Impera: Civilian Control of the Military in Ghana's Second and Third Republics," *Journal of Modern African Studies* 23/4 (1985), p. 632.
8. Valery Bennet, op. cit., p. 302.

9. Ibid., p. 305.
10. Eboe Hutchful, "A Tale of Two Regimes: Imperialism, the Military and Class in Ghana," *Review of African Political Economy* vol. 11 (1979), p. 36.
11. See *West Africa*, September 8, (1972).
12. See Eboe Hutchful, "Institutional Decomposition and Junior Ranks' Political Action in Ghana," in Eboe Hutchful and Abdoulaye Bathily (eds.), *The Military and Militarism in Africa* (Dakar: Cordesria, 1998), p. 220.
13. See "Why Revolution," *Daily Graphic*, June 30 (1979) p. 1.
14. Cited in Emmanuel Hanson and Paul Collins, "The Army, the State and the 'Rawlings Revolution' in Ghana," *African Affairs* 79/314 (1980), p. 15.
15. Jerry Rawlings, quoted in "Ghana's New Strong Man Gains Support," *West Africa*, June 18 (1979), p. 1,061.
16. Naomi Chazan, "Ghana: Problems of Governance and the Emergence of Civil Society," in Larry Diamond, et al (eds.), *Democracy in Developing Countries: Africa* (Boulder: Lynne Rienner, 1988), p. 110.
17. Denis Herbstein, "Broomstick Revolution," *West Africa*, August 13 (1979), p. 1,462.
18. See "Rawlings' View of Ghana's Future," *West Africa*, July 9 (1979), p. 1,197.
19. See Eboe Hutchful, "Institutional Decomposition," op. cit., p. 223.
20. See "World Reacts Unfavorably," *Daily Graphic*, June 29 (1979), p. 2.
21. The three executed former heads of state were Lt. Gen. A.A. Afrifa (former NLC Chairman), I.K. Acheampong (former Chairman SMC I), and F.W.K. Akuffo (former Chairman, SMC II). The other five executed senior officers were Rear Admiral Joy Amedume (former Navy Commander), Air Vice-Marshall George Boakye (former Air Force Commander), Major General Robert Kotei (former Chief of Defense Staff) Col. Roger Felli (former Commissioner of Foreign Affairs under Acheampong), and Major General E. K. Utuka (Commaner of the Border Guards Service). Aceheampong and Utuka were executed on June 16, 1979 while the remaining six were executed on June 30, 1979.
22. *West Africa*, August 27 (1979), pp. 1539–1541.
23. For a gendered account of the AFRC's attack on traders, especially market women, see Claire Robertson, "The Death of Makola and other Tragedies," *Canadian Journal of African Studies*, 17/3 (1983), pp. 469–497.
24. *West Africa*, July 2 (1979), p. 1,151.
25. See "Akuffo and Fifty Others Charged With Corruption," *West Africa*, June 25 (1979), p. 1,138.
26. See "No Compromise With Exploiters," *West Africa*, June 25 (1979), p. 1,138.
27. Elizabeth Ohene, "Death Not the Answer," reprinted in *West Africa*, July 16 (1979), p. 1,256.
28. See "Akuffo Assets Frozen," *West Africa*, June 18 (1979), p. 1,094.
29. See "Assets Committee," *West Africa*, August 27 (1979), p. 1,575.
30. See "More People Declare Assets," *West Africa*, July 23 (1979), p. 1,347 and "Judges Declare Assets," *West Africa*, August 13 (1979), p. 1,482.

31. See Richard Jefferies, "Leadership Commitment and Political Opposition to Structural Adjustment in Ghana," in Donald Rothchild (ed.), *Ghana: The Political Economy of Recovery* (Boulder: Lynne Rienner, 1991), p. 160.
32. See "Military Court Set Up," *Daily Graphic*, June 12, 1979, p. 1.
33. See "Students Back Secret Trials," *Daily Graphic*, July 3, 1979, p. 1.
34. See Kevin Shillington, *Ghana and the Rawlings Factor* (New York: St Martins, 1992), p. 54.
35. Dennis Austin, "The Ghana Armed Forces and Ghanaian Society," *Third World Quarterly*, 7/1 (January 1985), p. 94.
36. See "Election Conduct for Soldiers," *West Africa*, July 9 (1979), p. 1,241.
37. See "Parties Call For End to Executions," *West Africa*, July 9 (1979), p. 1,240.
38. Claire Robertson, op. cit., p. 469.
39. Ibid., pp. 476–77, 490.
40. See "Ghana: Election Go-ahead, But Handover Delayed," *West Africa*, June 18 (1979), p. 1,093.
41. Nii K. Bentsi-Enchill, "Ghana Revolution Loses Steam," *West Africa*, June 25 (1979), p. 1,105.
42. Richard Jeffries, "The Ghanaian Elections of 1979," *African Affairs*, 79/316 (1980), p. 397.
43. Ibid., p. 412.
44. Ibid.
45. Ibid., pp. 402–404.
46. Ibid.
47. Quoted in "PNP Heads For Majority," *West Africa*, June 25 (1979), p. 1,106.
48. See "Questions for Civilian Rule in Ghana," *West Africa*, September 10 (1979), p. 1,642.
49. Richard Jeffries, "Rawlings and the Political Economy of Underdevelopment," *African Affairs*, 81/324 (1982), p. 314.
50. Jon Kraus, "Rawlings Second Coming," *Africa Report*, 27/3 (1982), p. 64.
51. Richard Jefferies, "Rawlings and the Political Economy of Underdevelopment," op. cit., p. 314.
52. See "Legon Students in 7 Hour Demo," *Daily Graphic*, July 4, 1979, p. 1.
53. See "Foreign Exchange Permits Restricted," *West Africa*, August 27 (1979), p. 1,575.
54. See "Ghana's New Strong Man Gains Support," *West Africa*, June 18 (1979), p. 1,060.
55. See Naomi Chazan, in Larry Diamond et al. (eds.), op. cit., p. 111.
56. For perspectives on the AFRC's legacy, see Jon Kraus, "The Political Economy of Conflict in Ghana," *Africa Report* (March–April 1980), and Emmanuel Hansen, *Ghana Under Rawlings* (Lagos: Malthouse Press, 1991).
57. Quoted in *Africa*, March (1980), p. 20.
58. See "Rawlings Explains," *Daily Graphic*, January 6, 1982, p. 1.
59. See "Constitution is Suspended," *Daily Graphic*, January 4, 1982, p. 1.

60. Zaya Yeebo, *Ghana: The Struggle for Popular Power* (London: New Beacon Books, 1991), p. 36.
61. Ibid.
62. Ibid., p. 55.
63. Eboe Hutchful, "Insititutional Decomposition," op. cit., p. 229.
64. Ibid.
65. Naomi Chazan, "The Political Transformation of Ghana under the PNDC," in Donald Rothchild (ed.), *Ghana: The Political Economy of Recovery* (Boulder: Lynne Rienner, 1991) op. cit., p. 25.
66. Jerry Rawlings, quoted in *West Africa*, January 11 (1982), p. 69.
67. *Daily Graphic*, September 28 (1982).
68. Zaya Yeebo, op. cit., p. 61.
69. Roger Gocking, "Ghana's Public Tribunals: An Experiment in Revolutionary Justice," *African Affairs*, vol. 95 (1996) p. 218.
70. Ibid., p. 221.
71. Zaya Yeebo, op. cit., p. 62.
72. Ibid., p. 63.
73. Baffour Agyeman-Duah, "Ghana. 1982–1986: The Politics of the PNDC," *Journal of Modern African Studies*, 25/4 (1987), pp. 628–629.
74. See "Rawlings: I'm Incorruptible," *West Africa*, December 2-8 (1991), p. 2,022.
75. According to Zaya Yeebo, op. cit., p. 265, a total of 29 Ghanaians sought political asylum abroad in 1980, compared to 407 in 1982, 689 in 1983, 337 in 1984, 220 in 1986, and 155 in 1988.
76. Ibid., p. 255.
77. Quoted in Kevin Shillington, op. cit., p. 95.
78. Ibid., pp. 89–90.
79. Zaya Yeebo is the former PNDC member. See his book, op. cit., p. 254.
80. Ibid., p. 260.
81. Baffour Agyeman-Duah, op. cit., p. 620.
82. Quoted in *People's Daily Graphic*, January 6, 1983, p. 1.
83. See Jeff Haynes, "Sustainable Democracy in Ghana? Problems and Prospects," *Third World Quarterly*, 14/3 (1993).
84. PNDC Press Statement, 1982.
85. Ibid.
86. Eboe Hutchful, "Institutional Decomposition . . . ," op. cit., p. 239.
87. Zaya Yeebo, op. cit., pp. 73–74.
88. See Richard Jeffries and Clare Thomas, "The Ghanaian Elections of 1992," *African Affairs*, 92/368 (1993), p. 335.
89. See "Announcement of the Formation of a Broad-Based National Movement—The Movement for Freedom and Justice (MFJ)", in Kwame Ninsin (ed.), *Ghana's Political Transition: Selected Documents* (Accra: freedom Publications, 1996), p. 13.
90. See "Statement by the National Union of Ghana Students on the Political Future of Ghana," in Kwame Ninsin, Ibid., p. 27.

91. *West Africa*, November 18–24 (1991), p. 1,924.
92. See "Low Turn Out For Referendum," *West Africa*, May 11–17 (1992), p. 809.
93. For a discussion of Rawlings's options during the transition period, see Jeff Haynes, op. cit., p. 458.
94. For contrasting views on the conduct and outcome of the 1992 elections in Ghana, see Richard Jeffries and Clare Thomas, op. cit., pp. 331–366 and Mike Oquaye, "The Ghanaian Elections of 1992—A Dissenting View," *African Affairs* 94/375 (1995), pp. 259–275.
95. Daniel Green, "Ghana's 'Adjusted' Democracy," *Review of African Political Economy*, 22/66 (1995), p. 578.
96. Ibid.
97. Jeff Haynes, op. cit., p. 454.
98. E. Gyimah-Boadi, "Ghana's Uncertain Political Opening," *Journal of Democracy*, 5/2 (1994), p. 82.
99. Jon Kraus, "Rawlings' Second Coming," op. cit., p. 65.
100. Excerpt from a speech by Rawlings at Tamale (October 14, 1982). Speech is included in *A Revolutionary Journey: Selected Speeches of Flt.–Lt. Jerry John Rawlings*, vol. 1 (Accra: Ghana Publishing Corp.), p. 65.
101. Paul Nugent, "Educating Rawlings: The Evolution of Government Strategy Toward Smuggling," in Donald Rothchild (ed.), op. cit., p. 75.
102. See Kwasi Anyemedu, "The Economic Policies of the PNDC," in E. Gyimah-Boadi (ed.), *Ghana Under PNDC Rule* (Dakar: Codesria, 1993).
103. Trevor Parfitt, "Adjustment for Stabilization and Growth," *Review of African Political Economy*, no. 63 (1995), p. 56.
104. The comparative figures on rural poverty are from Daniel Green's "Ghana's Adjusted Democracy," op. cit., p. 581.
105. Jon Kraus, "The Political Economy of Stabilization and Structural Adjustment in Ghana," in Donald Rothchild (ed.), op. cit., p. 129.
106. Trevor Parfitt, op. cit., p. 57.

Chapter 5

1. Gus Liebenow, *Liberia: The Quest For Democracy* (Bloomington: Indiana University Press, 1987), p. 60
2. Quoted in Liebenow, Ibid., p. 182.
3. Christopher Clapham, "Liberia," in Donal B. Cruise O'Brien et al. (eds.), *Contemporaray West African States* (London: Cambridge University Press, 1989), p. 101.
4. Amos Sawyer, *The Emergence of Autocracy in Liberia* (San Francisco: ICS Press, 1992), p. 291.
5. Stephen Tolbert was killed in a plane crash in 1975, five years prior to the coup that ended TWP hegemony in Liberian politics.

6. The list of Tolbert family members in top positions was quite long. In addition to the Finance Minister and President Pro-Tempore of the Senate, who were brothers of President Tolbert, the following positions were also filled by close relatives: two of the president's daughters served as deputy ministers of Education and a son-in-law, M. Burleigh Holder, was minister of defense and later national Security; three nephews-in-law were appointed Army Chief of Staff, Director of the National Security Agency and Deputy Director of Police. For a sample listing of the offices held by relatives of President Tolbert from 1972–1980, see George Boley, *Liberia: The Rise and Fall of the First Republic* (London: Macmillan, 1983), p. 96. The author is also indebted to George Kieh for clarifying some of these relationships.
7. See "Dr. Doe Heals the Wounds," *West Africa*, August 2 (1982), pp. 1977–1978. The thirteen TWP officials executed by firing squad after the 1980 coup reportedly owned 144 houses.
8. See George Boley, op. cit.
9. Information on the links between MOJA and SUP is based on personal interview of Kwame Clements, a student leader at the University of Liberia in the early eighties.
10. See "Behind the Strike Call," *West Africa*, April 7 (1980), p. 605.
11. Amos Sawyer, op. cit., p. 290.
12. Ibid., p. 293.
13. George Kieh, "Causes of Liberia's Coup," *TransAfrica Forum*, 6/2 (Winter 1989), pp. 37–38.
14. See "Death of a Liberian Regime," *West Africa*, April 21 (1980), p. 687.
15. Quoted in Gus Liebenow, op. cit., p. 209.
16. See "Liberia One Year After the Coup," *West Africa*, 13 April (1981), p. 839.
17. See "Threat to Teachers," *West Africa*, October 3 (1983), p. 2,325.
18. See Blaine Harden, "Who Killed Liberia? We Did," *Washington Post* (National Weekly Edition) June 3–9, (1996), p. 24.
19. See "Quiwonkpa Breaks His Silence," *West Africa*, June 17 (1985), p. 1204.
20. *New York Times*, April 23 (1980), p. 1.
21. *West Africa*, August 18 (1980), p. 1,542.
22. *West Africa*, December 1 (1980), p. 2,400.
23. *West Africa*, June 16 (1980), p. 1,092.
24. *West Africa*, June 23 (1980), p. 1,156.
25. Stephen Ellis, "Liberia 1989–1994: A Study of Ethnic and Spiritual Violence," *African Affairs* 94/375 (1995), p. 176.
26. Bill Berkeley, "Liberia: Between Repression and Slaughter," *The Atlantic*, 270 (December 1992), p. 54.
27. Stephen Ellis, op. cit., p. 176.
28. Christopher Clapham, op. cit., p. 108.
29. See "The Flanzamaton Affair," *West Africa*, May 13 (1985), pp. 929–930.
30. Amos Sawyer, "Effective Immediately: Dictatorship in Liberia 1980–1986," Liberia Working Group (Paper 5), Bremen, p. 8.

31. Max Sesay, "Civil War and Collective Intervention in Liberia," *Review of African Political Economy*, 67 (1995), p. 36.
32. See "Quiwonkpa Breaks His Silence," op. cit., p. 1,204.
33. Lawyers' Committee For Human Rights, *Liberia: A Promise Betrayed* (New York: 1986), p. 52.
34. Ibid.
35. Ibid., p. 57.
36. See "How Quiwonkpa and Gbenyon Died," *West Africa*, December 30, 1985.
37. Yekepa was one of the towns that had prematurely erupted in celebration at the news of Doe's downfall. Charles Julu initially went into hiding and only resurfaced after Doe regained control.
38. Lawyers' Committee, op. cit., p. 72.
39. Ibid., p. 157.
40. Much of this information is based on conversations with Alaric Tokpa in Jos, Nigeria, 2000.
41. Lawyers Committee, op. cit. p. 157.
42. Ibid., p. 143.
43. Ibid., p. 7.
44. *West Africa*, June 6 (1980), p. 1,092.
45. See "Quiwonkpa Breaks His Silence," op. cit., p. 1,202
46. Laywers Committee, op. cit., p. 109.
47. Gus Liebenow, op. cit., p. 277.
48. Lawyers' Committee, op. cit., p. 119.
49. In the words of Douglas Kline, a high ranking official at the Monrovia Office of the USAID, the United States "funded the election, we organized it, we supervised the voting and then when Doe stole it, we didn't have the guts to tell him to get his ass out of the mansion." Quoted in Blaine Harden, "Who Killed Liberia," op. cit., p. 24.
50. *West Africa*, January 13 (1986), p. 56.
51. Ibid.
52. West Africa, April 22 (1985), p. 809.
53. West Africa, August 19 (1985), p. 1,719.
54. Tunji Lardner, "An African Tragedy," *Africa Report*, Nov/Dec. (1990), p. 15.
55. See Blaine Harden, op. cit., p. 24.

Chapter 6

1. Quoted in Guy Martin, "Ideology and Praxis in Thomas Sankara's Populist Revolution of 4 August 1983 in Burkina Faso," *Issue*, 15 (1987), p. 78.
2. Thomas Sankara, *Thomas Sankara Speaks: The Burkina Faso Revolution 1983–1987* (New York: Pathfinder, 1988), p. 18.
3. See Claude Welch, "Obstacles to Disengagement and Democratization: Military Regimes in Benin and Burkina Faso," in Constantine Danopoulos (ed.), *The*

Decline of Military Regimes: The Civilian Influence (Boulder: Westview Press, 1988), pp. 30–31.

4. Pierre Englebert, *Burkina Faso: Unsteady Statehood in West Africa* (Boulder: Westview Press, 1996), p. 47.
5. Ibid., p. 48.
6. Ibid., p. 50.
7. Richard Vengroff, "Africa's New Hope For Democracy," *Africa Report* (July–August 1978), p. 59.
8. Pierre Englebert, op. cit., pp. 50–51.
9. Ibid., p. 52.
10. Press Conference of June 28, 1983, *Carrefour Africain*, 758 (1 July 1983), p. 10.
11. See Rene Otayek, "The Revolutionary Process in Burkina Faso: Breaks and Continuities," in John Markakis and Michael Waller (ed.), *Military Marxist Regimes in Africa* (London: Frank Cass, 1986), p. 87.
12. Thomas Sankara, op. cit., p. 21.
13. Ibid., p. 22.
14. Ibid., p. 25.
15. Ibid., p. 42.
16. Ibid., pp. 40–41.
17. Ibid., pp. 11–20.
18. Rene Otayek, op. cit., p. 89.
19. Thomas Sankara, op. cit., p. 78.
20. Thomas Sankara, quoted in an interview with *Newsweek*, November 19 (1984), p. 68.
21. See "Upper Volta: The Language of the Revolution," *West Africa*, September 19 (1983), pp. 2,167–2,168, for an account of this policy.
22. Thomas Sankara, op. cit., p. 48.
23. Ibid., p. 48.
24. Ibid., p. 50.
25. Ibid., p. 49.
26. Quoted in Lyse Doucet, "Ca Va la Revolution," *West Africa*, June 17 (1985), p. 1,217.
27. Ibid.
28. Ibid., p. 1,218.
29. Elliot Skinner, "Sankara and the Burkinabe Revolution," *Journal of Modern African Studies*, 26/3 (1988), p. 499.
30. Ibid.
31. See "Burkina Salary Cuts," *West Africa*, January 13 (1986), p. 100.
32. See "Burkinabe Officials Sent Back to the Land," *African Business*, October (1985), p. 68.
33. Thomas Sankara, op. cit., p. 56.
34. Ibid., p. 57.
35. Victoria Brittain, "Introduction to Sankara and Burkina Faso," *Review of African Political Economy*, 32 (1985), p. 46.

36. Rene Otayek, "Burkina Faso: Between Feeble State and Total State, the Swing Continues," in Donal Cruise O'Brien et al., *Contemporary West African States* (London: Cambridge University Press, 1989), p. 26.
37. Quoted in Michael Wilkins, "The Death of Thomas Sankara and the Rectification of the People's Revolution in Burkina Faso," *African Affairs*, 88/352 (1989), p. 383.
38. Thomas Sankara, op. cit., p. 40.
39. Rene Otayek, "The Revolutionary Process in Burkina Faso," op. cit., p. 91.
40. G. Bourke, "Burkina Faso's Revolution Loses its Way," *The Independent*, August 4, 1988.
41. Rene Otayek, "Burkina Faso: Between Feeble State and Total State," op. cit., pp. 23-24.
42. Quoted in B.P. Bamouni, *Carrefour africain*, 888, June 21 (1985), p. 10.
43. See "Sankara Consolidates," *West Africa*, August 20 (1983), p. 2030.
44. *Thomas Sankara Speaks*, p. 43.
45. Ibid., pp. 135–136.
46. Ibid.
47. Pierre Englebert, op. cit., p. 59.
48. Ernest Harsch, "A Revolution Betrayed," *Africa Report*, 33/1, February (1988), p. 37.
49. Ibid., p. 37.
50. Pierre Englebert, op. cit., p. 61.
51. See Guy Martin, op. cit., p. 82.
52. *Thomas Sankara Speaks*, p. 51
53. Sally Lyall Grant, "A Railway by Volunteer Labor" *West Africa*, July 1 (1985), p. 1,338.
54. After building a third of the rail line up to Kaya, the project was discontinued in 1990.
55. See Lyse Doucet, "Reaching Understanding," *West Africa*, June 3 (1985), p. 1,105.
56. *Thomas Sankara Speaks*, op. cit., pp. 66–67.
57. Ibid., pp. 122–123.
58. Joan Baxter and Keith Sommerville, "Burkina Faso," in Chris Allen et al (eds.), *Benin, the Congo, Burkina Faso* (London: Pinter Publishers, 1989), p. 267.
59. Guy Martin, op. cit., p. 82.
60. Yves Lacoste, "Developpement: la Course d'obstacles," *Actuel Developpement*, 67, Juillet (1985), p. 41.
61. Michael Wilkins, op. cit., p. 386.
62. Ernest Harsch, op. cit., 39.
63. Russell Geekie, "Compaore's Campaign," *Africa Report*, 36/5, October (1991), p. 56.
64. Francois Mitterand, quoted in *Jeune Afrique*, 1399, October 28 (1987), p. 35.

Chapter 7

1. This count excludes the palace coup of January 1996, which resulted in the removal of Valentine Strasser as head of state and his replacement by Julius

Maada Bio. Unlike the other coups in the country's history, this brief changing of the guard at the top represented a coup within, rather than against, the NPRC.

2. Quoted in Thomas Cox, *Civil–Military Relations in Sierra Leone* (Cambridge: Harvard University Press, 1976), p. 85.
3. The other seven officers were Captains Sheku Tarawallie, Falawa Jawara and A Seray-Wurie; Lieutenants Abu Noah, E. Caulker, A.O. Kamara, and F.S. Josiah. With the exception of Noah, Caulker and Josiah, all the other arrested officers were northerners. Five NCOs rounded the list of officers detained.
4. Anton Bebler, *Military Rule in Africa: Dahomey, Ghana, Sierra Leone and Mali* (New York: Praeger Publishers, 1973), p. 68.
5. Ibid., p. 69.
6. Ibid.
7. *Daily Mail*, April 19 (1968), p. 1.
8. See *The Rising Sun: A History of the All People's Congress Party of Sierra Leone* (Freetown: APC Publications, 1982), p. 96.
9. Thomas Cox, op. cit., p. 209.
10. See "Ex-Army Boss Comes Clean," *West Africa*, April 3–9 (1995), p. 499.
11. *West Africa*, October 28–3 November 1996, p. 1,676.
12. Elizabeth Rubin, "An Army of One's Own," *Harpers Magazine* (February 1997), p. 47.
13. "The Sierra Leone Coup," *West Africa*, May 11–17 (1992), pp. 788–789.
14. Joe Opala, "Ecstatic Revolution: Street Art Celebrating Sierra Leone's 1992 Revolution," *African Affairs*, 93/371 (1994).
15. See Chris Simpson, "Exit the Fat Man," *West Africa*, May 11–17 (1992), p. 786.
16. "The Sierra Leone Coup," *West Africa*, Ibid., p. 789.
17. "Setback For Democracy?," *West Africa*, Ibid., p. 789.
18. Ibid.
19. Quoted in *Unity Now*, July 18 (1994), p. 2.
20. Foday Sankoh, quoted in an interview with *New African*, June (1995), pp. 12–13.
21. *The Vision* Newspaper, January 6–13 (1994), p. 1.
22. Arthur Abraham served as the first Minister of Education in the NPRC government. For this citation, see Arthur Abraham, "War and Transition to Peace: A Study of State Conspiracy in Perpetuating Armed Conflict," *Africa Development*, vol XXII, 3/4 (1997), p. 109.
23. Joseph Opala, "Sierra Leone: The Politics of State Collapse," Paper Presented at SAIC Conference on Irregular Warfare in Liberia and Sierra Leone, Denver, Colorado, July 30–August 1 (1998), p. 14.
24. Personal interview of Julius Maada Bio by author, Alexandria, Virginia, USA, July 2000.
25. Stephen Riley and Max Sesay, "Sierra Leone: The Coming Anarchy," *Review of African Political Economy*, 72 (1997), p. 124.
26. Amnesty International, *Sierra Leone: Human Rights Abuses in a War Against Civilians*, AFR 51/05/95 (London: 13 September, 1995), p. 7.
27. Ibid.

28. *Unity Now*, July 18 (1994), p. 1.
29. See *White Paper on the Report of the Justice Laura Marcus-Jones Commission of Inquiry* (Freetown: Government Printers, January 1993), p. 1.
30. See *Reports of the National Commission for Unity and Reconciliation and the Government White Paper Thereon, July 1996-September 1997* (Freetown: Government Printers, 1997).
31. Ibid., pp. 7–8.
32. Abdul Karim Koroma, a former APC minister, makes this claim in his book *Sierra Leone: The Agony of a Nation* (Freetown: Andromeda Publications, 1996), p. 213.
33. Elizabeth Rubin, op. cit., p. 46.
34. See "Redeemers or Villains,"*New Breed*, October 13 (1993), p. 1.
35. Quoted in "It is a Tough Job," *West Africa*, November 15–21 (1993), p. 2,065.
36. Information on how this scheme was operated by junta members is based on personal interviews of Bank of Sierra Leone officials during the Summer of 1994.
37. Joseph Opala, "The Politics of State Collapse," op. cit., p. 23.
38. Steve Riley and Max Sesay, "Sierra Leone: The Coming Anarchy," op. cit., p. 123.
39. See *Sierra Leone Gazette Extraordinary*, CXXV, no. 12, March 4, 1994 (Freetown: Government Printers, 1994), pp. 1–4.
40. These are the words of Thaimu Bangura, first Finance Minister of the Second Republic, as quoted in *Sierra Leone Progress*, August (1996), p. 4.
41. See "Why I Joined the AFRC Government," *Daily Mail* (Special Supplement), September 10, 1997, p. 3.
42. Elco Krijn was a Dutch volunteer doctor working in the area. For details of these murders see, "The Panguma Tragedy" in *Sierra Leone Catholic* XI/3 (1994), pp. 2–3.
43. *The Sierra Leone Catholic*, XI/4 (1994), p. 7.
44. *New Shaft*, July 19–25 (1994), p. 1.
45. See Amnesty International, op. cit., p. 11.
46. See Richard M'Bayo, "The Beleaguered Press," *West Africa*, May 5–11 (1997), pp. 718–719.
47. Quoted in *West Africa*, May 18–24 (1992), p. 840.
48. James Jonah, quoted in *West Africa*, February 28–6 March (1994), p. 346.
49. Based on personal interview of James Jonah by author, July 1994, Freetown.
50. *Concord Times*, June 23 (1995), p. 1.
51. Quoted in "Born Again Politicians Want to Rape Again," *Unity Now*, January 18 (1996), p. 5.
52. See "Rumors Versus Strasser," *Concord Times*, January 16 (1996), p. 3.
53. Karefa Kargbo, quoted in "Will Bio Allow Elections?," *Unity Now*, January 18 (1996), p. 1.
54. To this day, Bio denies the charge that his attempt to postpone the elections had anything to do with his desire to prolong his stay in power. He sees the aftermath of the elections as vindication of his position that the war should have been

ended before holding elections. What this view ignores, however, is that the NPRC had four years to end the war during which it failed to do so. Bio's views on the elections and the rebel war are based on personal interviews and conversations with the former NPRC leader by the author.

55. See "To Be or not To Be," *West Africa*, February 12–18 (1996), p. 223.
56. See "International Community to Isolate Sierra Leone," *New Citizen*, January 15 (1996), pp. 1–2.
57. For an account of this election, see Jimmy Kandeh, "Transition Without Rupture: Sierra Leone's Transfer Election of 1996, *African Studies Review*, 41/2 (1998), pp. 91–111.
58. *African Development Report 1997* (London:Oxford University Press, 1997).
59. "The Sierra Leone Coup," *West Africa*, May 11–18 (1992), p. 788–789.
60. *The World Bank Atlas: 1995* (Washington, DC: The World Bank), p. 19.
61. *African Development Report 1997*, op. cit.
62. West Africa, August 21–27 (1995), p. 1,323.
63. *World Economic Outlook: May 1997* (International Monetary Fund, 1997), p. 138.
64. Economist Intelligence Unit, *Country Profile: Guinea, Sierra Leone, Liberia, 1997/98*, p. 43.
65. William Reno, "Ironies of Post-Cold War Structural Adjustment in Sierra Leone", *Review of African Political Economy*, 67 (1996), p. 13.
66. Olu Awoonor-Gordon, "A Nation Held Hostage," *For Di People*, June 12 (1997), p. 2.
67. *The Democrat*, April 16 (1998), p. 1.
68. See "Court Martial: Gborie Fingers Omrie Golley," *The Democrat*, August 7 (1998), pp. 1 & 4.
69. See "17 Soldiers Planned AFRC Coup," *The Democrat*, August 7 (1998), p. 4.
70. See "We Planned Mutiny, Not Coup," *The Democrat*, August 13 (1998), p. 4.
71. See Stephen Riley, "Sierra Leone: The Militariat Strikes Again," *Review of African Political Economy*, no. 72 (1997), p. 287.
72. Rice was sold to the army at Le1,000 per bag, compared to Le 23,000 on the open market.
73. For an account that blames the AFRC coup on the loss of military privileges and rivalry with the Kamajors, see A.B. Zack-Williams, "Kamajors, 'Sobels' and the Militariat", *Review of African Political Economy*, 73 (1997), pp. 373–398.
74. See "How Coup Was Staged," *Daily Mail*, August 7 (1998), p. 1.
75. Stephen Riley, "The Militariat Strikes Again," op. cit., p. 287.
76. See "Coup in Freetown," *West Africa*, June 2–8 (1997), pp. 887–888.
77. See "I Will Not Hand Over to a Demon," *We Yone*, November 11 (1997), p. 1.
78. See "Mass Looting at Rutile," *Unity Now*, February 13 (1995), pp. 1, 7.
79. See "Charles Taylor Plotted the May 25 Coup," *The Democrat*, May 2 (1998), p. 3.
80. See "Court Martial: Gborie Fingers Golley", op. cit., pp. 1 & 4.
81. Based on personal interview of Johnny Paul Koroma by author, Freetown, July 2001. To be the leadership preference of subalterns does not, however, imply

masterminding subaltern agency. That Musa was the choice of those who staged the coup is beyond dispute; what is not clear is that Musa, while in England, orchestrated the coup.

82. Alex Tamba Brima (alias Gullit), one of the leaders of the 1997 coup, confirmed Johnny Paul Koroma's claim that Musa, not Koroma, was the insurgent subaltern's sentimental choice as leader. This information is based on personal interview of Brima by author in Freetown, July 2001.
83. Johnny Paul Koroma claimed Musa was not content to play second fiddle to him and tried on numerous occasions to kill him (Koroma).
84. *West Africa*, June 2-8 (1997), p. 888.
85. Personal interview of Desmond Luke, Chief Justice of Sierra Leone (1998–2002), by author in Freetown, September 1998.
86. See "Alieu Kamara's Interview Provokes Concern," *Concord Times*, October 27 (1997), p. 1.
87. Quoted in "In Praise of What," *The Democrat*, January 15 (1998), p. 2.
88. Quoted in Joseph Opala, "Sierra Leone: The Politics of State Collapse," op. cit., p. 19.
89. See "AFRC Coup: What the Diplomats Say," *Unity Now*, June 16 (1997), p. 1.
90. See "Spur Loop Theft: Major Koroma Takes Responsibility," *The Vision*, September 16 (1997), p. 1.
91. See "The Armed Forces Revolutionary Council (Anti-Looting Decree), 1997, *Supplement to the Sierra Leone Gazette*, Vol. CXXVIII, No. 63 (Freetown: Government Printing Department, 1997), pp. 3–4.
92. Ibid., p. 6.
93. Ibid.
94. See "Gborie Burnt Down Treasury Building," *The Democrat*, August 5 (1998), p. 1.
95. See "Armed Men Strip Embassy," *The Democrat*, January 6 (1998), p. 1.
96. *The Democrat*, January 17 (1997), p. 1.
97. See "Sojas Loot EU Hondas," *The Democrat*, October 28 (1997), p. 4.
98. See, for example, "Junta SOS on Selling Spree," *The Democrat*, October 23 (1997), p. 4.
99. See "Tejan Kabba's Lodge Looted," *Daily Mail*, August 29 (1998), p. 1.
100. See "Gunmen Loot Bishop," *The Democrat*, October 14 (1997), p. 4.
101. See "Sojas Plunder Displaced People," *The Democrat*, September 26 (1997), p. 1.
102. See "How SLPP Secretary-General Was Killed," *The Democrat*, September 11 (1998), p. 1. The specifics of this incident were recounted to the author during an interview with Mrs Caulker, the victims mother, in September 1998.
103. Amnesty International, op. cit., p. 3.
104. See "Tough Time for Journalists," *The Democrat*, October 14 (1997), p. 1.
105. See "Three Journalists Released," *Concord Times*, October 27 (1997), p. 1.
106. "BBC Reporter Detained in Bo," *The Democrat*, October 16 (1997), p. 4.
107. *The Democrat*, January 17 (1997), p. 1.

108. *The Democrat*, November 14 (1997), p. 1.
109. *The Democrat*, October 7 (1997), p. 1.
110. *The Democrat*, September 23 (1997), p. 4.
111. Sierra Leoneans took to referring to Johnny Koroma as "foot of state" to underscore their view of him as an impostor unfit to occupy the highest political office in the country.
112. See "Child Soldiers: The Misery, the Deprivation," *The Democrat*, November 14 (1997), p. 1.
113. See "Go and Show Kabba," *Vision*, May 9 (1998), p. 1.
114. See "I will not Handover to a Demon," *We Yone*, op. cit., p. 1.
115. *Concord Times*, October 27 (1997), p. 1.
116. See "Coup in Freetown?," *West Africa*, June 2–8 (1997), p. 888.
117. *West Africa*, April 14–20 (1997), pp. 594–596.
118. See *Government Budget and Statement of Economic and Financial Policies for the Financial Year 1998* (Freetown: Government Printing Department, 30th June 1998), pp. 2–3.
119. See "Remedy the Economy," *Unity Now*, January 5 (1998), p. 2.
120. This information is based on personal interviews of senior bank officials in 1998 and 1999.
121. See "America Freezes Sierra Leone's Account," *Independent Observer*, December 2 (1997), p. 1.
122. See "Lebanese Cut Junta's Tail," *The Democrat*, October 16 (1997), p. 1.

Chapter 8

1. Chris Allen, "Understanding African Politics," *Review of African Political Economy*, 65 (1995), p. 305.
2. For excellent accounts of this coup, see Arnold Hughes "The Attempted Gambian Coup d'etat of 27 July 1981", in Arnold Hughes (ed.) *The Gambia: Studies in Society and Politics* (Birmingham: African Studies Series 3, 1991) pp. 92–106; and John Wiseman, "Attempted Coup in The Gambia: Marxist Revolution or Punk Rebellion," *Journal of Communist Affairs*, vol. 1 (1982), pp. 434–443.
3. Arnold Hughes, Ibid., p. 99.
4. For a discussion of some of the issues involved in the collapse of this confederation, see Arnold Hughes, "The Collapse of the Senegambian Confederation," *Journal of Commonwealth and Comparative Politics*, vol. 30, no. 2 (July 1992), pp. 200–222.
5. Ibid., p. 105.
6. Alhaji A.E. Cham Joof, "July 1981 Revisited," *Weekend Observer*, July 29–31 (1994), p. 17.
7. Zaya Yeebo, *State of Fear in Paradise: The Military Coup in The Gambia and its Implications for Democracy* (London: Africa Research and Information Bureau, 1995), p. 3.

8. See "Army Coup in Gambia," *Daily Observer*, July 25 (1994), p. 1.
9. See "We are not Promising Miracles," *Daily Observer*, August 8 (1994), pp. 1 & 10.
10. Ibid., p. 1.
11. Abdoulaye Saine, "The Coup d'Etat in The Gambia, 1994: The End of the First Republic," *Armed Forces and Society*, 23/1 (Fall 1996), pp. 97–111.
12. John Wiseman, "Military Rule in The Gambia: An Interim Assessment," *Third World Quarterly*, 17/5 (1996), p. 931.
13. Ibid., p. 920.
14. Ibid.
15. Abdoulaye Saine, op. cit., p. 103.
16. See "Why I Took Over," *Daily Observer*, July 25 (1994), p. 9.
17. Wassa Fatty, a local political activist, quoted in Zaya Yeebo, op. cit., p. 44.
18. See "Workers Support for AFPRC is Conditional," *Daily Observer*, July 28 (1994), p. 13.
19. See "Dibba Endorses Army Coup," *Daily Observer*, August 4 (1994), pp. 1 & 10.
20. See "Step Down Immediately," *Daily Observer*, November 9 (1994), pp. 1 & 10.
21. *The Point*, November 3 (1994).
22. See "2,500 British Subjects Leave Gambia," *Weekend Observer*, November 25–27 (1994), p. 1.
23. *West Africa*, January 9–15 (1995), p. 11.
24. See "Danes Warned to Avoid Gambia," *Daily Observer*, November 29 (1994), p. 1. An estimated 9,000 tourists from Denmark visited Gambia annually before the coup.
25. See "USAID to Close Down," *The Point*, September 8 (1994), p. 1.
26. See "EU Suspends Some Aid to Gambia," *Daily Observer*, October 13 (1994), p. 1.
27. *West Africa*, March 13-19 (1995), pp. 386-387.
28. *New Citizen*, September 30 (1994), p. 1.
29. See "We are Prepared to Die," *Daily Observer*, September 27 (1994), p. 12.
30. See "No Compromise for Sovereignty," *Daily Observer*, October 19 (1994), p. 12.
31. Zaya Yeebo, op. cit., p. 45.
32. *Daily Observer*, July 25 (1994), p. 8.
33. *Daily Observer*, October 10 (1994), p. 1.
34. See "No Mercy for the Corrupt," *Daily Observer*, October 10 (1994), pp. 1 & 10.
35. See "23 Officials Get their Assets Frozen," *Daily Observer*, December 12 (1994), p. 13.
36. See "Commissions of Inquiry Members Sworn In," *Daily Observer*, November 10 (1994), pp. 1 & 10.
37. John Wiseman, op. cit., p.930.
38. Abdoulaye Saine, op. cit., pp. 97–111.
39. John Wiseman, op. cit., p. 932.
40. *Daily Observer*, October 10 (1994), p. 4.
41. *Daily Observer*, July 11 (1995), pp. 1 & 10.

42. Amnesty International, *The Gambia: Erosion of Human Rights Safeguards Continues*, AFR 27/002/1996 (January 26, 1996).
43. See "My Husband Was Never a High Blood Patient," *The Point*, June 8 (1995), pp. 1, 12.
44. See "Finance Minister Dies Mysteriously," *Daily Observer*, June 26 (1995), p. 1.
45. *West Africa*, August 14 (1994), p. 1,388.
46. *Weekend Observer*, August 18–20 (1995), p. 1.
47. *The Point*, November 28 (1994), p. 1.
48. See "Observer Boss Deported," *Daily Observer*, October 31 (1994), pp. 1 & 10.
49. See "Observer Reporter Picked Up," *Daily Observer*, October 11 (1994), p. 1.
50. See "VOA Banjul Stringer Deported from Gambia," *Daily Observer*, April 24 (1996), p. 1.
51. See "Reporters Sans Frontiers Calls for Prosecution of Soldiers," *Daily Observer*, November 9 (1994), p. 1.
52. For a detailed account of the circumstances surrounding these violations, see Amnesty International, *The Gambia: Democratic Reforms Without Human Rights*, AFR 27/04/97.
53. See "The AFRC Indemnity Clause in the Constitution," *Daily Observer*, September 16 (1996), p. 6.
54. See "We Will Not Accept Democracy," *Daily Observer*, December 28 (1994), p. 1 & 12.
55. *Daily Observer*, July 25 (1994), p. 8.
56. *Daily Observer*, September 22 (1994), p. 1.
57. "Why We Took Over," *Daily Observer*, July 25 (1994), p. 9.
58. See "Return to the Barracks: European Union Tells AFPRC," *Daily Observer*, July 28 (1994), p. 1.
59. See, for example, "Bar Association Maintains Stance on Timetable," *Daily Observer*, November 7 (1994), pp. 1 & 10.
60. John Wiseman, "Military Rule in The Gambia," op. cit., p. 935.
61. See "AFPRC Bans PPP, NCP, GPP From Contesting Elections," *Daily Observer*, August 19 (1996), p. 1.
62. See "Ban On My Party Does Not Surprise Me," *Daily Observer*, August 19 (1996), p. 1.
63. *Daily Observer*, August 19 (1996), p. 12.
64. See "Gambians Endorse Revised Draft Constitution," *Weekend Observer*, August 10–11 (1996), pp. 1 & 10.
65. *Weekend Observer*, September 13–15 (1996), p. 9.
66. See "UDP Leader Lambasts AFPRC," *Daily Observer*, September 10 (1996), pp. 1, 10.
67. See "NRP Leader Hamat Bah Speaks Out," *Weekend Observer*, September 13–15 (1996), p. 11.
68. See "NRP Formally Launched in Gunjur," *Daily Observer*, September 11 (1996), p. 1.

69. *Daily Observer*, Sept. 5 (1996), p. 6.
70. World Bank Report, 1995.
71. Quoted in "Donor Pullout Will Not Affect Salary Payment," *Daily Observer*, September 19 (1994), p. 10.

Conclusion

1. Thomas Sankara, "Political Orientation Speech", in *Thomas Sankara Speaks* (New York: Pathfinder, 1988), p. 48.
2. Patrick Chabal and Jean-Pascal Daloz, *Africa Works: Disorder as Political Instrument* (Oxford: James Curry, 1999), pp. 83–84.
3. Barry Schutz, "The Heritage of Revolution and the Struggle for Governmental legitimacy in Mozambique," in I. William Zartmann (ed.), *Collapsed States* (Boulder: Lynne Rienner, 1995), p. 109.
4. Robert Jackson, *Quasi-States: Sovereignty, International Relations and the Third World* (New York: Cambridge University press, 1990), p. 22.

Bibliography

Abdullah, Ibrahim. "Bushpath to Destruction: The Origin and Character of the Revolutionary United Front (RUF/SL)," *Africa Development* 22/3–4 (1997), pp. 45–76.

Aboagye, Festus. *The Ghana Army: A Concise Contemporary Guide to its Centennial Regimental History, 1897–1999*. Accra: Sedco, 1999.

Abraham, Arthur. "War and Transition to Peace: A Study of State Conspiracy in Perpetuating Armed Conflict," *Africa Development*, 22/3–4 (1997), pp. 101–116.

Adekson. J. 'Bayo. "On the Theory of Modernizing Soldier: A Critique, *Issue*, August (1978), pp. 28–41.

Afrifa, Akwasi, *The Ghana Coup: 24th February 1966*. London: Frank Cass, 1966.

Agyeman, O. "Setbacks to Political Institutionalization by Praetorianism in Africa," *Journal of Modern African Studies*, 26/3 (1988), pp. 403–435.

Agyeman-Duah, Baffour. "Ghana, 1982–1986: the Politics of the PNDC," *Journal of Modern African Studies*, 25/4 (1987), pp. 613–642.

Ake, Claude. Address to the Annual Meeting of the Nigerian Political Science Association, reprinted in *West Africa* May 25 (1981), pp. 1,162–1,623.

Allen, Chris. "Understanding African Politics," *Review of African Political Economy*, vol. 65 (1995), pp. 301–320.

Anderson, Perry. "The Antinomies of Antonio Gramsci," *New Left Review*, vol. 100 (1977), pp. 1–79.

Anyemedu, Kwasi. "The Economic Policies of the PNDC," in E. Gyimah-Boadi (ed.), *Ghana Under PNDC Rule*. Dakar: Codesria, 1993.

Arendt, Hannah. *On Violence*. New York: Harcourt, Brace, Jovanovich, 1970.

Arnold, David. "Gramsci and Peasant Subalternity in India," *Journal of Peasant Studies*, 11/4 (1984), pp. 155–177.

Austin, Dennis. "The Ghana Armed Forces and Ghanaian Society," *Third World Quarterly*, 7/1 (1985), pp. 90–101.

Austin, Dennis and Robin Luckham (eds). *Politicians and Soldiers in Ghana*. London: Frank Cass, 1975.

Awoonor, Kofi. *Ghana: A Political History*. Accra: Sedco Publishing, 1990.

Bangura Yusuf. "Understanding the Political and Cultural Dynamics of the Sierra Leone Civil War: A Critique of Paul Richards's Fighting for the Rain Forest," *Africa Development*, 22/3–4 (1997), pp. 117–148.

Baxter, Joan and Keith Sommerville. "Burkina Faso," in Christopher Allen et al (eds.), *Benin, The Congo, Burkina Faso*. London: Pinter Publishers, 1989. pp. 239–287.

Bayart, Jean-Francois, et al. *The Criminalization of the State in Africa*. London: James Currey, 1999.

Bayart, Jean-Francois. *The State in Africa: The Politics of the Belly*. London: Longman, 1993.

Bayly, C.A. "Rallying Around the Subaltern," *Journal of Peasant Studies*, 16/1 (1988), pp. 110–120.

Baynham, Simon. "The Subordination of African Armies to Civilian Control: Theory and Praxis," *Africa Insight*, 22/4 (1992), pp. 259–263.

Baynham, Simon. "Security Issues in Africa: The Imperial Legacy, Domestic Violence and the Military," *Africa Insight*, 21/3 (1991), pp. 180–189.

Baynham, Simon. "Divide et Impera: Civilian Control of the Military in Ghana's Second and Third Republics," *Journal of Modern African Studies*, 23/4 (1985), pp. 623–642.

Bebler, Anton, *Military Rule in Africa: Dahomey, Ghana, Sierra Leone and Mali*. New York: Praeger, 1973.

Beckman, Bjorn. "The Military as Revolutionary Vanguard: A Critique," *Review of African Political Economy*, vol. 37 (1986), pp. 50–62.

Bentsi-Enchill, Nii K. "Ghana Revolution Loses Steam," *West Africa*, 25 June (1979), pp. 1, 105–1, 106.

Bennet, Valery. "Epilogue: Malcontents in Uniform," in Dennis Austin and Robin Luckham (eds.), op. cit.

Berkeley, Bill. "Liberia: Between Repression and Slaughter," *The Atlantic*, 270, December (1992), pp. 52–64.

Berry, Sara. *Fathers Work for their Sons: Accumulation, Mobility and Class Formation in an Extended Yoruba Community*. Berkeley: University of California Press, 1985.

Bienen, Henry. "Populist Military Regimes in West Africa," *Armed Forces and Society*, 11/3 (1985) pp. 357–377.

Blackey, Robert. "Fanon and Cabral: A Contrast in Theories of Revolution for Africa," *Journal of Modern African Studies*, 12/2 (1974), pp. 191–209.

Boley, George. Liberia: *The Rise and Fall of the First Republic*. London: Macmillan, 1983.

Bratton, Michael and Nicholas van de Walle. "Neopatrimonial Regimes and political Transitions in Africa," in Peter Lewis (ed.), *Africa: The Dilemmas of Development and Change*. Boulder: Westview, 1988.

Brittain, Victoria. "Ghana's Precarious Balance," *New Left Review*, vol. 140 (July–August 1983), pp. 50–61.

Brittain, Victoria. "Introduction to Sankara and Burkina Faso," *Review of African Political Economy*, vol. 32 (1985), pp. 39–47.

Cabral, Amilcar. *Revolution in Guinea*. New York: Monthly Review Press, 1969.

Callaghy, Thomas. *The State-Society Struggle: Zaire in Comparative Perspective*. New York: Columbia University Press, 1984.

Cartwright, John. *Politics in Sierra Leone: 1947–1967.* Toronto: University of Toronto Press, 1970.

Chabal, Patrick and Jean-Pascal Daloz. *Africa Works: Disorder as Political Instrument.* London: James Currey, 1999.

Chatterjee, Partha. "Caste and Subaltern Consciousness," *Subaltern Studies*, vol. 6 (1989), pp. 169–209.

Chazan, Naomi. "The Political Transformation of Ghana Under the PNDC," in Donald Rothchild (ed.), *Ghana: The Political Economy of Recovery*. Boulder: Lynne Rienner, 1991.

Chazan, Naomi. "Ghana: Problems of Governance and the Emergence of Civil Society," in Larry Diamond et al (eds.), *Democracy in Developing Countries: Africa.* Boulder: Lynne Rienner, 1988.

Chazan, Naomi. "Ethnicity and Politics in Ghana," *Political Science Quarterly*, 97/3 (1982), pp. 461–485.

Chilcote, Ronald. "The Political Thought of Amilcar Cabral," *Journal of Modern African Studies*, 6/3 (1968), pp. 3,373–3,388.

Chipman, John. *French Power in Africa*. London: Basil Blackwell, 1989.

Cirese, Alberto Maria. "Gramsci's Observations of Folklore," in A.S Sasson (ed.), *Approaches to Gramsci*. London: Writers and Readers, 1982.

Clapham, Christopher (ed.), *African Guerrillas*. Oxford: James Currey, 1998.

Clapham, Christopher. "Liberia," in Donal Cruise O'Brien et al (eds.), *Contemporary West African States*. Cambridge: Cambridge University Press, 1989.

Clayton, Anthony and David Killingray. *Khaki and Blue: Military and Police in British Colonial Africa*. Athens: Ohio University Press, 1989.

Coleman, James and Belmont Brice. "The Role of the Military in Subsaharan Africa," in John Johnson (ed.), *The Role of the Military in Underdeveloped Countries*. Princeton: Princeton University Press, 1962.

Collier, David (ed.). *The New Authoritarianism in Latin America*. Princeton: Princeton University Press, 1979.

Collier, Paul. "Doing Well Out of War," in Mats Berdal and David Malone (eds.), *Greed and Grievance: Economic Agendas in Civil Wars*. Boulder: Lynne Rienner, 2000.

Conteh-Morgan, Earl. "The Military and Human Rights in a Post-cold war Africa," *Armed Forces and Society*, 21/1 (1994), pp. 69–87.

Cox, Thomas. *Civil-Military Relations in Sierra Leone: A Case Study of African Soldiers in Politics*. Cambridge: Harvard University Press, 1976.

Crocker, Chester. "Military Dependence: The Colonial Legacy in Africa," *Journal of Modern African Studies*, 12/2 (1974), pp. 265–286.

Davidson, Basil. *The Black Man's Burden*. New York: Times Books, 1992.

Davis, Shelby. *Reservoirs of Men: A History of the Black Troops of French West Africa*. Geneva: Libraire Kundig, 1934.

Decalo, Samuel. "Not By Democracy Alone," *Journal of African Policy Studies* 1/3 (1995), pp. 99–106.

Decalo, Samuel. "The Process, Prospects and Constraints of Democratization in Africa," *African Affairs*, 91/362 (1992), pp. 7–36.

Decalo, Samuel. *Coups and Army Rule in Africa: Studies in Military Style.* New Haven: Yale University Press, 1976.

Dhanagare, D.N. "Subaltern Consciousness and Populism: Two Approaches in the Study of Social Movements in India," *Social Scientist*, 16/11, November (1988), pp. 18–35.

Dhareshwar, Vivek and R. Srivatsan. "Rowdy-Sheeters: An Essay on Subalternity and Politics," *Subaltern Studies*, vol. 9 (1996), pp. 201–231.

Dieke, Peter. "The Political Economy of Tourism in The Gambia," *Review of African Political Economy*, no. 62 (1994), pp. 611–627.

Dolgoff, Sam (ed.). *Bakunin on Anarchy: Selected Works.* New York: Alfred A. Knopf, 1972.

Dowse, Robert. "Military and Police Rule," in Dennis Austin and Robert Luckham (ed.), op. cit.

Echenberg, Myron. *Colonial Conscripts: The Tirailleurs Senegalais in French West Africa, 1857–1960.* London: James Currey, 1991.

Ellis Stephen. *The Mask of Anarchy: The Destruction of Liberia and the Religious Dimension of an African Civil War.* New York: New York University Press, 1999.

Ellis, Stepen. "Liberia 1989–1994: A Study of Ethnic and Spiritual Violence," *African Affairs*, 94/375 (1995), pp. 165–198.

Engels, Frederick. *The Peasant War in Germany.* New York: International Publishers, 1976.

Englebert, Pierre. *Burkina Faso: Unsteady Statehood in West Africa.* Boulder: Westview Press, 1996.

Esseks, John. "Economic Policies," in Dennis Austin and Robert Luckham (eds.), op. cit.

Fanon, Frantz. *The Wretched of the Earth.* New York: Grove Weidenfeld, 1963.

Fatton, Robert. *Predatory Rule in Africa.* Boulder: Lynne Rienner, 1992.

Fatton, Robert. "Bringing the Ruling Class Back In: Class, State and Hegemony in Africa," *Comparative Politics*, 20/3 (1988), pp. 253–264.

Feaver, Peter. "The Civil-Military Problematique: Huntington, Janowitz and the Question of Civilian Control," *Armed Forces and Society*, 23/2 (1996), pp. 149–178.

Finer, Samuel. "The Man on Horseback," *Armed Forces and Society*, 1/1 (1974), pp. 5–27.

First, Ruth. *Power in Africa.* New York: Penguin, 1971.

Fyfe, Christopher. *A History of Sierra Leone.* London: Cambridge University Press, 1962.

Fyle, C. Magbaily." The Military and Civil Society in Sierra Leone: the 1992 Military Coup D'etat," *Africa Development*, 19/2 (1994), pp. 127–146.

Fyle, C. Magbaily (ed.). *The State and Provision of Social Services in Sierra Leone Since Independence, 1961–1991* (Dakar: Codesria, 1993).

Gberie, Lansana. "The May 25 Coup d'etat in Sierra Leone: A Militariat Revolt," *Africa Development*, 22, 3/4 (1997), pp. 149–170.

Geekie, Russell. "Compaore's Campaign," *Africa Report*, 36/5 (1991), pp. 55–58.

Gershoni, Yekutiel. "War Without End and an End to War: The Prolonged Wars in Liberia and Sierra Leone," *African Studies Review*, 40/3, (1997), pp. 55–76.

Gershoni, Yekutiel. "The Changing Pattern of Military Takeovers in Sub-Saharan Africa," *Armed Forces and Society*, 23/2, (1996), pp. 235–248.

Gocking, Roger. "Ghana's Public Tribunals: An Experiment in Revolutionary Justice," *African Affairs*, vol. 95 (1996) pp. 197–223.

Goldsworthy, David. "Civilian Control of the Military in Black Africa," *African Affairs*, 80/318 (1981), pp. 49–74.

Graf, William. *The Nigerian State*. Portsmouth: Heinemann, 1988.

Gramsci, Antonio. *Selections from the Prison Notebooks*. New York: International Publishers, 1971.

Green, Daniel. "Ghana's Adjusted Economy," *Review of African Political Economy*, 22/66 (1995), pp. 577–585.

Grundy, Kenneth. *Conflicting Images of the Military in Africa*. Nairobi: East African Publishing House, 1968.

Gutteridge, William. *Military Regimes in Africa*. London: Methuen, 1975.

Gyimah-Boadi, E. "Ghana's Uncertain Political Opening," *Journal of Democracy*, 5/2 (1994), pp. 75–86.

Gyimah-Boadi, E. (ed.). *Ghana Under PNDC Rule*. Dakar: Codesria, 1993.

Gyimah-Boadi, E. and Rothchild, Donald. "Rawlings, Populism and the Civil Liberities Tradition in Ghana," *Issue*, 12/3–4 (1982), pp. 64–69.

Hansen, Emmanuel. *Ghana Under Rawlings*. Lagos: Malthouse, 1991.

Hansen, Emmanuel and Collins, Paul. "The Army, The State, and the 'Rawlings Revolution' in Ghana", *African Affairs*, 79/314 (1980), pp. 3–23.

Harden, Blaine. "Who Killed Liberia?," *Washington Post* (National Weekly Edition), June 3–9, 1996, p. 24.

Harsch, Ernest. "A Revolution Betrayed," *Africa Report*, 33/1 (1988), pp. 56–51.

Hayward, Fred and Jimmy, Kandeh. "Perspectives on Twenty-Five Years of Elections in Sierra Leone," in Fred Hayward (ed.), *Elections in Independent Africa*. Boulder: Westview, 1987.

Haywood, A. and F.A.S., Clarke. *The History of the Royal West African Frontier Force*. Aldershot: Gale and Polden, 1964.

Haynes, Jeff. "Sustainable Democracy in Ghana? Problems and Prospects," *Third World Quarterly*, 14/3 (1993), pp. 451–467.

Herbst, Jeffrey. *The Politics of Reform in Ghana, 1982–1991*. Berkeley: University of California Press, 1993.

Hooper, Jim. "Sierra Leone—the War Continues," *Jane's Intelligence Review*, 8/1 (January 1996).

Hirsch, John. *Sierra Leone: Diamonds and the Struggle for Democracy*. Boulder: Lynne Rienner, 2001.

Hughes, Arnold. "The Attempted Gambian Coup d'etat of 27 July 1981," in Arnold Hughes (ed.), *The Gambia: Studies in Society and Politics*. London: Birmingham African Studies Series 3, 1991.

Hughes, Arnold. "The Collapse of the Senegambian Federation," *Journal of Commonwealth and Comparative Studies*, 30/2 (1992), pp. 200–222.

Huntington, Samuel. *The Soldier and the State: The Theory and Politics of Civil–Military Relations*. New York: Vintage Books, 1964.

Hutchful, Eboe. "Military Issues in the Transition to Democracy," In Eboe Hutchful and Abdoulaye Bathily (eds.), *The Military and Militarism in Africa*. Dakar: Codesria, 1998.

Hutchful, Eboe. "Institutional Decomposition and Junior Ranks' Political Action in Ghana," in Hutchful and Bathily (eds.), op. cit.

Hutchful, Eboe. "Trends in Africa," *Alternatives*, 10/1 (1984), pp. 115–137.

Hutchful, Eboe. "A Tale of Two Regimes: Imperialism, the Military and Class in Ghana," *Review of African Political Economy*, vol. 11 (1979), pp. 36–55.

Hyden, Goran. *No Shortcuts to Progress*. Berkeley: University of California Press, 1983.

Ihonvbere, Julius. "Are Things Falling Apart: The Military and the Crisis of Democratization in Nigeria," *Journal of Modern African Studies*, 34/2 (1996), pp. 193–225.

Jeffries, Richard and Clare Thomas. "The Ghanaian Elections of 1992," *African Affairs*, 92/368 (1993), pp. 331–366.

Jeffries, Richard. "Urban Popular Attitudes Towards The Economic Recovery Program and the PNDC Government in Ghana," *African Affairs*, 91 (1992), pp. 207–226.

Jeffries, Richard. "Leadership Commitment and Political Opposition to Structural Adjustment in Ghana," in Donald Rothchild (ed.), *Ghana: The Political Economy of Recovery*. Boulder: Lynne Rieneer, 1991.

Jeffries, Richard. "Rawlings and the Political Economy of Underdevelopment in Ghana," *African Affairs*, 81/324 (1982), pp. 307–317.

Jeffries, Richard. "The Ghanaian Elections of 1979," *African Affairs*, 79/316 (1980), pp. 397–414.

Kandeh, Jimmy. "Ransoming the State: Elite Origins of Subaltern Terror in Sierra Leone," *Review of African Political Economy*, vol. 81 (September 1999), pp. 349–366.

Kandeh, Jimmy. "Transition Without Rupture: Sierra Leone's Transfer Elections of 1996," *African Studies Review*, 41/2 (1998), pp. 91–111.

Kandeh, Jimmy. "What Does the Militariat Do When it Rules: Military Regimes in The Gambia, Sierra Leone and Liberia," *Review Of African Political Economy*, vol. 69 (September (1996), pp. 387–404.

Kandeh, Jimmy. "Contradictory Class Functionality of the 'Soft' State," *Review of African Political Economy*, vol. 55 (November 1992), pp. 30–43.

Kaplan, Richard. "The Coming Anarchy," *The Atlantic Monthly*, 273/2, pp. 44–76.

Kasfir, Nelson (ed.). *State and Class in Africa*. London: Frank Cass, 1984.

Keen, David. "Incentives and Disincentives for Violence," in Mats Berdal and David Malone (eds.), *Greed and Grievance: Economic Agendas in Civil Wars*. Boulder: Lynne Rienner, 2000.

Khadiagala, Gilbert. "The Military in Africa's Democratic Transitions," *Africa Today*, 42/1–2 (1995), pp. 61–74.

Kieh, George. "Causes of Liberia's Coup," *Transafrica Forum* (Winter 1989), pp. 37–47.

Killingray, David. "Labor Exploitation for Military Campaigns in British Colonial Africa 1870–1945," *Journal of Contemporary History*, vol. 24 (1989), pp. 483–501.

Killingray, David. "The Idea of a British Imperial African Army," *Journal of African History*, 20/3 (1970), pp. 421–436.

Kilson, Martin. *Political Change in a West African State: A Study of the Modernization Process in Sierra Leone*. Cambridge: Harvard University Press, 1968.

Koroma, Abdul Karim. *Sierra Leone: The Agony of a Nation*. Freetown: Andromeda Publications, 1996.

Kpundeh. Sahr. "Limiting Administrative Corruption in Sierra Leone," *Journal of Modern African Studies*, 32/1 (1994), pp. 139–157.

Kraus, Jon. "The Political Economy of Stabilization and Structural Adjustment in Ghana", in Donald Rothchild (ed.), *Ghana: The Political Economy of Recovery*. Boulder: Lynne Rienner, 1991.

Kraus, Jon. "The Political Economy of Conflict in Ghana," *Africa Report*, 25/2 (March–April, 1980), pp. 9–16.

Kraus, Jon. "Rawlings Second Coming," *Africa Report*, 27/3, (1982), pp. 59–66.

Lardner, Tunji. "An African Tragedy," *Africa Report*, (Nov./Dec. 1990), pp. 13–16.

Levy, Marion. *Modernization and the Structure of Society*. Princeton: Princeton University Press, 1966.

Liebenow, Gus. *Liberia: The Quest for Democracy*. Bloomington: Indiana University Press, 1987.

Liebenow, Gus. "The Military Factor in African Politics: A Twenty Year Perspective," in Gwendolen Carter and Patrick O'Meara (eds), *African Independence: The First Twenty Five Years*. Bloomington: Indiana University Press, 1986.

Lofchie, Michael. "The Uganda Coup—Class Action by the Military," *Journal of Modern African Studies*, 10/1 (1972), pp. 19–35.

Lonsdale, Jon. "Political Accountability in African History," in Patrick Chabal (ed.), *Political Domination in Africa*. Cambridge: Cambridge University Press, 1986.

Luanda, Nestor. "The Tanganyika Rifles and the Mutiny of January 1964," in Eboe Hutchful and Abdoulaye Bathily (eds.), op. cit.

Luckham, Robin. "Taming the Monster: Democratization and Militarization," in Eboe Hutchful and Abdoulaye Bathily (eds.), op. cit.

Luckham, Robin. "The Military, Militarization and Democratization in Africa: A Survey of Literature and Issues," *African Studies Review*, 35/2 (1994), pp. 13–76.

Luke, David and Stephen Riley. "The Politics of Economic Decline in Sierra Leone", *Journal of Modern African Studies*, 27/1 (1989), pp. 133–142.

Mamdani, Mahmood. *Citizen and Subject: Contemporary Africa and the Legacy of Late Colonialism*. Princeton: Princeton University Press, 1996.

Mamdani, Mahmood. *When Victims Become Killers: Colonialism, Nativism and the Genocide in Rwanda*. Princeton: Princeton University Press, 2001.

Manning, Patrick. *Francophone Subsaharan Africa 1880–1985*. London: Cambridge University Press, 1988.

Martin, Guy. "Francophone Africa in the Context of Franco-American Relations," in John Harbeson and Donald Rothchild (ed.), *Africa in World Politics: Post-Cold War Challenges*. Boulder: Westview Press, 1995.

Martin, Guy. "Ideology and Praxis in Thomas Sankara's Populist Revolution of 4 August," *Issue*, vol. 15 (1987), pp. 77–90.

Marx, Karl and Frederick Engels. *Collected Works*, vol. 10. New York: International Publishers, 1978.

Mbaku, John. "Military Coups as Rent-Seeking Behavior," *Journal of Political and Military Sociology*, vol. 22 (1994), pp. 241–284.

Mazrui, Ali. "The Lumpen Proletariat and the Lumpen Militariat: African Soldiers as a new Political Class," *Political Studies*, 21/1 (1973), pp. 1–12.

McGowan, Patrick. "African Military Coups d'etat, 1956–2001: Frequency, Trends and Distribution," *Journal of Modern African Studies*, 41/3 (2003), pp. 339–370.

McGowan, Patrick and Thomas Johnson. "Sixty Coups in Thirty years- Further Evidence Regarding African Military Coups d'Etat," *Journal of Modern African Studies*, 24/3 (1986), pp. 539–546.

Mkandawire, Thandika. "The Terrible Toll of Post-Colonial 'Rebel Movements' in Africa: Towards an Explanation of the Violence Against the Peasantry," *Journal of Modern African Studies*, 40/2 (2002), pp. 181–215.

Muana, Patrick. "The Kamajoi Militia: Violence, Internal Displacement and the Politics of Counter-Insurgency," *Africa Development*, 22/3–4 (1997) pp. 77–1000.

Mukonweshuro, E. G. *Colonialism, Class Formation and Underdevelopment in Sierra Leone*. Lanham: University Press of America, 1993.

Murray, Roger. "Militarism in Africa," *New Left Review*, vol. 38 (July/August, 1966), pp. 35–59.

Newitt, Malyn. *Portugal in Africa*. London: C Hurst & Co., 1981.

Nicol, Abioseh. "West Indians in West Africa," *Sierra Leone Studies*, vol. 13 (June 1960), pp. 14–23.

Ninsin, Kwame (ed.). *Ghana's Political Transition: Selected Documents*. Accra: Freedom Publications, 1996.

Ninsin, Kwame. "Ghanaian Politics After 1981: Revolution or Evolution,"*Canadian Journal of African Studies*, 20/1, 1987, pp. 17–37.

Nordlinger, Eric. "Soldiers in Mufti: The Impact of Military Rule Upon Economic and Social Change in the Non-Western States," *American Political Science Review*, vol. 64 (1970), pp. 1,131–1,148.

Nugent, Paul. "Living in the Past: Urban, Rural and Ethnic Themes in the 1992 and 1996 Elections in Ghana," *Journal of Modern African Studies*, 37/2 (1999), pp. 287–319.

Nugent, Paul. "Educating Rawlings: The Evolution of Government Strategy Toward Smuggling," in Donald Rothchild (ed.), *The Political Economy of Recovery*, op. cit.

Ocran, A.K. *A Myth is Broken*. London: Longmans, 1968.

Offe, Claus and Helmut Wiesenthal. "Two Logics of Collective Action: Theoretical Notes on Social Class and Organizational Form," in Maurice Zeitlin (ed.), *Political Power and Social Theory*, vol. 1. Greenwich, Conn: JAI Press, 1980, pp. 67–115.

Opala, Joseph. "Sierra Leone: The Politics of State Collapse," Paper presented at SAIC conference on Irregular Warfare in Liberia and Sierra Leone, Denver, Colorado, July 30–August 1, 1998.

Opala, Joseph. "Ecstatic Revolution: Street Art Celebrating Sierra Leone's 1992 Revolution," *African Affairs* 93/371, (1994), pp. 195–218.

Oquaye, Mike. "The Ghanaian Elections of 1992—A Dissenting View," *African Affairs*, 94/375 (1995), pp. 259–275.

Otayek, Rene. "The Revolutionary Process in Burkina Faso: Breaks and Continuities," in Markakis, John and Michael Waller (eds.), *Military Marxist Regimes in Africa*. London: Frank Cass, 1986.

Othman, Shehu. "Classes, Crises and Coups: The Demise of Shagari's Regime," *African Affairs*, 83/333 (1984), pp. 441–461.

Owusu, Maxwell. "Custom and Coups: a Juridical Interpretation of Civil Order and Disorder in Ghana," *Journal of Modern African Studies*, 24/1 (1986), pp. 69–99.

Parfitt, Trevor. "Adjustment for Stabilization and Growth: Ghana and The Gambia," *Review of African Political Economy*, no. 63 (1995), pp. 55–72.

Perlmutter, Amos. *The Military and Politics in Modern Times*. New Haven: Yale University Press, 1977.

Pitcher, Anne. *Politics in the Portuguese Empire*. Oxford: Oxford University Press, 1993.

Pye, Lucien. "Armies in the Process of Political Modernization," in John Johnson (ed.), *The Role of the Military in Underdeveloped Countries*. Princeton: Princeton University press, 1962.

Rapoport, David. "The Praetorian Army: Insecurity, Venality and Impotence," in Roman Kolkowicz and Andrej Korbonski (eds.), *Soldiers, Peasants and Bureaucrats*. London: Allen and Unwin, 1982.

Rashid, Ismail. "Subaltern Reactions: Lumpen, Students, and the Left," *Africa Development*, 22/3–4 (1997), pp. 19–44.

Reno, William. *Corruption and Politics in Sierra Leone*. Cambridge: Cambridge University Press, 1995.

Reno, William. *Warlord Politics and African States*. Boulder: Lynne Rienner, 1998.

Reno, William. "Privatizing War in Sierra Leone," *Current History* (May 1997), pp. 227–230.

Richards, Paul. *Fighting for the Rain Forest: War, Youth and Resources in Sierra Leone*. London: James Currey, 1996.

Riley, Stephen. "Sierra Leone: The Militariat Strikes Again," *Review of African Political Economy*, no. 72 (1997), pp. 287–292.

Riley Stephen and Sesay, Max. "Sierra Leone: The Coming Anarchy," *Review of African Political Economy*, 22/63 (March 1995), pp. 121–126.

Robertson, Claire. "The Death of Makola and other Tragedies," *Canadian Journal of African Studies*, 17/3 (1983), pp. 469–495.

Rubin, Elizabeth. "An Army of One's Own: In Africa, Nations Hire a Corporation to Wage War," *Harpers Magazine*, February (1997), pp. 44–55.

Rudebeck, Lars. "Reading Cabral in 1993," *Review of African Political Economy*, vol. 58 (1993), pp. 63–70.

Saine, Abdoulaye. "The Coup d'Etat in The Gambia, 1994: The End of the First Republic", *Armed Forces and Society*, 23/1 (1996), pp. 97–111.

Sallah, Tijan. "Economics and Politics in The Gambia," *Journal of Modern African Studies*, 28/4 (1990), pp. 621–648.

Sankara, Thomas. *Thomas Sankara Speaks*. New York: Pathfinder, 1988.

Sawyer, Amos. *The Emergence of Autocracy in Liberia*. San Francisco: ICS Press, 1992.

Sawyer, Amos. "Effective Immediately: Dictatorship in Liberia, 1980–1986," *Liberia Working Group* (Paper 5), Bremen, (1987).

Sawyer, Amos. "The Making of the 1984 Liberian Constitution: Major Issues and Dynamic Forces," *Liberian Studies Journal*, 12/1 (1987), pp. 1–15.

Schiff, Rebecca. "Civil-Military Relations Reconsidered: A Theory of Concordance," *Armed Forces and Society*, 22/1 (1995), pp. 7–24.

Sesay, Max. "Civil War and Collective Intervention in Liberia," *Review of African Political Economy*, Vol 67 (1995) pp. 35–52.

Shillington, Kevin. *Ghana and the Rawlings Factor*. New York: St. Martin's Press, 1992.

Skinner, Elliot. "Sankara and the Burkina Revolution: Charisma and Power, Local and External Dimensions," *Journal of Modern African Studies*, 26/3 (1988), pp. 437–455.

Sklar, Richard. "The Nature of Class Domination in Africa," *Journal of Modern African Studies*, 17/4 (1979), pp. 531–552.

Sivaramakrishnan, K. "Situating the Subaltern: History and Anthropolgy in the Subaltern Studies Project," *Journal of Historical Sociology*, 8/4 (1995), pp. 395–429.

Spivak, Gayatri. "Can the Subaltern Speak," in Gary Nelson and Lawrence Grossberg (ed.), *Marxism and the Interpretation of Culture*. Urbana: University of Illinois Press, 1991.

Stallybrass, Peter. "Marx and Heterogeneity: Thinking the Lumpenproletariat," *Representations*, vol. 31 (1990), pp. 69–95.

Stevens, Siaka. *What Life Has Taught Me*. London: Kensal House, 1984.

Tilly, Charles. "War Making and State Making as organized Crime," in Peter Evans et al (eds.), *Bringing the State Back In*. Cambridge: Cambridge University Press, 1985.

Valenzuela, Arturo. "A Note on the Military and Social Science Theory," *Third World Quarterly*, 7/1 (1985), pp. 132–143.

Vengroff, Richard. "Africa's New Hope for Democracy," *Africa Report* (July–August 1978), pp. 59–64.

Wedgwood, Josiah. *Memoirs of a Fighting Life*. London, 1941.

Welch, Claude. "Obstacles to Disengagement and Democratization: Military Regimes in Benin and Burkina Faso," in Constantine Danopoulos (ed.), *The Decline of Military Regimes: The Civilian Influence*. Boulder: Westview Press, 1988.

Welch, Claude. "Military Disengagement from Politics: Lessons from West Africa," *Armed Forces and Society*, 9/4 (1985) pp. 541–554.

Wilkins, Michael. "The Death of Thomas Sankara and the Rectification of the People's Revolution in Burkina Faso," *African Affairs*, 88/352 (1989), pp. 375–388.

Wiseman, John. "Letting Jammeh Off Lightly," *Review of African Political Economy*, No. 72 (1997), pp. 265–269.

Wiseman, John. Military Rule in The Gambia: An Interim Assessment," *Third World Quarterly*, 17/5 (1996), pp. 917–940.

Wiseman, "Attempted Coup in The Gambia: Marxist Revolution or Punk Rebellion?," *Journal of Communist Affairs*, vol. 1 (1982), pp. 434–443.

Wolseley, Garnet. "The Negro as a Soldier," *Forthnightly Review*, December (1888), pp. 84–94.

Yeebo, Zaya. *State of Fear in paradise: The Military Coup in The Gambia*. London: Africa Research and Information Bureau, 1995.

Yeebo, Zaya. *Ghana: The Struggle for Popular Power*. London: New Beacon Books, 1991.

Young, Crawford. *The African Colonial State in Comparative Perspective*. New Haven: Yale University Press, 1994.

Zack-Williams, Alfred. "Kamajors, 'Sobels' and the Militariat," *Review of African Political Economy*, 24/73 (September 1997), pp. 373–380.

Zack-Williams, Alfred. *Tributors, Supporters and Merchant Capital: Mining and Underdevelopment in Sierra Leone*. Aldershot: Avebury Press, 1995.

Zack-Williams, Alfred and Stephen Riley. "Sierra Leone: The Coup and its Consequences," *Review of African Political Economy*, 20/56 (March 1993), pp. 91–98.

Zack-Williams, Alfred. "Sierra Leone: Crisis and Despair," *Review of African Political Economy*, 17/49, (Winter 1990), pp. 22–33.

Zartman, I. William (ed.). *Collapsed States: The Disintegration and Restoration of Legitimate Authority*. Boulder: Lynne Rienner, 1995.

Newspapers and News Journals

Concord Times (Freetown)
Daily Mail (Freetown)
Daily Graphic (Accra)
Daily Observer (Banjul)
Democrat (Freetown)
For Di People (Freetown)
Foroyaa (Banjul)
Independent Observer (Freetown)
New Citizen (Banjul)
New Shaft (Freetown)

New York Times (New York)
People's Daily Graphic (Accra)
Sierra Leone Progress (New York)
The Point (Banjul)
The New Pioneer (Freetown)
Unity Now (Freetown)
Vision (Freetown)
Washington Post (Washington, DC)
We Yone (Freetown)
Weekend Observer (Banjul)
West Africa (London)

Index